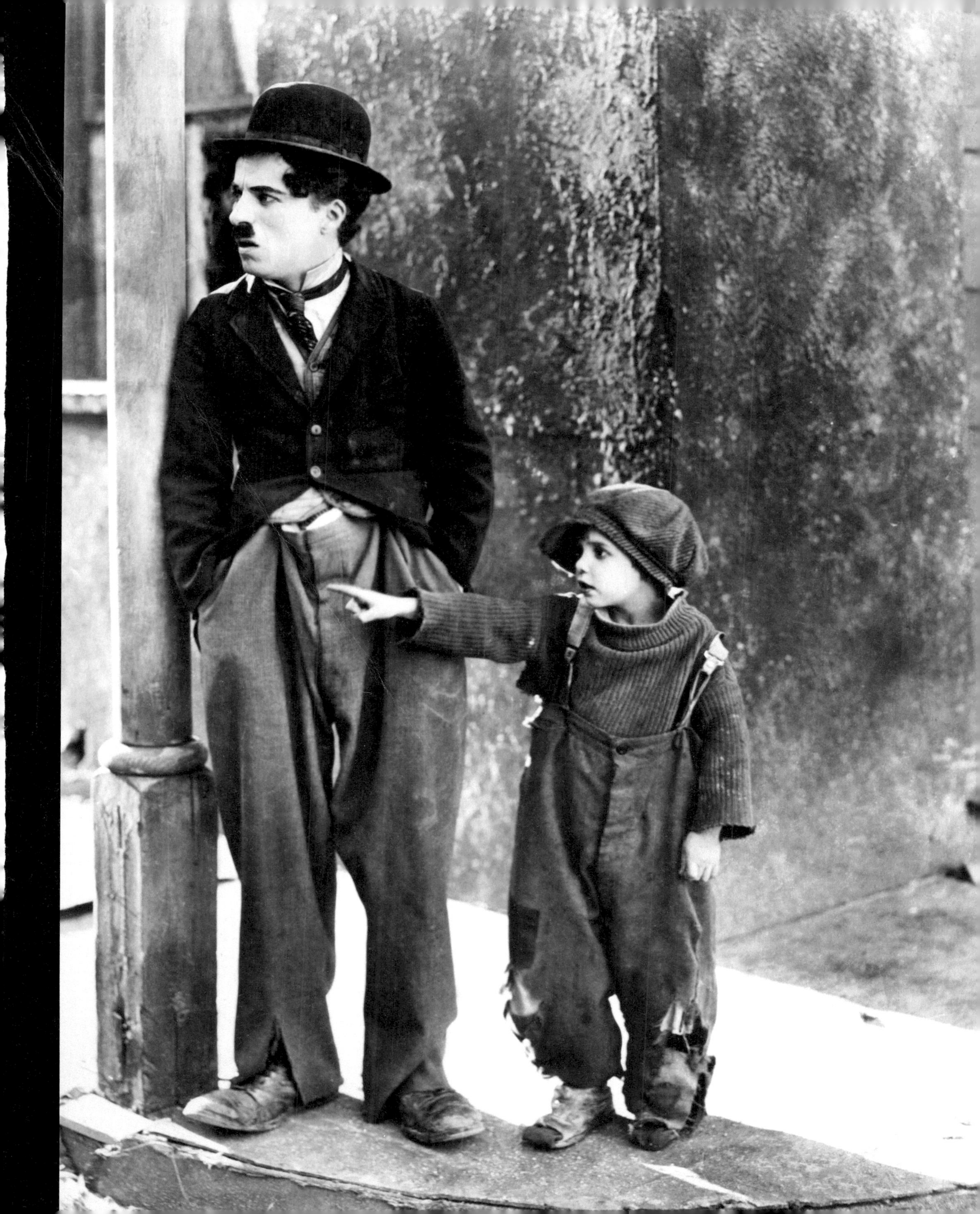

Starlight – 100 Years of Film Stills

Edited by Michael Juul Holm and Mette Marcus
Sub Editor: Jeanne Rank

Graphic design: Steen Heide
Translations from the Danish: James Manley
Printed at Rosendahls Bogtrykkeri, Esbjerg
ISBN 87-91607-31-0
Printed in Denmark 2006

This catalogue is published on the occasion of the exhibition
STARLIGHT – 100 YEARS OF FILM STILLS
13 October 2006 – 25 January 2005
Curated by Mette Marcus and Michael Juul Holm
Exhibition Coordinator: Eva Lund and Birgit Flügge
Exhibition Consultants: Charlotte Sprogøe and Christina Christensen
Exhibition Design: Gudrun Krabbe and Anne Schnettler

Louisiana Museum of Modern Art
DK-3050 Humlebæk, Denmark
Tel: +45 4919 0719
Fax: +45 4919 3505
E-mail: museumshop@louisiana.dk
www.louisiana.dk
Opening hours: Daily 10-17, Wednesdays 10-22

Cover illustration: *Kill Bill*, 2003. Quentin Tarantino. Courtesy of Miramax Film Corp. All Rights Reserved © Uma Thurman
Back cover: *Vivre sa vie*, 1982. Jean-Luc Godard. In the picture: Anna Karina © Les Films Du Jeudi
Page 1: *The Kid*, 1921. Charles Chaplin. In the picture: Charles Chaplin, Jackie Coogan © Roy Export Establishment Company
Page 96: *Pulp Fiction*, 1994. Quentin Tarantino. In the picture: Uma Thurman
Courtesy of Miramax Film Corp. All Rights Reserved © Uma Thurman

The exhibition has been organised in collaboration with The Danish Film Institute and The National Film School of Denmark
The exhibition is supported by The Greater Copenhagen Authority, HUR

DONG energy
Main sponsor of exhibitions at Louisiana

Realdania
The Foundation Realdania. Sponsor of architectural exhibitions at Louisiana

Nykredit
Sponsor of Louisiana Contemporary

STARLIGHT

100 YEARS OF FILM STILLS

PREFACE

"It was just like being in a film...," we sometimes tell one another – and what do we mean by that? We say it when an event, an incident, a detail perhaps, suddenly stands out with a clarity that comes from somewhere else than the event itself. The event in which we may be involved takes on the appearance or feel of a motif, an image, a scene. You say goodbye – and in the same instant a flock of birds rises, the light falls in a particular way, accompanying sounds are heard; it's all coincidental, but it fits the situation, which suddenly seems pre-arranged – and thus just like a film. For we read films as pictures too. We are alert, sitting there in the dark, we keep an eye on what is happening and how it all looks. We aren't simply sucked into the realism of the film, its evocative magic; distance and empathy go hand in hand, and that is why we talk about 'scenes' in a film, not just a flow of action. It's the scenes that stick with us and survive as the types or patterns or models that later make us exclaim: "It was just like being in a film...".

The twentieth century has been called the century of film, and there is no doubt that film as a medium has changed our culture in a whole range of ways. It has affected our way of telling stories, our way of seeing the world, our knowledge of the world outside our own little circle, the formation of our identities and thus our behaviour on the large and small scale.

Film – because of its global distribution – is probably our strongest shared cultural reference: perhaps the only one that really *is* common to us all?

Such a visual medium inevitably interests an institution like Louisiana. For Louisiana is and has always been interested in investigating and showing the media that carry our ideas about the world, whether they are the classic arts or other kinds of cultural achievements. And of course what is particularly interesting in connection with the images of film is the points at which the film images interface directly with the museum's core areas – visual art, architecture and photography.

What are the images of film? Of course anyone could say that the images in films are those that move; that is, the flow of images in the cinema where it all seems to come together in one great image – the film – only interrupted by cuts that take the viewer from angle to angle, from scene to scene. But film also involves other kinds of images – those that stick in the mind. They no longer move, they are frozen moments of great clarity; they are the decisive moments that contain more than the split second they depict. They are in a certain sense representative of both what has gone before and what comes after; as when Bogart and Bergman say goodbye on the airport apron in Casablanca, for that image can be run back and forwards in the mind of anyone who has seen the film. And yet it is also an independent image of a classic scene: departure.

The images we are talking about are called 'stills' in the world of film itself. They have their own history. Once it was a special discipline to take these pictures during filming, now the pictures are often taken from the actual film and allowed to stand. We know them from the display cases in the old days and from film books, film magazines and reviews – that is, all the places where the film has to stand still for a moment to be remembered.

It is about 700 of these stills, ranging over the whole century of film, that Louisiana is now showing in the major exhibition *Starlight – 100 years of film stills*. There are small pictures and giant pictures, backlit and on paper, there are Chaplin and Nicole Kidman, Clint Eastwood and Peter Sellers, there are divas and baddies and goodies, there are kisses and burning cars, shudders and horrors and moments of great beauty – all gathered in a grand tour of the imaginings of the twentieth century.

In fact it is something of an experiment, since no museum has done this sort of thing before. On the other hand it's such an obvious idea that it just had to be realized. And it is in fact being realized Louisiana-style, that is with the focus on the viewer and his or her chance to enter into a labyrinth of images that evoke both recognition and surprise. *Starlight – 100 years of film stills* is our history – so everyone will find something or other that impinges on their lives and dreams. The mass medium links up with the personal narrative – hardly anyone can fail to be affected.

Where do you go to find these pictures? Surprisingly enough not so far if you live in Humlebæk, for the Danish Film Institute in Gothersgade, Copenhagen, in fact has one of the world's finest and most comprehensive collections of film stills from the whole history of the medium – some 2.3 million pictures. So Louisiana has had an excellent collaboration with the Danish Film Institute, which has long had a fervent wish to mount an exhibition of this art, and in that connection we would like to thank its director Henning Camre, and Dan Nissen, director of the Cinemateque and Museum. We owe special thanks to Madeleine Schlawitz, head of the Film Institute Stills & Poster Archive, for her great efforts and commitment to the exhibition. Our warmest thanks also to the exhibition architects Gudrun Krabbe and Anne Schnettler for their design work, commitment and enthusiasm. Finally we thank the still photographer Rolf Konow, who tells us in the exhibition and in the catalogue about his work on Danish and international film productions; as well as the other writers in the catalogue and the copyright owners – actors, photographers and production and distribution companies – for their good will and understanding of the use of the pictures in the exhibition context. Besides the Danish Film Institute, Louisiana has also collaborated in connection with the exhibition with the National Film School of Denmark. Our thanks to the principal, Poul Nesgaard and to Tina Sørensen, head of the Professional Training Department, who have contributed important input. La Cinémathèque Française, Svenska Filminstituttet, British Film Institute and Deutsches Filminstitut have provided crucial information and we thank them for their generous cooperation.

The Greater Copenhagen Authority (HUR) has made an important contribution to the realization of the project, and the museum's principal sponsor, DONG, has helped to make this kind of extraordinary exhibition at all possible at Louisiana.

Mette Marcus
Michael Juul Holm
Exhibition directors

Poul Erik Tøjner
Director

ETERNITY IS IN LOVE WITH THE PRODUCTIONS OF TIME

ON FILM STILLS, HUMAN CURIOSITY AND THE IMAGE MACHINE THAT RUNS CONSTANTLY IN THE SKULL

By **Michael Juul Holm**

On 14th April 1912 the Danish polar explorer Knud Rasmussen wrote at the beginning of his diary of the First Thule Expedition: "Fine weather at last, warm sun, travelling weather! We break camp at ten, 35 sledges with a total of 350 dogs [...] Sledge after sledge slides out from the little settlement, forming a bridge across the ice; shouts and cheerful hubbub fill the day [...] Our ascent, with the many sledges in train and the surging teams that brought the glacier to life wherever we arrived, looked splendid. The magnificent picture had the effect of an Arctic gala parade. We forced the glacier in an easy ascent, and showers of good humour continued to rain down on our heads. I stopped to take a picture, and as the sledges filed past I heard Freuchen's strong voice raised in song: 'Napoleon's march over the Alps!'"

Late that same evening, a few hundred nautical miles due south in the strait that separates Greenland from America, one of history's worst ship disasters, at all events the best known, took place when the luxury liner Titanic went down off Newfoundland after a collision with an iceberg. 1522 passengers perished. There were no other witnesses than those on board; no one "stopped to take a picture".

All the same we see it vividly – the sinking of the Titanic, the hull slowly tilting, breaking and sinking in two parts; the Atlantic waves that carry the all too few lifeboats with passengers primarily from first class, the unfortunates who never get out of the ship or cry in vain for help before being swallowed up by the sea – and the photograph that Rasmussen took of the 'Arctic gala parade' after such a lively description of the circumstances. We even have no problem envisaging Napoleon's march over the Alps. Why is that? How do we manage to imagine something we have never seen? How has it come about that we can converse about more or less anything in this whole magically complex world we live in – and clearly see it all in our mind's eye, or write images into one another's heads, as I have just done here?

Each of the two encounters with the ice on this spring day in 1912 testifies in its own way to a time that had put speed, motion, the desire for new worlds on the agenda of the great public sphere. When globalization is used today as a buzzword, and we are inclined to believe with the arrogance of the moment that we are facing something radically new, that we are at a cultural watershed, we overlook the fact that actual, practical globalization (if we wish to accept the term at all, that is) comes on the heels of a long-since completed globalization in the sphere of the imagination. There are no blank spots left on our internal map of the world, or any other map, almost regardless of the degree of detail. We know what it is like diving beneath the ice sheet sheathed in a small submarine; we know what it looks like inside a luxurious penthouse apartment in New York, in the palace of the Tsar a hundred years ago, how Paris looks from the air, how the pilot experiences flying just above the treetops to avoid enemy radar, what it's like when the most beautiful woman – or man – in the world comes on to you. We know it all from films (and the later spin-offs TV, video and the Internet). That doesn't mean that what we see would be the same as reality if we were to put it to the test one day.

La Dolce Vita,1960
Director: Federico Felini
In the picture: Anita Ekberg
© Société Pathé Cinéma

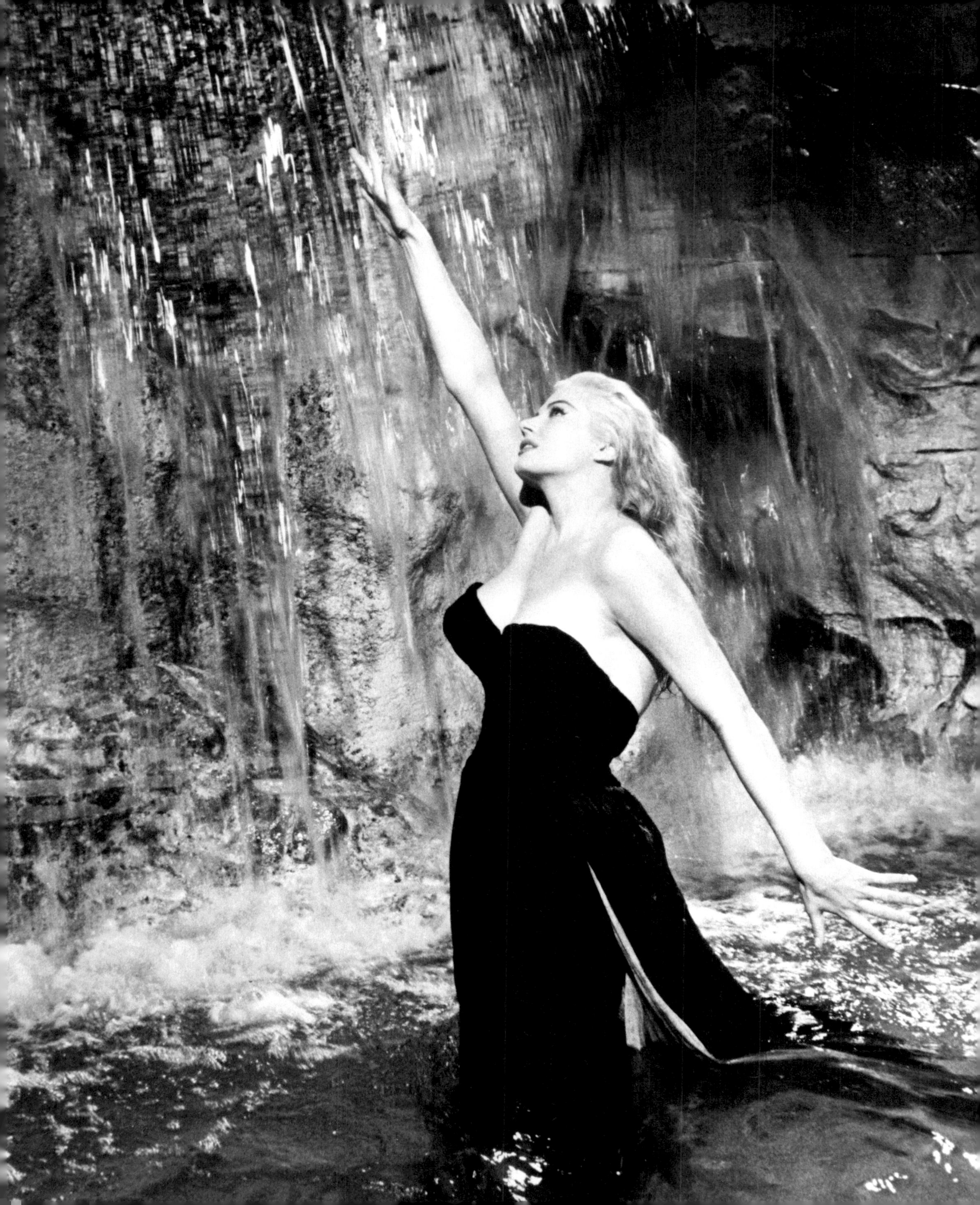

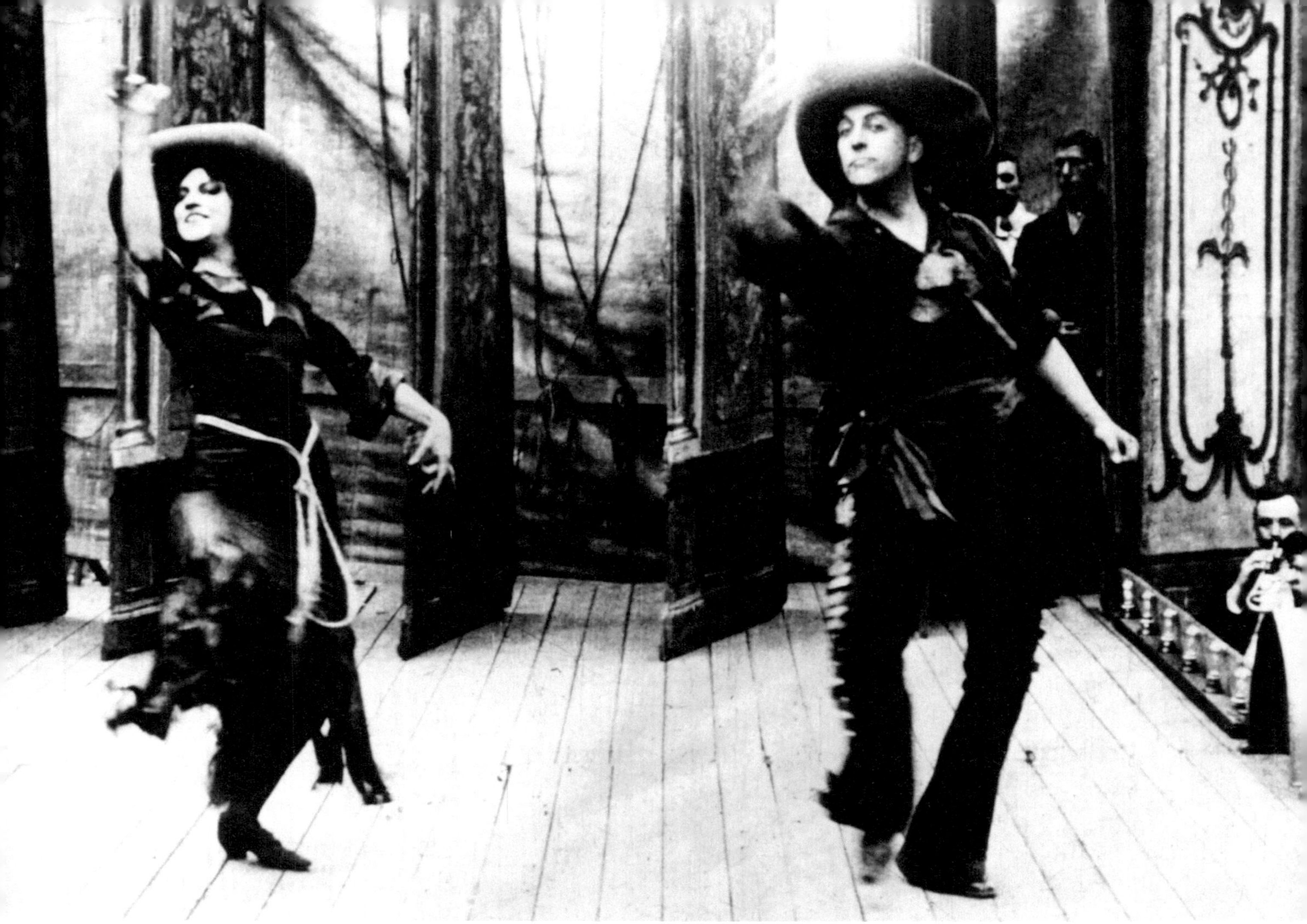

Afgrunden, 1910 (The Abyss). Director: Urban Gad. In the picture: Asta Nielsen, Poul Reumert © Nordisk Film. Danish Film Institute

But we see *something*, and that something is one of the things the following pages will be about.

Among the Greenlandic legends and myths that Knud Rasmussen collected on his expeditions from the trading station Thule, a single quotation could stand as a kind of credo for both the restless polar traveller himself and the time of which he was a part: "This time I will leave my dwelling-place and seek new sights in a foreign region...," says the legend of the Great Hunter from Aluk (whose heart burst when he saw the sun over his settlement – already we see it for ourselves!).[1] 'New sights' could be understood as a metaphor for the period in general – in the words of the philosopher Nietzsche a *revaluation of all values*, the modern showdown with hidebound norms and conformist evaluations of the moral, aesthetic, political etc. Here, though, it will mostly be about the more straightforward meaning: new sights, new images of the world. That the two things are in fact closely connected is something we can dismiss or note for further reflection according to temperament.

In all its simplicity, it is about curiosity. Mankind is by nature both a visual and a visionary being; visual inasmuch as an immense part of our brain capacity is used to process visual impressions; visionary in the sense that we simply can't help envisaging things.[2] Our access to the world, whether linguistically or auditively linked, goes through our sense of vision: everything becomes pictures in our heads. The smaller the world becomes, the more images we must have of it to make our way in it. The twentieth century brought a deluge of new images with it.

The new images of the world were already well on their way to imprinting themselves on ordinary people's

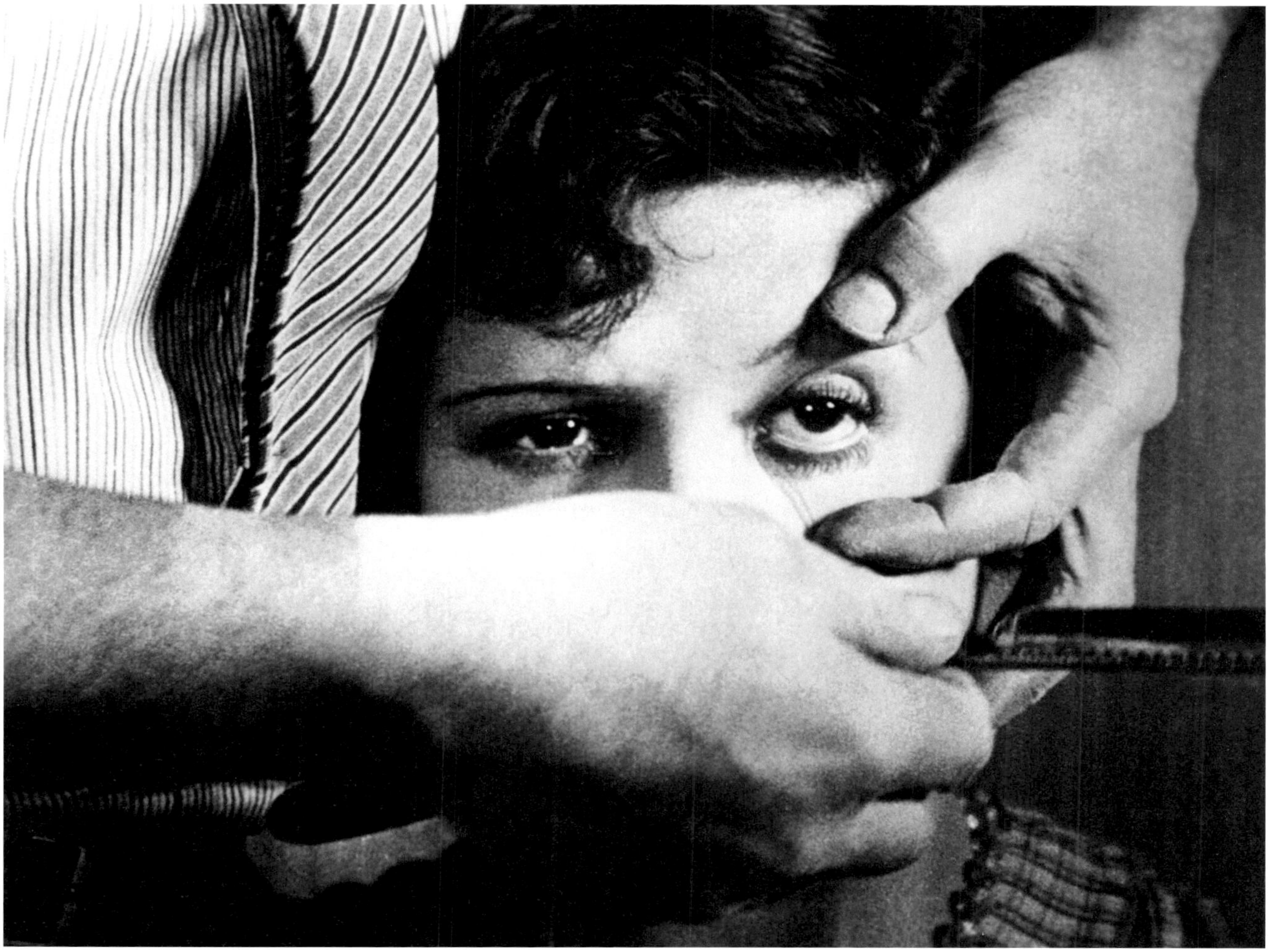

Un Chien Andalou, 1940 (An Andalousian Dog). Director: Luis Buñuel © Les grands films classiques, Paris F

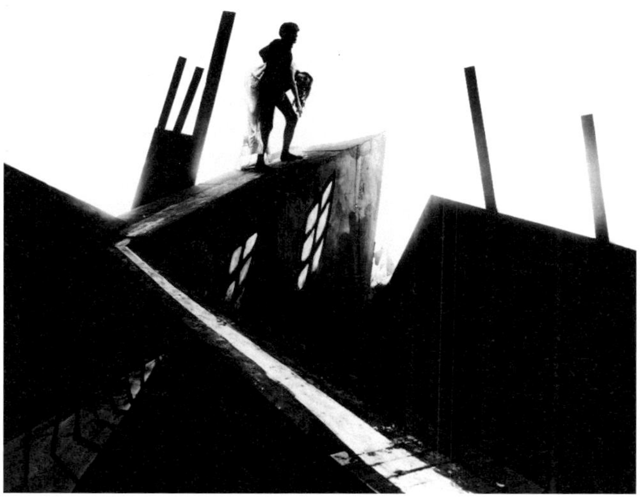

minds some time before the film came to play a role in earnest. This is not the place to unravel the whole history of mentalities that followed in the wake of industrialization, the depletion of the rural population and the corresponding growth of the cities, the relative improvement in living conditions, the growing self-awareness of the bourgeoisie etc., etc. But if we want to understand the 'little history' of the importance of film images to the formation of the new way of *thinking* in pictures, we must dwell on at least two technical pre-

Das Cabinet des Doktor Caligari, 1919
(The Cabinet of Dr. Caligari)
Director: Robert Wiene. Still photographer: Karl-Heinz Vogelman. © Friedrich-Wilhelm-Murnau-Stiftung
Distributor: Transit Film GmbH

cursors of the moving picture – two inventions, each of which in its own way blazed a new trail for the eye: the railway and photography.

With the development of the rail network in both Europe and the USA from the mid-nineteenth century, ordinary people could for the first time be transported through the landscape as easily as they had earlier moved on foot through their own rooms or the small towns they typically lived in. What had once been experienced as physical (and arduous) motion in time now became aesthetic motion in space: you could drive out of town, follow a curve up a range of hills and then a moment later experience the town in miniature viewed half from above. Within a few hours you could pass rivers and wilderness and forests and fields, and then suddenly see the city towering up ahead.[3]

Within more or less the same span of years in the second half of the last century, people gradually grew accustomed to looking at photographs (or prints from photographs) from foreign places, other countries; at interiors they would never have been grand enough to visit for themselves – even at pictures from the chambers of royalty or government. In newspapers and other printed matter they could simply see for themselves: new sights from foreign regions. They grew used to viewing the world at second hand, but at the same time to understanding these 'views' as authentic experiences. The American writer and physician Oliver Wendell Holmes called the photograph a "mirror with memory" and wrote in 1859 that in the future "... image would become more important than the object itself and would in fact make the object disposable."[4] Besides being the immediate precursors of film as technical innovations, the two breakthroughs – the factual one of the train and the vicarious one of the photograph – also supplied direct mental preparation for understanding

The Elephant Man, 1980. Director: David Lynch. In the picture: John Hurt
Still photographer: Frank Connor © Canal+Image UK Ltd.

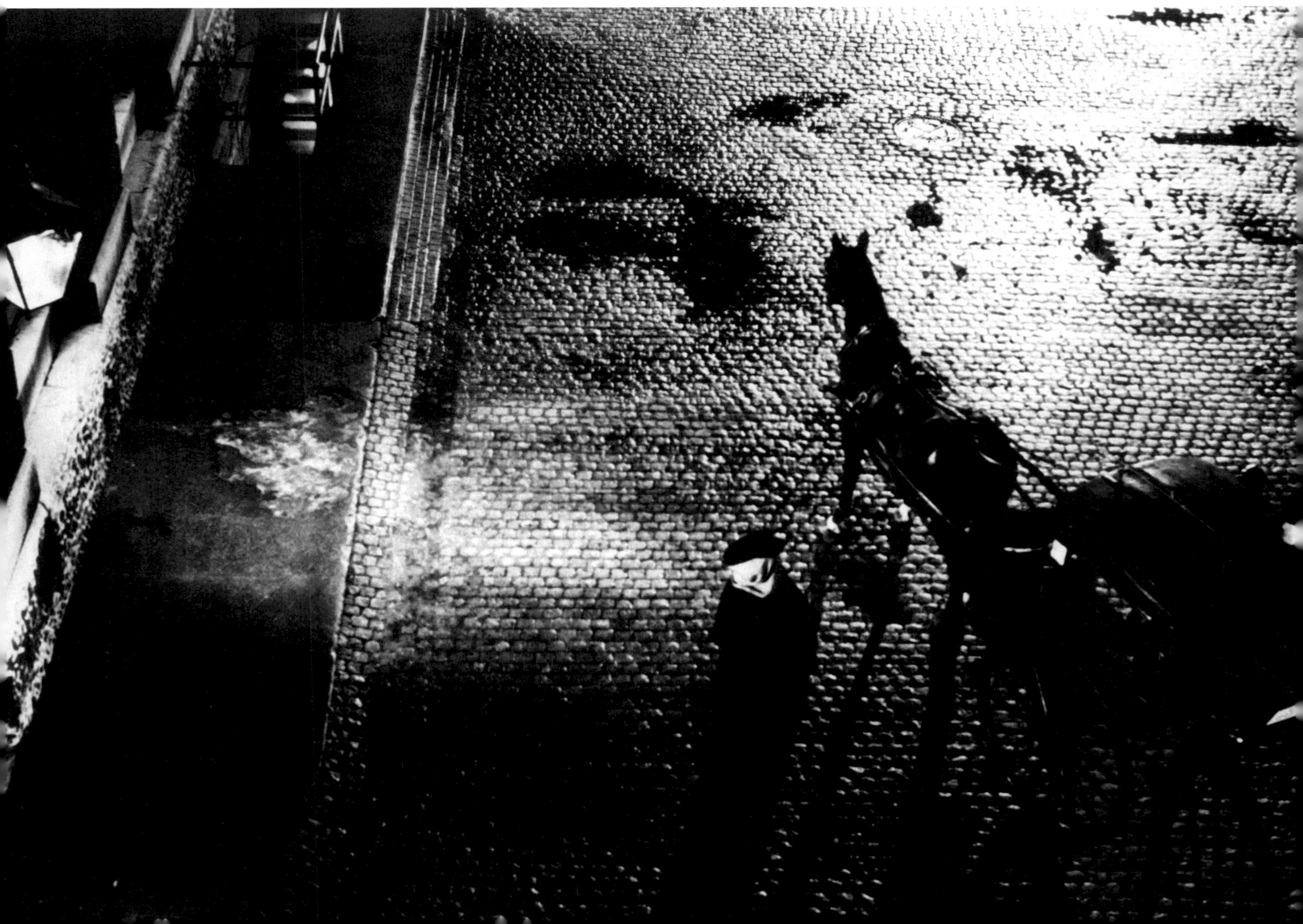

shifting points of view, quick cuts and fluid transitions, and trained the ability to identify with what one did not oneself come from or was a part of.

However, the true explosion, the total turbocharging of the imagery in everyone's internal image bank, only came with film. From the moment the feature film became a mass medium and ousted the serialized novel, the church, the theatre, the circus and all the other fun of the fair as the most important purveyor of dreams, entertainment, shock-and-horror and edification, the world, as a field of images we effortlessly exchange with one another, had definitively changed. In this field, five evenings in the cinema correspond to a whole life of train travel and leafing through newspapers (not that the latter should be neglected!).

And if we want to put a date to when the images of film really became common currency for people in the western world, the year of the Titanic and the Thule Expedition, 1912, is perhaps as good as any. That year there were no fewer than two films of the Titanic drama – so people could see what they had already heard and read about. The first, a short film lasting ten minutes, came just a month after the event the second, a German film entitled *In Nacht und Eis*, was three times as long and is considered the world's first disaster film. It was also the year when the first film serial was released; the year the first gangster film was premiered (D.W. Griffith's *The Musketeers of Pig Alley*); the year the first true feature film was premiered in the USA (*Oliver Twist*); while in Europe the Italian Enrico Guazzoni produced the first feature film lasting more than two hours, *Quo Vadis*. Not least, it was the year when three of the film industry giants were founded: Universal Pictures, Fox Film Foundation (later 20th Century Fox) and Technicolor. And thus the basis had been laid for the shift in the balance of power in the American film

Citizen Kane, 1941. Director: Orson Welles. In the picture: Orson Welles
© Still photographer: Alexander Kahle. RKO/Aries

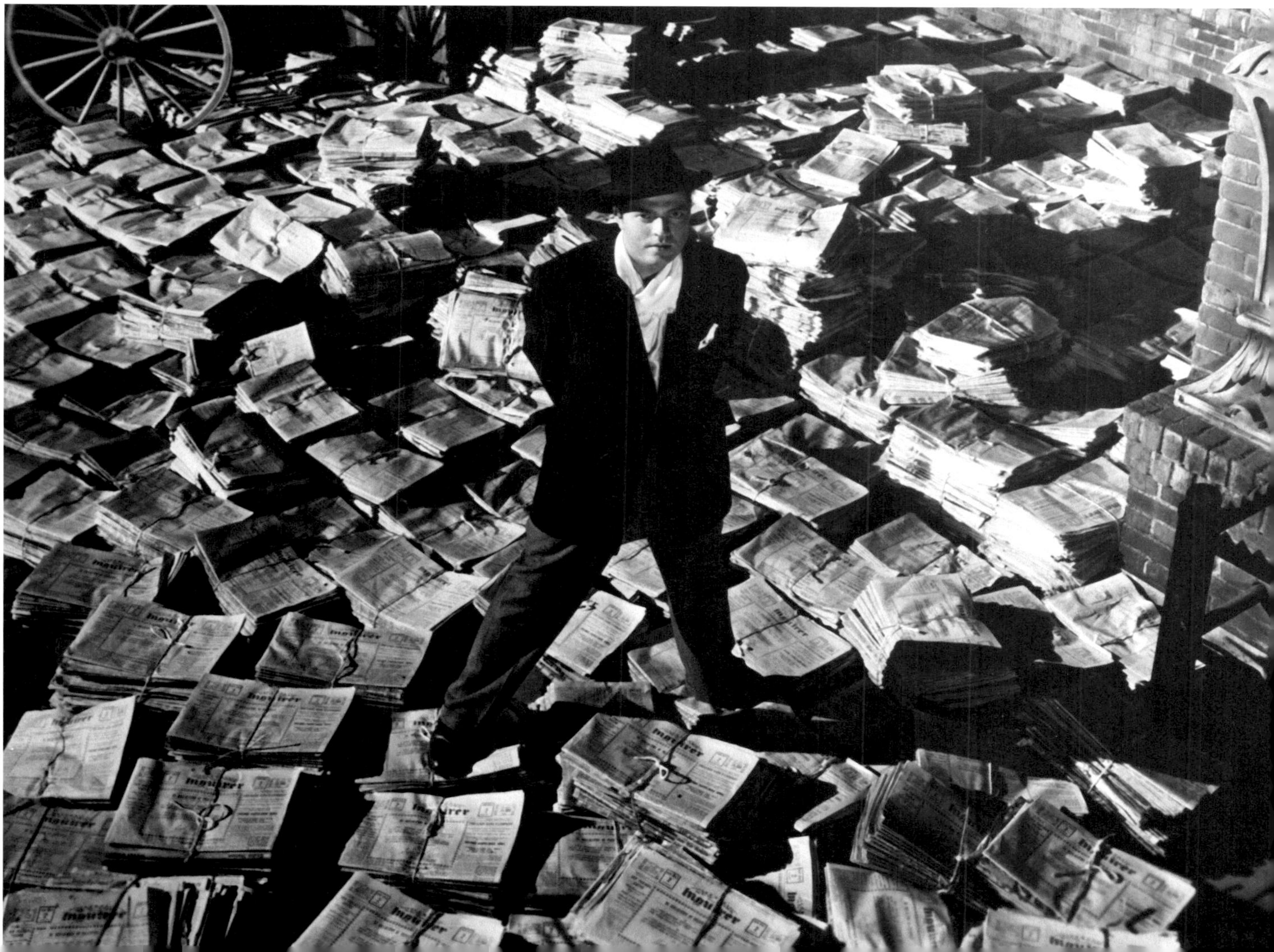

industry from the east to the west coast and the foundation of Hollywood's so far undisputed special status. The best indicator that film had now really taken hold of the big audiences was however that the first fan magazine was launched: *Photoplay*, with small film-based short stories, stills and star portraits, was the pioneer of the whole starstruck glamour cult and the celebrity hysteria that has endured, with small adjustments for the changing fashions of the times, until today. But that's another story.

II

Everyone has one or more stills in his or her head that are unforgettable for personal reasons – we have our soft spots for this or that genre, person, time or atmosphere. It may be the picture of a luscious young Elizabeth Taylor standing barefoot on Rock Hudson's shoes in *Giant*; Clint Eastwood as "Dirty" Harry Callahan alone in the Yankee Stadium; Dr. Caligari on his way through the insanely distorted futuristic city in his head, or perhaps Marilyn Monroe with her skirt up around her ears in *The Seven Year Itch*. During the preparation for the exhibition *Starlight – 100 years of film stills* we have looked through more than 120,000 stills from about 1400 films. That is only a microscopic part of all those that exist: in the Copenhagen archives alone there are more than 2.3 million photos, and these are only from films that have been premiered in Denmark. In practice we can regard the number of existing film stills as infinite, for no human being could manage to see them all, even if there were nothing else at all to spend one's life on.

All the same the problem is not insuperable. After all, the material is first and foremost photographs: you quickly distinguish the good from the less good – either it grabs you and works, or it doesn't. In fact it isn't just a matter of taste; among the people who have been involved in the process, there has hardly been any disagreement when it came to the pictures that were considered good in one way or another. There are many things you can fall for: an expression, a surface, a particular wealth of detail, the way the picture is composed, the interplay among the actors. The rare sight. The less good pictures tend to fade out. Something that was originally meant to indicate a point in the film or just to draw attention to the participation of an actor often pales when viewed as a picture in its own right. And once you've been through a couple of thousand photos from all the genres and periods of film history, you discover that a taxonomy, a principle of classification, forces itself upon you among the few from each film that you have laid aside. The pictures choose one another in categories. Quite regardless of whether we are looking at American comedies from the thirties, Neoimpressionist Italian films from the fifties, French New Wave films, brand new Danish and international action dramas, the entertainment industry or the art cinema, related pictures will appear in large numbers.

On the one hand the taxonomy generates a little typology of basic human conditions: when you lay out the pictures you end up with some piles that together describe the most important emotions, states and situations in a human life: the meeting, the departure, the exercise of power, the spontaneous expression of joy, the affirmation of comradeship; betrayal, fear, attraction, caring, resistance, opposition, flight, resignation, abandonment, sex and death. Briefly put.

And then you discover that a smaller but still important number of pictures group themselves according to quite different criteria: they are related as subjects but not necessarily because they describe the same (emotional) content. It isn't the same thing when Anne Frank stands beneath a skylight and when we see the Marx brothers or Kirk Douglas (bare-chested) in the same situation; it isn't the same when Woody Allen, Ebbe Rode, Grace Kelly or Ingrid Bergman, at a crucial point in the film, seizes the telephone. And there is no direct connection between all the stairways, railway stations and conversations in cars that appear again and again in stills. But it is the same motif: the still has its own history of motifs. Elsewhere in this catalogue you can read how its roots lie in among other places the history of painting and the other visual arts.

The film's reservoir of pictures functions as an inexhaustible stock of references to important experiences in one's personal life, common denominators for the identity of a whole generation, vehicles for idiosyncrasies (we can agree on hating or loving a particular character, actors, a kind of film) and emblems that sum up whole periods. More anonymously, as an overall mass, they represent a plethora of possible ways of

Hard Target, 1993. Director: John Woo

Foreign Correspondent, 1940
Director: Alfred Hitchcock
Still photographer: William Walling

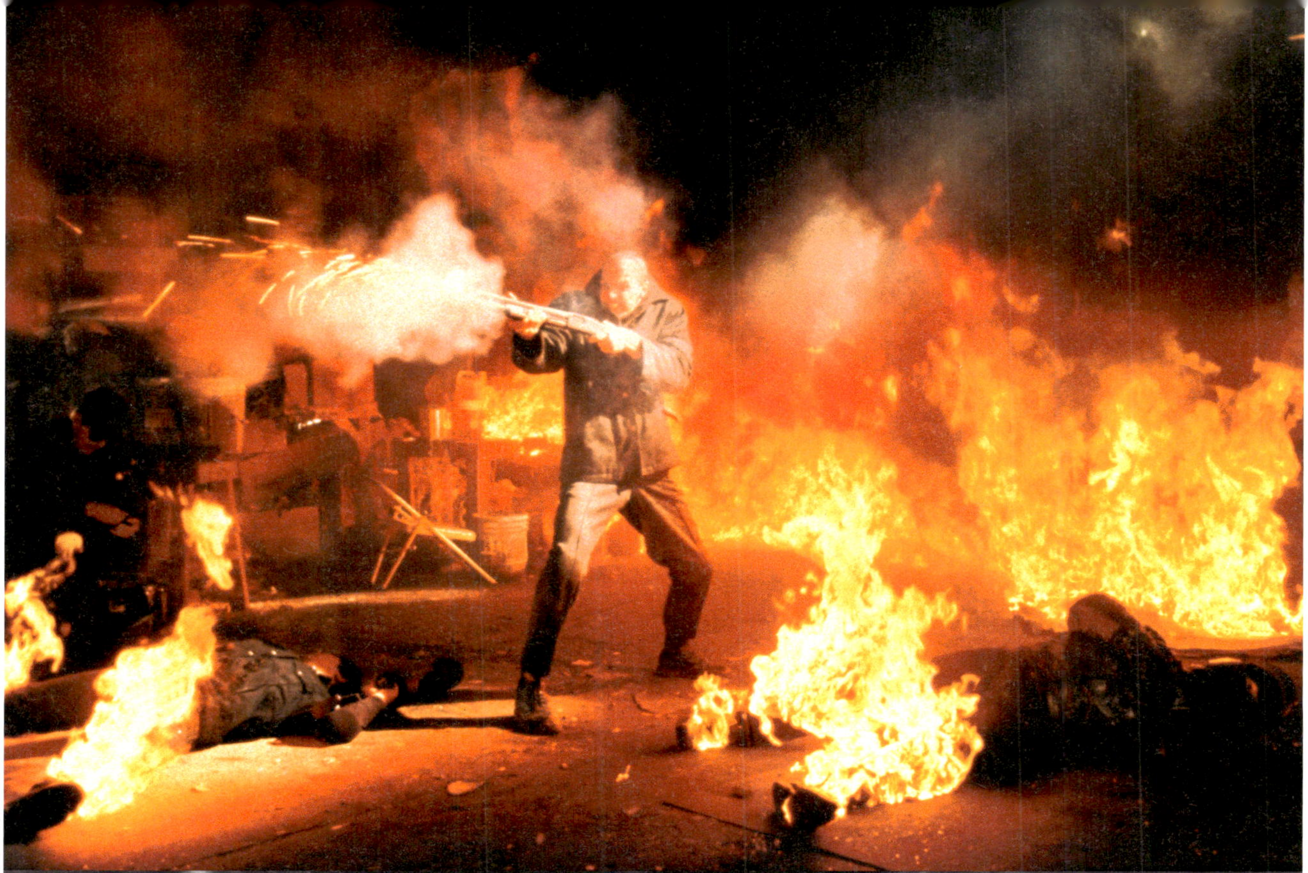

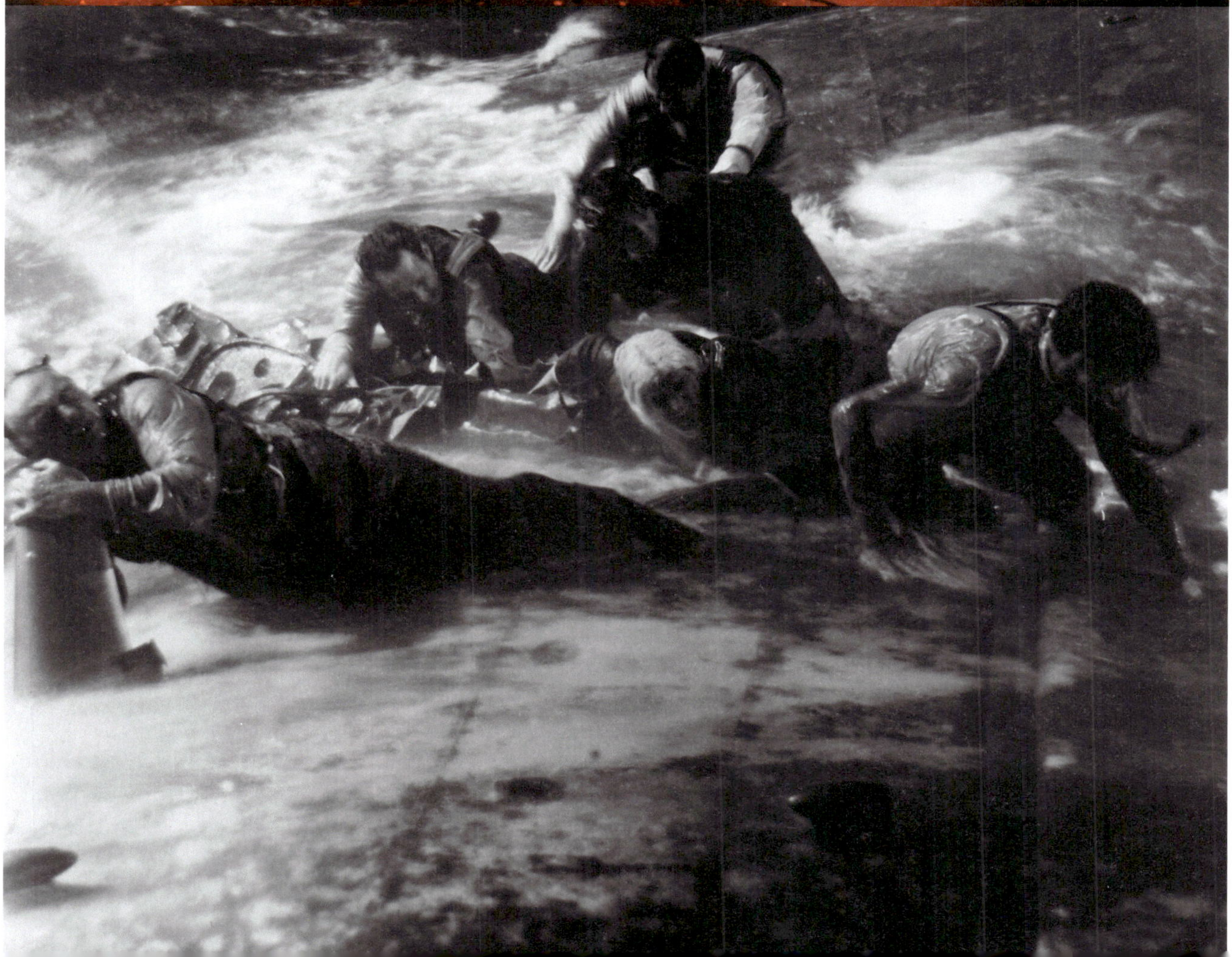

seeing, of conceivable situations, of places, moods, social roles – in these pages, for example, you will find a mini-history of women in pictures: women can't drive; but women can stand up for their rights; women are objects of desire; women are *beaten back* by the black cross of the patriarchy. In that sense the stills function as the film's vicarious templates for ways of acting, or just as bearers of Utopian dreams of a different reality from the one in which we happen to find ourselves. The most frequent criticism of the film industry and the culture of the image in general throughout the century of the film has been precisely that it veils reality (with its real conflicts of interest); that it is the opium of the people, escapism, false consciousness, etc.[5] Much as one's finer sensitivities urge suitable opposition to the lowbrow speculation and the untalented abuse of the medium that have always taken up plenty of the filmic landscape, it must be said the criticism is naïve. It is naïve because of its implicit assumption that people glut themselves indiscriminately on all that they see. That is not the case. And it isn't because there's anything wrong with the face value of the film image – the thing that directly sticks in our minds. The best of them are sheer masterpieces in which we can immerse ourselves and of which we never tire. But the face value is only one side of the coin.

III

If we are to approach an understanding of the effect of the film and especially of its individual images in a wider – I am tempted to say sociological – context, we must first commit a small fatal error, as they say in the computer dialogue boxes. We must do something that according to all aesthetic theory is wrong – that is, we must separate form and content. While the specific *content of* the stills has fed us with information about how the world looks (could look / once looked / perhaps will look in the future); has given us an infinity of detailed descriptions of things, places, people's attitudes, costumes, architecture etc., their *form* – lighting, point

Holiday Inn, 1942. Director: Mark Sandrich. In the picture: Virginia Dale, Marjorie Reynolds
Still photographer: John Ellis © 1942 Paramount Pictures, Inc.

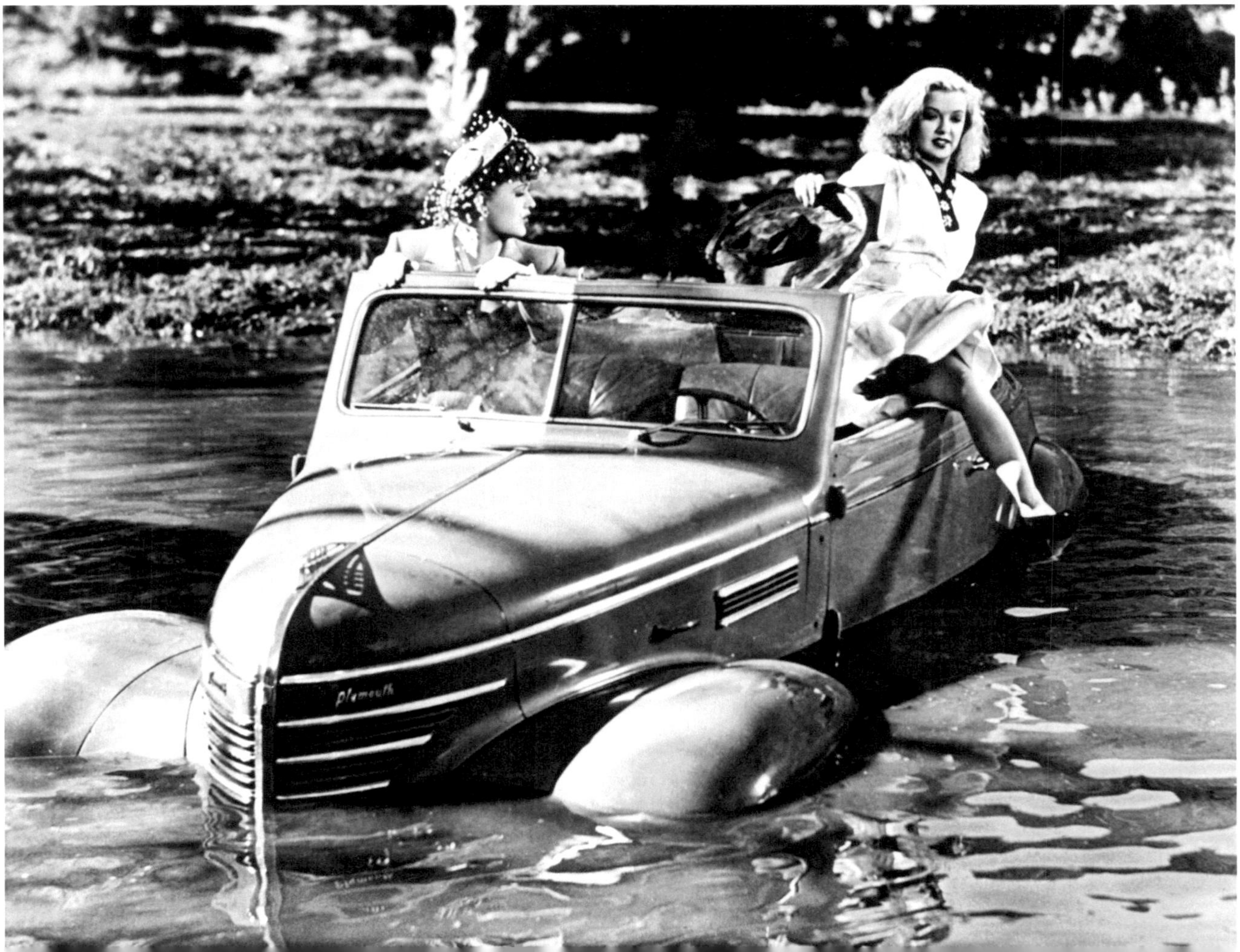

of view, framing, depth, degree of contrast, resolution, focus etc. – has rather helped to upgrade our internal projector at a more functional level. Once installed, all these *ways* of imagining something will always be available for other types of content; they are like a toolbox for the imagination that we can add to all the ways we already know from *real* reality.

The images of film have thus made us a great deal wiser about the world. When I say the images of film, and not just film, it is because we rarely think in moving pictures. Of course we have all experienced the internal film that runs when we dream or daydream, when we anticipate or remember particular events. But usually it is the fixed picture that remains as the concentrate of a particular scene. As in dreams, there is a compaction of the sequence: it is all held together, as when the great history painters captured the essence of a battle of the Napoleonic Wars (or Napoleon's march over the Alps) in one image. The stills from films play a special role in this respect: you could say that the photographer's job is to do some of the work that we would otherwise do by ourselves – that is to store something mentally in an economical way. At all events this is true for the individual viewer when there actually is a direct connection between the experience of a film still and the film to which it refers.

But often this is precisely *not* the case: just think of all the films you have never seen, or those you have only seen after close scrutiny of the stills from them in books, cinema foyers or display cases. Personally, for example, I have never seen Steve McQueen in the racing car film *Le Mans* from 1971 – it was prohibited for children under 12, and I was only 11 then – but I have spent several half-afternoons looking at the stills in the display case in front of the Imperial Cinema down on the corner, and so I know quite a lot about how you get quickly into a racing car, how a totally concentrated person looks seconds before the race starts, and how it looks when a human body flies out of a burning car. What the still does here is not help us to remember; hardly even predict what we are to experience later. The twelve stills in the display case may have been very carefully selected by someone who wanted to sell us the film, to suck us into it. But each of them also, in its static singularity, represents an *emancipation* from the film's all-absorbing possession of the senses and thus the director's or the production's controlling intentions: film stills, in their individual framing, make themselves available for all sorts of personal further elaborations which are in principle and often also in practice irrelevant to the film.

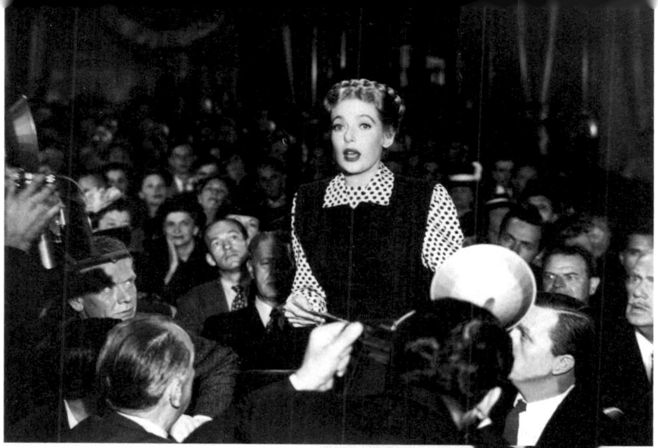

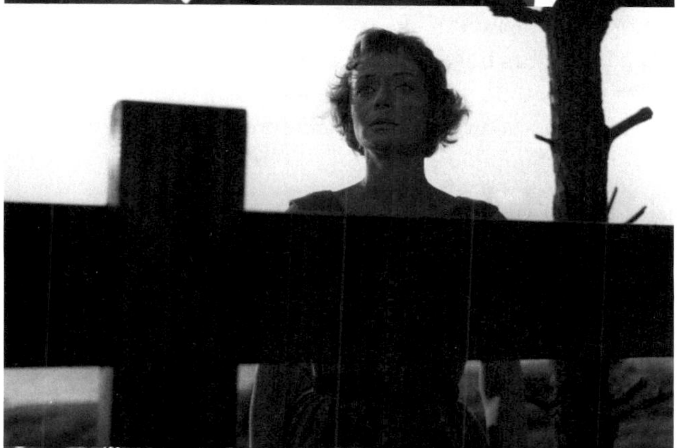

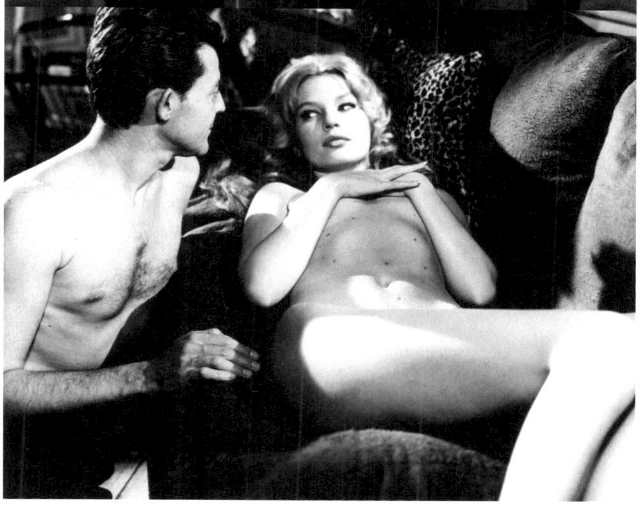

The Farmer's Daughter, 1947. Director: H. C. Potter
In the picture: Loretta Young © 1940 Universal Pictures

En Fremmed Banker På, 1959 (A Stranger Knocks)
Director: Johan Jacobsen.
In the picture: Birgitte Federspiel. Still photographer: Gergely Szabo © Rialto Film/Preben Philipsen ApS

Les Liaisons Dangereuses, 1960 (Dangerous Liaisons)
Director: Roger Vadim. In the picture: Annette Vadim, Gérard Philipe. Still photographer: Serge Beauvarlet
© 1960 TF1 International

The best film stills are fantastic images of the world as it has been conceived and staged by particularly gifted directors, cameramen and still photographers using the best, most expressive actors and the whole crew of people who are involved in the production of the motion picture fictions. Together they share with us an overview of the diversity of life that we could never collect for ourselves as lived experience. All the way from Heaven – Anita Ekberg in the Trevi Fountain in a moment of sublime life-fulfilment – to Hell: the situations we could never experience ourselves, for the simple reason that we would not survive them; like the stills in the preceding pages from John Woo's *Hard Target* and Hitchcock's rather neglected early film *Foreign Correspondent*, where the escalating drama of a whole film is summed up in the struggle for life of a group of men on something that looks like the Raft of the Medusa or later the hull of the Titanic just before the final plunge. When the individual photographs are best, they are great photographic art; but taken as a whole, as a genre, or perhaps one should just say as a field of photography, they are first and foremost a fantastic source of concentrated impressions of the multiplicity of the world and the humanly possible. It is all here: *The Good, the Bad and the Ugly*.

One of the masterpieces of the English poet (and visual artist) William Blake is called *The Marriage of Heaven and Hell*. There is a good deal of mysticism and true romanticism at play in the work, which includes a great many of his frequently quoted 'one-liners' (there is something of Sam Spade – Bogart's character in *The Maltese Falcon* – in Blake, when the inspiration strikes him ... or the other way round, rather). In the section called *Proverbs of Hell*, the poet takes us on a procession past a row of inscriptions with truths from the mouth of the Devil. For in this strange marriage the devil can tell us truths we would be unable to hear from his better half. One of the finest is "Eternity is in Love with the Productions of Time". We can only understand and speak of truly great, epoch-making, eternal matters in life by relating them to the thronging, richly detailed differences that this world has to offer.

I have earlier spoken of mankind as a visionary being. Normally we reserve the word visionary for people like Blake – the seer, the prophetic poet – or the masters among the film artists: people who can envision the unseen and materialize it as works. But the reality is that we are all, always, visionaries. Otherwise we would be unable to talk together, to write so we can understand one another, or even make our everyday life in all its triviality hang together. What we do incessantly is mix images we already have in our heads with one another so that new images are born.[6] Anyone can imagine Chaplin on board the Titanic, Anita Ekberg beside the ladykiller Knud Rasmussen, in sealskins on her way up over the ice cap. Or any other amalgamation of something real and personally experienced, something 'second-hand' like film stills and something that has arisen inside our own heads. Where the image machine keeps running.

Le Salaire de la peur, 1953 (The Wages of Fear)
Director: Henri-Georges Clouzot
© Still photographer: Lucienne Chevert, Jean Clouzot
1952 - TF1 International - Vera Films - Pathé - Fono Roma

Jules et Jim, 1962 (Jules and Jim)
Director: Francois Truffaut
In the picture: Jeanne Moreau, Oskar Werner, Henri Serre
© Still photographer: Raymond Cauchetier. Studio Canal
Les Films du Carrosse. Sédif Productions

1 The author Tor Nørretranders made the quotation the motto for a series of publications about scientific breakthroughs that he edited for the publisher Munksgaard in the 1990s.

2 Curiosity appears not only to be a cognitive and psychological precondition of knowledge and thus in the broader perspective of survival, but a mechanism already determined at the physical level; research by among others Markus Meister at Harvard University has shown that the retinal ganglion cells of the eye react directly to changes in the familiar patterns and environments. In the scientific periodial Nature (July 2005) he formulates it as follows: "Apparently our thirst for novelty begins in the eye itself." A quick googling of the name Markus Meister will lead anyone interested to both this and other articles on the subject.

3 Railways and photography are not only historical precursors of film, they are also very often motifs in them. Film is historically linked with a number of other technical advances such as the car, the phone and the phonograph – broadly speaking there is hardly a feature film without a car chase, a telephone scene or a filmed musical sequence. But the train and the photograph play a quite special role as metaphors of motion and stillness respectively. As a textbook example of the linkage of the train, the still photo and the fascination of the new, modern world, one can for example watch the introductory

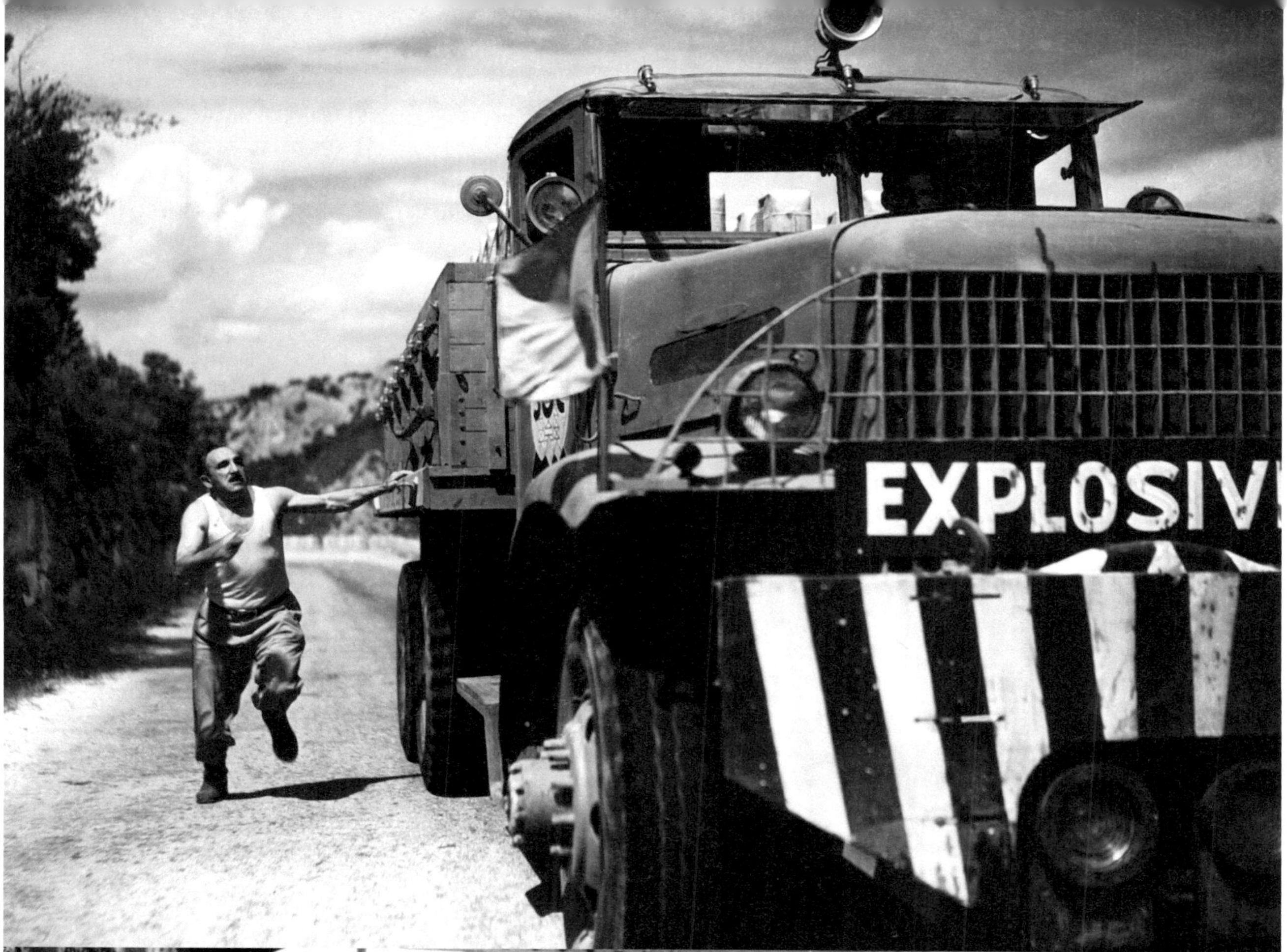
EXPLOSIV

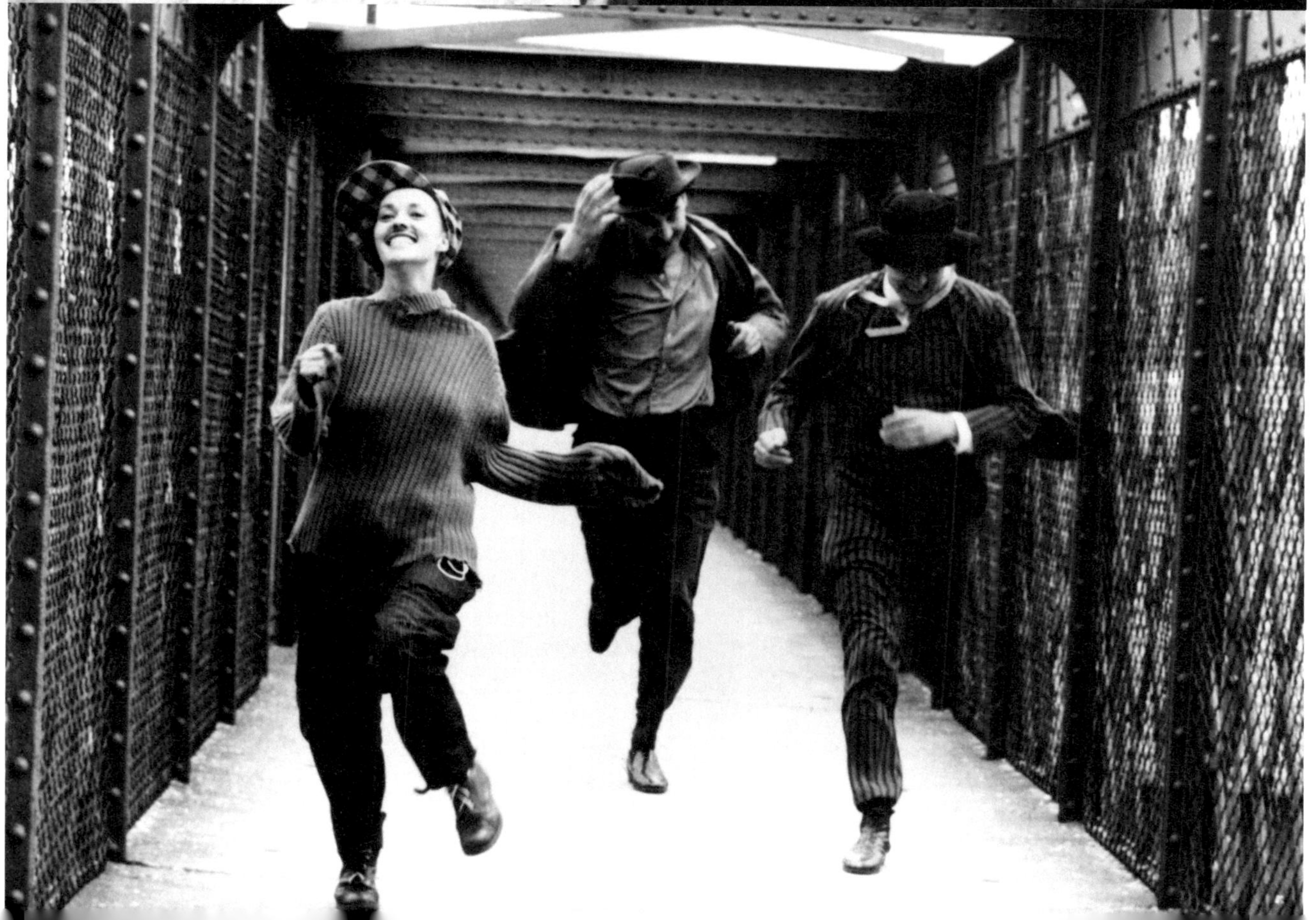

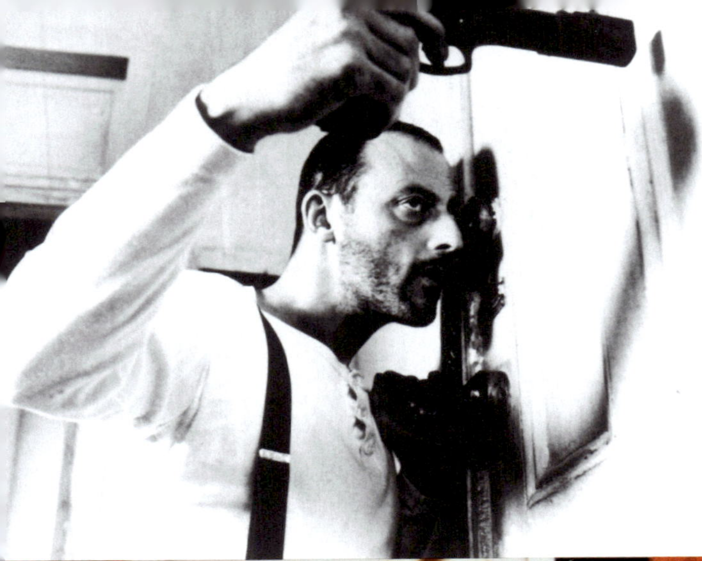

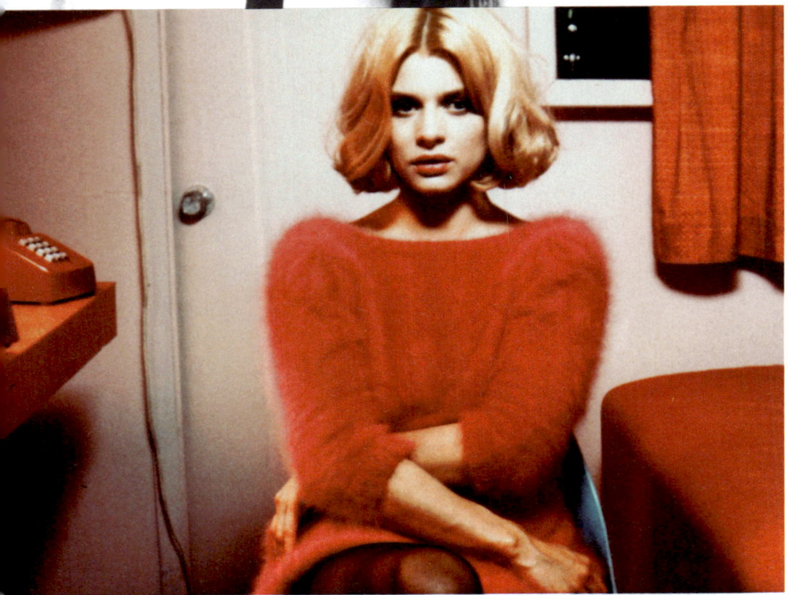

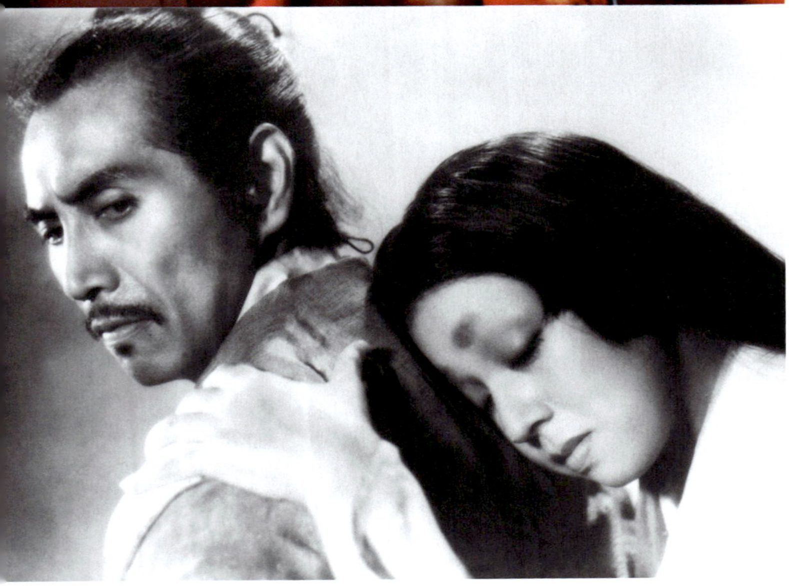

sequence in the German director Walter Ruttmann's *Berlin – die Sinfonie der Großstadt* (1927), where we move on a train through the landscape in towards Berlin. The views from the train, first rural areas, later more and more urban landscapes, and finally the mighty industrial complexes on the edge of the city – are cross-cut with the train's power transmission details: the engine, the couplings, the locomotive. When we have arrived in the city and the train has stopped, we first see a series of lingering, fixed camera shots of the city in a bird's-eye view, before the first people and the first motion appear. For further reading, see Wolfgang Schievelbuschs' *Geschichte der Eisenbahnreise*, Fischer Verlag 1977.

[4] "The Stereoscope and The Stereograph", in *Atlantic Monthly* no. 3, June 1859.

[5] I will refrain from offering examples of all the doomy prophecies published over the years on the theme that "we are heading for the new Middle Ages", only noting that even gifted and knowledgeable critics like Susan Sontag have expressed concern about the capacity of the photograph to undermine our sense of reality. A fine exhibition of film stills in Switzerland fifteen years ago was called *Emotions Made in Hollywood* – the title captured the criticism, the sense of the Utopian potential and respect for distinctiveness of the profession: the still photographer as our vicarious memory and experience engine.

[6] In cognitive linguistics the phenomenon is called conceptual integration or 'double-scope blending'; the leading researchers in the field are Gilles Fauconnier and Mark Turner. Anyone particularly interested can start with this website: http://markturner.org/

Léon, 1994
Director: Luc Besson
In the picture: Jean Reno
Still photographer: Patrick Camboulive
© 1994 Gaumont

Paris, Texas, 1984
Director: Wim Wenders
In the picture: Nastassja Kinski
Still photographer: Robin Holland
© Road Movies
Courtesy Reverse-Angle GmbH

Rashomon, 1951.
Director: Akira Kurosawa.
In the picture: Masayuki Mori, Machiko Kyo
© Kadokawa Herald Pictures, Inc.

Mr. Smith Goes to Washington, 1939
Director: Frank Capra
In the picture: Jean Arthur og James Stewart
Still photographer: Irving Littman
© 1939, renewed 1967 Columbia Pictures Industries, Inc.
All Rights Reserved
Courtesy of Columbia Pictures

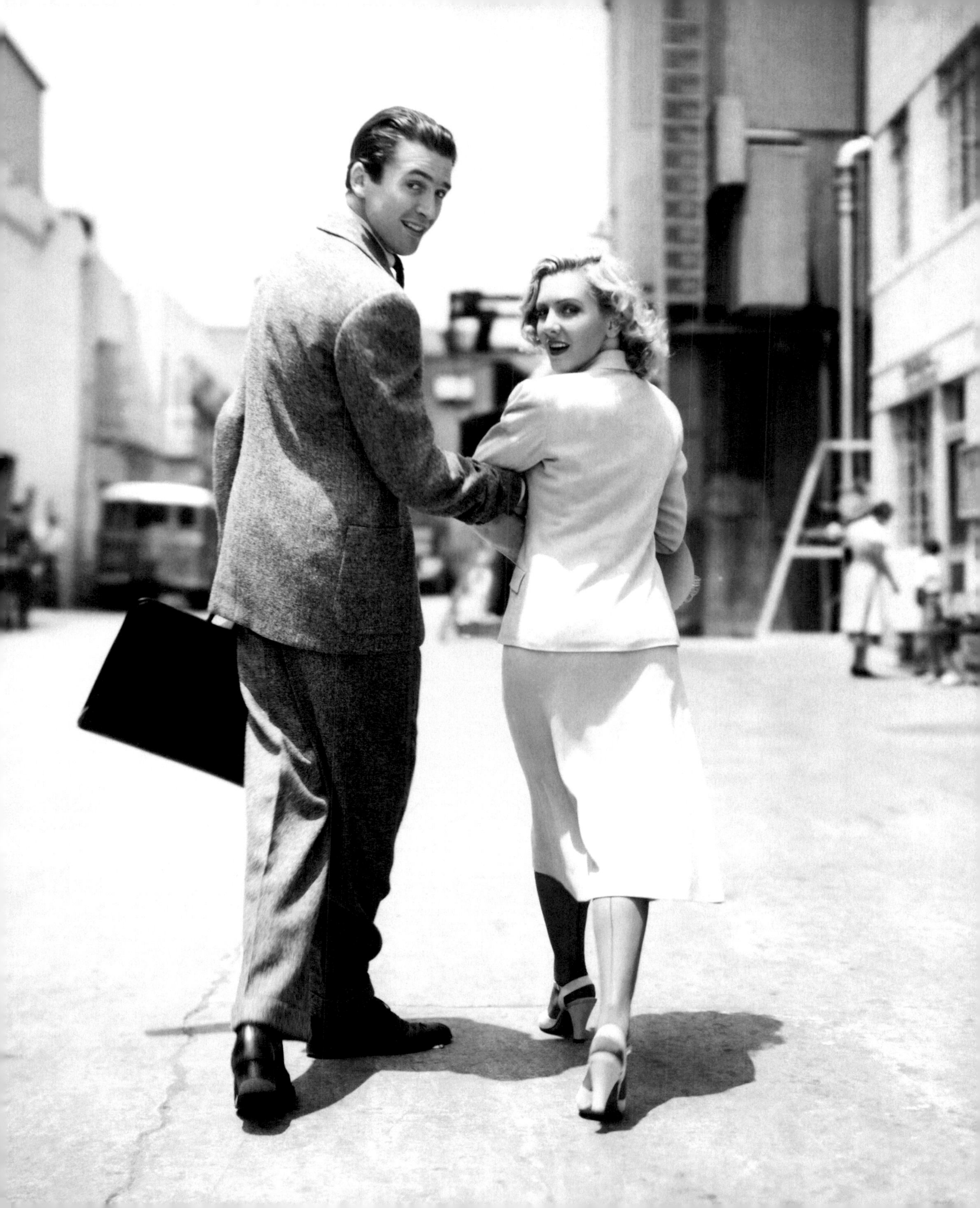

THE USUAL SUSPECTS

THE STILL IN THE HISTORY OF FILM

BY **MADELEINE SCHLAWITZ**

DFI/Stills & Posters Archive, which is part of the Danish Film Institute, houses one of the world's finest collections of stills from the whole history of the film medium. Since the Film Act of 1962 Danish distributors have had a statutory obligation to submit the material to what was then the Danish Film Museum, which means that the collection in the archive in Gothersgade has stills from more or less all Danish and foreign films that have been premiered in Denmark. With the more than 2.3 million stills in Filmhuset in Gothersgade, Copenhagen is therefore an important focus for everyone with an interest in the field: collectors, publishers, photo and film historians. Over the past ten years the archive has been headed by Madeleine Schlawitz, who talks here about the history of the film still.

"Louis, I think this is the beginning of a beautiful friendship" – most people will recognize the concluding remark in one of the world's most watched and loved films, *Casablanca* from 1942. The images and feelings that well up in our minds when the talk or the gaze turns to the film are not necessarily determined by whether we have seen it or not. For we have all at one time or another seen pictures from it, the so-called *stills*: for example the photograph of Humphrey Bogart outside Rick's club, or the picture from the final scene, where Ilsa (Ingrid Bergman), for the sake of a higher cause, must leave Rick (Bogart) to go with her husband Victor Laszlo. Both these motifs have passed into history (or at least into film history) as emblematic visualizations of great human dramas. And it is often just this that is characteristic of film stills. They are exactly the 'shots' that have come to stand for posterity as the epitome of a particular film. Ideally they show not only the frozen moment captured by the shutter, but the essence of a whole course of events; a whole atmosphere and meaning played out over time in the narrative of the film. While films are movies, as the Americans say, these classic photos with their roots in the history of photography are *stills* – they stand still while the film moves, and they have arisen as independent products during the rehearsals for or the actual shooting of the film, in America normally in the standard format 8 x 10", in Europe in 23 x 30 cm. We all know them from the display cases and foyers of the cinemas and from the newspapers, where they have typically been used as illustrations of the reviews. The main still from the film, that is the picture that has been chosen to sum up the film, its atmosphere, plot and character, is also used as an integral part of the film *poster*. Thus an isolated still or portrait is given the job of epitomizing all the expectations of the public with regard to the film and its content. Many people will perhaps remember that the posters for both *Pelle the Conqueror* and *Babette's Feast*, the two Danish Oscar-winners from the 1980s, were created according to this model.

Compared with the film still, it is rather easier to see that a film poster is something 'other' than the film

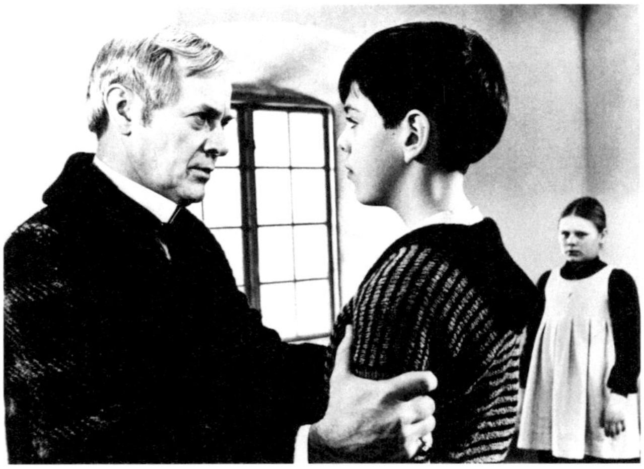

Fanny och Alexander, 1982. (Fanny and Alexander)
Director: Ingmar Bergman
In the picture: Jan Malmsjö, Bertil Guve
Still photographer: Arne Carlsson
© Svenska Filminstitutet (SFI)

itself. In this case you immediately register that an artistic temperament or at least an intention has been involved. And the poster doesn't look just like the film in the same way as the still; there is a much greater difference in the medium and the aesthetics. One thing that may have contributed to the failure to focus on the still as an independent work is its inherent status as a 'consumer disposable' that was never intended to have a lifetime beyond the period when the film was advertised in the display cases to tempt people into the cinema. Film students and film historians have both hitherto viewed the still in the same way as laymen, as a pure and simple 'illustration' of a given film. In so doing they have quite overlooked the fact that the still is a statement about the film with a unique, entirely independent value. The good still is never just an illustration of a film. It both is the film and at the same time is itself – a striking photographic statement that says: "This is what is important" or "This is what you should notice".

THE CLASSIC HOLLYWOOD STILL

Since the dawn of the age of film it has been possible to see stills related to the production of films – there are in fact documentary photos showing the still photographer at work as far back in time as 1903. Since about 1910 more or less all feature film productions have employed a still photographer. That was the time when film began to make its impact as a mass medium, and newspapers and magazines really began to demand

Les quatre cents coups, 1959. Director: François Truffaut. In the picture: Jean-Pierre Léaud, Albert Rémy
Still photographer: André Dino © Les Films du Carosse. Sédif Productions

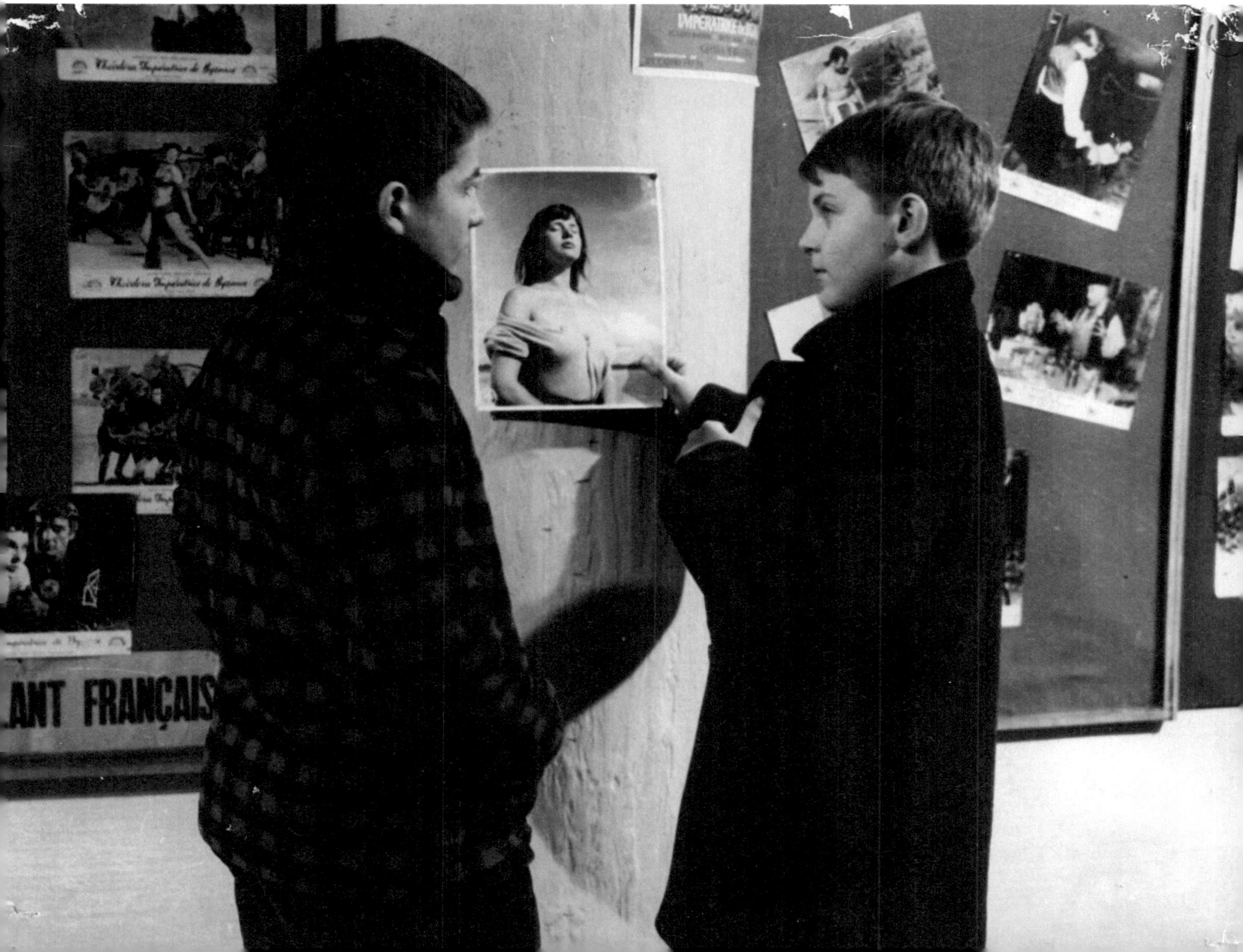

still photographs – which were also used on posters and in decided fan magazines. The history of film stills is of course inextricably linked with the history of film in general; from short films to feature films, the whole explosive development of the film industry and the rapidly growing audiences. In the great days of Hollywood, all the big film companies like MGM, Universal and RKO had a decided stills departments with a host of photographers who often had their own specialties and (as is in fact still the case today) were incredibly able photographers – Virgil Apger, Eric Carpenter and Bud Graybill from Metro Goldwyn Mayer; Jack Freulich and Ray Jones from Universal; Elmer Fryer and Bert Longworth from Warner Brothers; Madison Lacy, Al St. Hilaire, Scotty Welbourne, and a string of other photographers, all of whom have experienced the professional honour of seeing their pictures survive while their own names are known only to colleagues and the real nerds in the field. Something of a special status is enjoyed by Clarence Bull, who for forty years simply was MGM's stills department – today he is best known as *The Man Who Shot Garbo* – the apt title of his biography. If you look today at a picture of the great star, the mysterious Greta Garbo, it is probably one of his pictures you have in front of you; he is said to have been the only photographer she trusted. Bull also photographed stills for *The Wizard of Oz* and a number of other well known films from the 20s, 30s and 40s.

However, other photographers also had outstanding careers, extending over decades and beyond the normal range of subjects. The photographer Ruth Harriet Louise was able to make a name for herself in a profession that was otherwise completely male-dominated. Harriet Louise too was associated with MGM and photographed a number of well known films from the 20s including *The Big Parade* from 1925 and *Flesh and the Devil* from 1926 with Greta Garbo in the starring role. She managed to become MGM's official photographer in the years 1925-1930, a period when the company's prestige was at its highest and its stars were Hollywood's biggest. Over a five-year period she photographed more than 100,000 stills and portraits, and today she is often compared to the other great photographer of the era, George Hurrell. Together they were at the forefront of the development of the photographic genre that goes under the name of 'glamour photography'. Glamour photography is more an aesthetic style than an actual technique, and is also often called 'the Hurrell Style'. In the typical, classic Hollywood portraits – for example the double portrait of Cary Grant and Katherine Hepburn in *Bringing up Baby* from 1938 – you immediately see the technique in use and you understand what it is that constitutes the glamorous.

FROM PROGRAMME NOTE TO NOUVELLE VAGUE

The content of a typical set of stills for a film has of course changed over the more than 110 years that have passed since 1894, when the world first made the acquaintance of the phenomenon of film. In the prime of the Danish silent film from 1900 until the end of the 1920s the pictures were to a great extent meant to illustrate the printed programme that belonged to each film show. The films were still without sound, so the plot could sometimes be difficult to grasp for the moviegoers of the day, even when they had the sporadically inserted screen texts to read. The point of departure was thus a text that had to be illustrated. So all the crucial plot twists had to be acted over again and photographed so no one could be in any doubt about what was happening on the screen. Sometimes you can even see from the Danish Film Institute's collection that *everything* is thoroughly photographed – you can simply lay the stills end to end and work out the plot in detail. At the same time there is a wealth of cast portraits – that is, pictures of the actors in costume – but these are unlikely to have been used as anything but reference material during the filming. At all events portraits are extremely rare in the silent film programmes.

Later in the history of film, right up until the 1940s, stills from both Danish and foreign films continued to look more or less like that. It is of course difficult as a museum of cultural history to say what kind of material originally existed – we know what we have, but we don't know what we *could* have had. Looking at our collections today, there is every indication that there were very considerable quantities of pictures, and that in the course of time the pictures change in character and bear witness to social and economic shifts within the industry. For example we can note that in the forties the *director* has become an important person – there are often several pictures of the director, both in dialogue with the principal actors and during shooting. You can also see that pictures are now taken on location; the genesis of the film becomes more important, interest in the processual in the world of film grows.

This tendency is clear all the way up to the end of

Bringing up Baby, 1938
Director: Howard Hawks
In the picture: Cary Grant, Katharine Hepburn

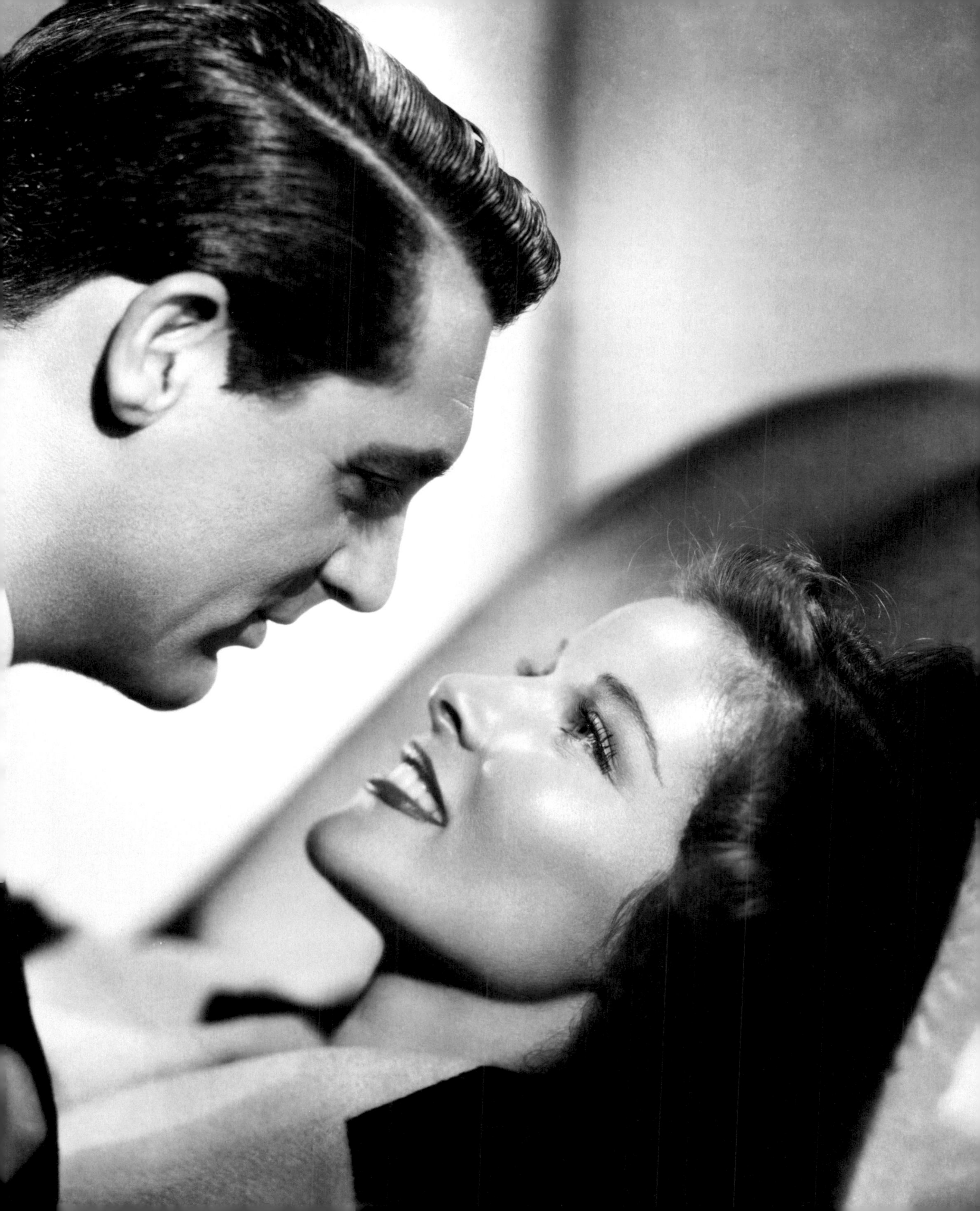

the 1950s, but then something happens: a brand new type of subject emerges in the course of the 1960s: pictures that can be described as inciting appetizers rather than simple markers of parts of the action of the film, spot reports from the narrative sequence. These are literally thought-provoking pictures: what is happening here? Rather than trying to render vividly the instant the photographer has seen through the viewfinder, the stills arouse a desire in the viewer to find out what the plot of the film actually is. What does it tell us, make us experience or make us think about? The still becomes more ambivalent and shifts further and further away from the directly illustrative. This tendency is most clearly played out in French films. A good example is stills from the French New Wave films, for example *Pierrot le Fou* by Jean-Luc Godard from 1965 (see the picture in this catalogue, p. 39).

STILLS AS DOCUMENTATION

The still photograph is often the only visible proof – apart from the film itself – that the film project has in fact taken place. The stills from the film are in that sense historical source material. Film stills share this documentary quality with all other photographs under the sun: photos always involve an underlying statement that what you see here has actually taken place. More conscious use of the documentary function can be found in the case of a whole succession of film titles from the 1950s and 1960s – especially the American ones. Many of the great photographers of the period 'discovered' the still as an artistic idiom, or at least that filming offered an interesting range of subjects. The best example is probably the international photography group MAGNUM's project with John Huston's film *The Misfits* from 1961. During the shooting a string of the

Shichinin no samurai, 1954 (Seven Samirai). Director: Akira Kurosawa. In the picture: Takashi Shimura, Yukiko Shimazaki
Still photographer: Masao Fukuda © 1954 Toho Co. Ltd.

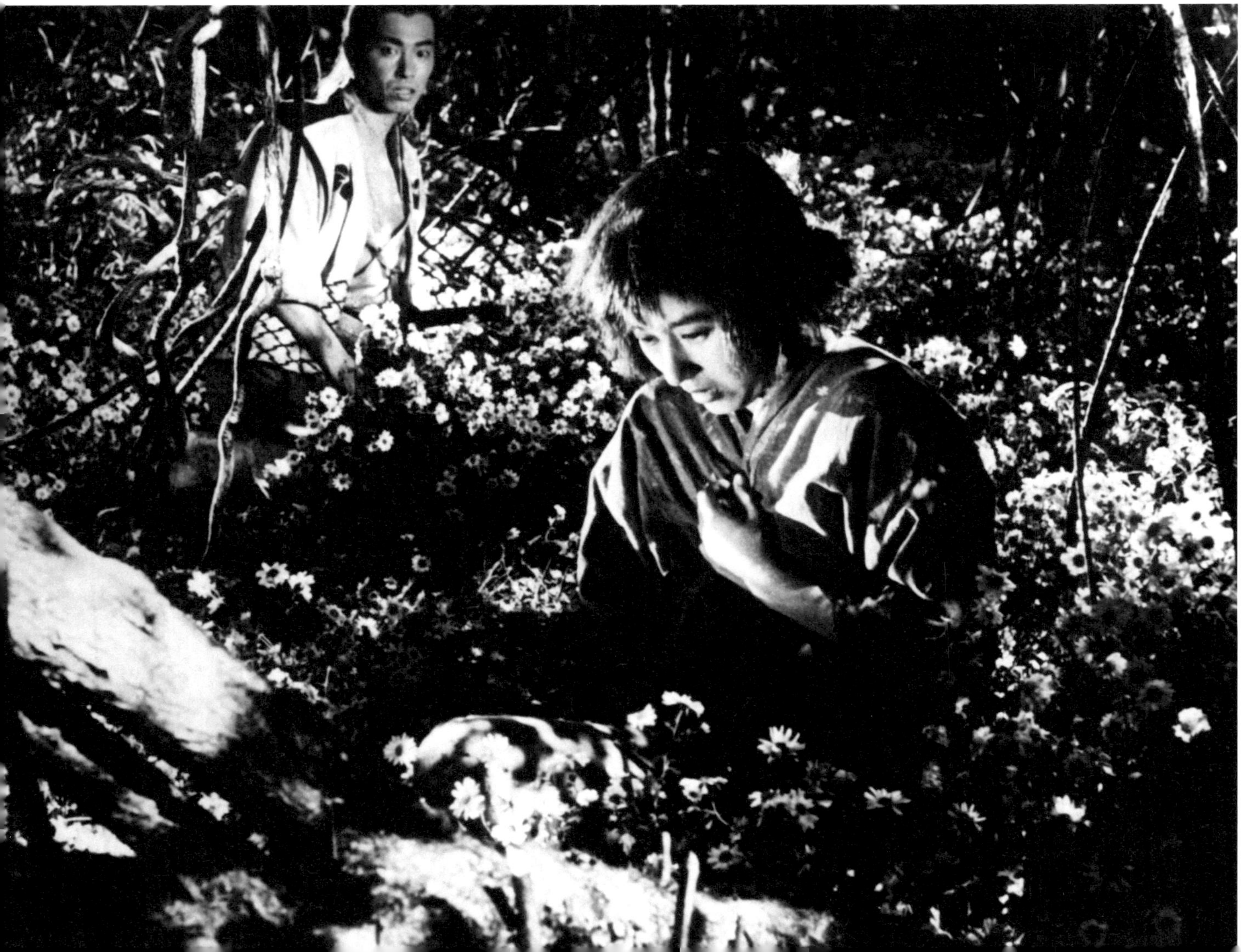

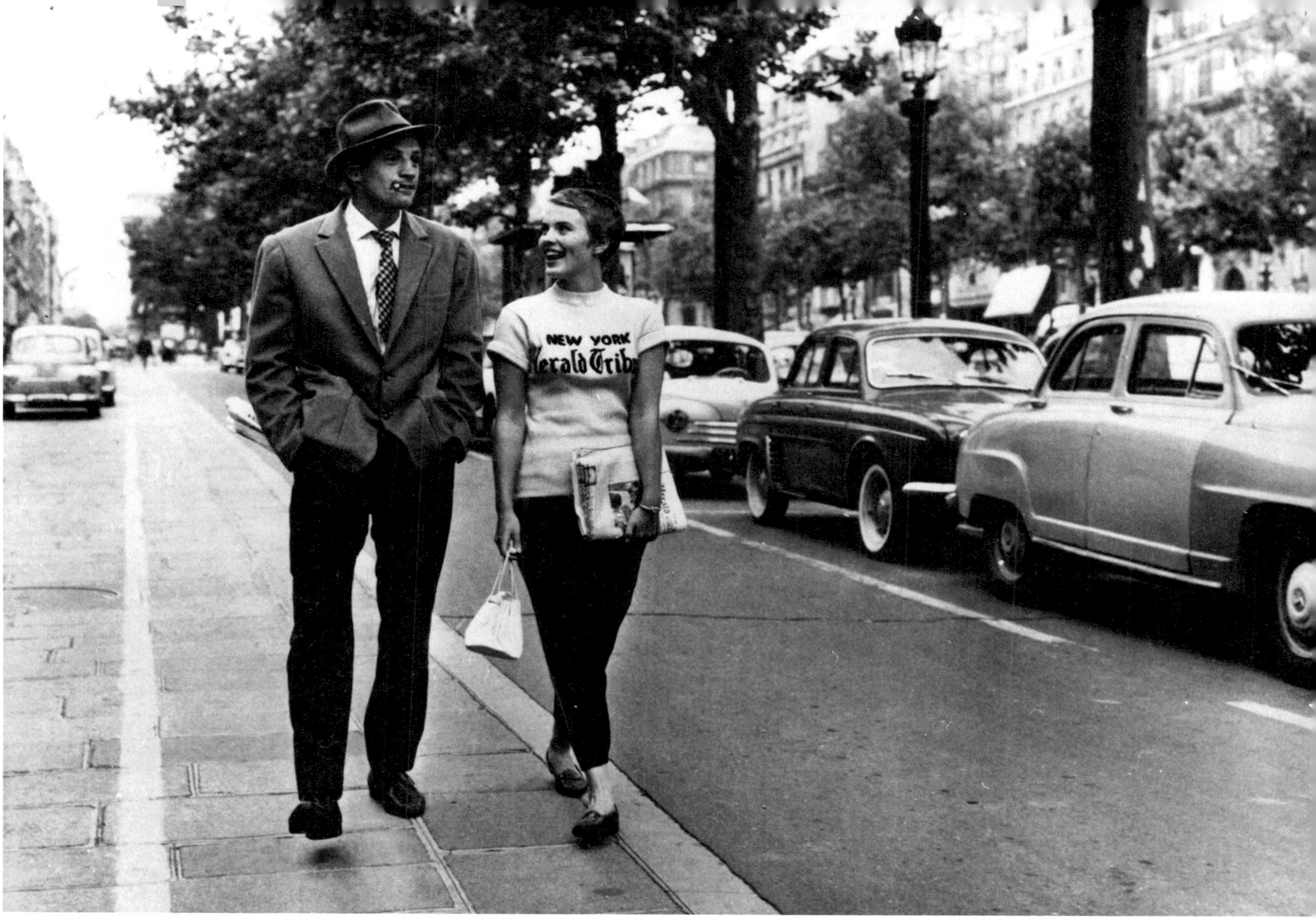

À bout de souffle, 1960. Director: Jean-Luc Godard. In the picture: Jean-Paul Belmondo, Jean Seberg
© Still photographer: Raymond Cauchetier. StudioCanal France

group's photographers visited the set and took hundreds of pictures. The world-famous photographer Henri Cartier-Bresson led the expedition; the photographers arrived on the set in pairs and took turns to cover the events two weeks at a time. The result of this experiment, where one of the best film directors of the time, some of the best and most charismatic actors, and world-class photographers from the outside worked together, can be studied today in detail on the Internet,[1] and the pictures provide rare insight into what can happen when top-class film and photography meet. The pictures from this film are surrounded by a special magic and mystery, partly because they have a quite unique quality and a different character from many contemporary film stills, and partly because *The Misfits* was to be the last film of both the Hollywood legend Clark Gable and one of the world's most beautiful and most photographed women, Marilyn Monroe.

Amidst a world of fictions – quite literally because we work in the film industry, but also in the broader sense of the fictionalization of reality – both we at the Danish Film Institute Stills & Posters Archive and our colleagues in the institutions with which we collaborate are experiencing an exponential growth in interest in background stills and production stills. For an average American film production, at least until around 1960, there are often several thousand pictures that document the production process in all its details. After 1960, on the other hand, the archives typically only have the pictures from the film production that were used as press pictures, and a similar development can be seen in Denmark.

THE STILLS OF THE FUTURE

In recent years the tendency has changed once again. A set of stills for the typical mainstream Hollywood film will normally be an official press set – the pictures that have been approved for use in the specific country where the film is premiered. Among these pictures, typically 6-8 stills, there will also be the picture we call the main still, i.e. the one that has been selected by the production top to be the 'face' of the film. Often it is precisely this, or at least the same very few pictures, that you see reproduced everywhere in the media when the film is premiered. One of the most important parameters to consider in the promotion of a film is *recognizability*, while at the same time – at any rate according to the still photographers themselves – there is no longer the same focus on and respect for the importance of their work as there once was. From the point of view of the archivist – or let us say more generally the museum, the contemporary historian, posterity – this is an impoverishment. The stills whose bottom-line justification is to sell the film become important historical source material even in the medium term. Film stills are an important key to the understanding of the fascination of film art – the still is after all often the first thing we see, if not *from* the film, at least *of* it, whether it is on the DVD cover, on the cinema poster or at the film's official website.

Of course it is still immensely important for the PR people for a given film to have the right stills available when the film is to have coverage in the media and people are to be tempted into the cinema. But with the

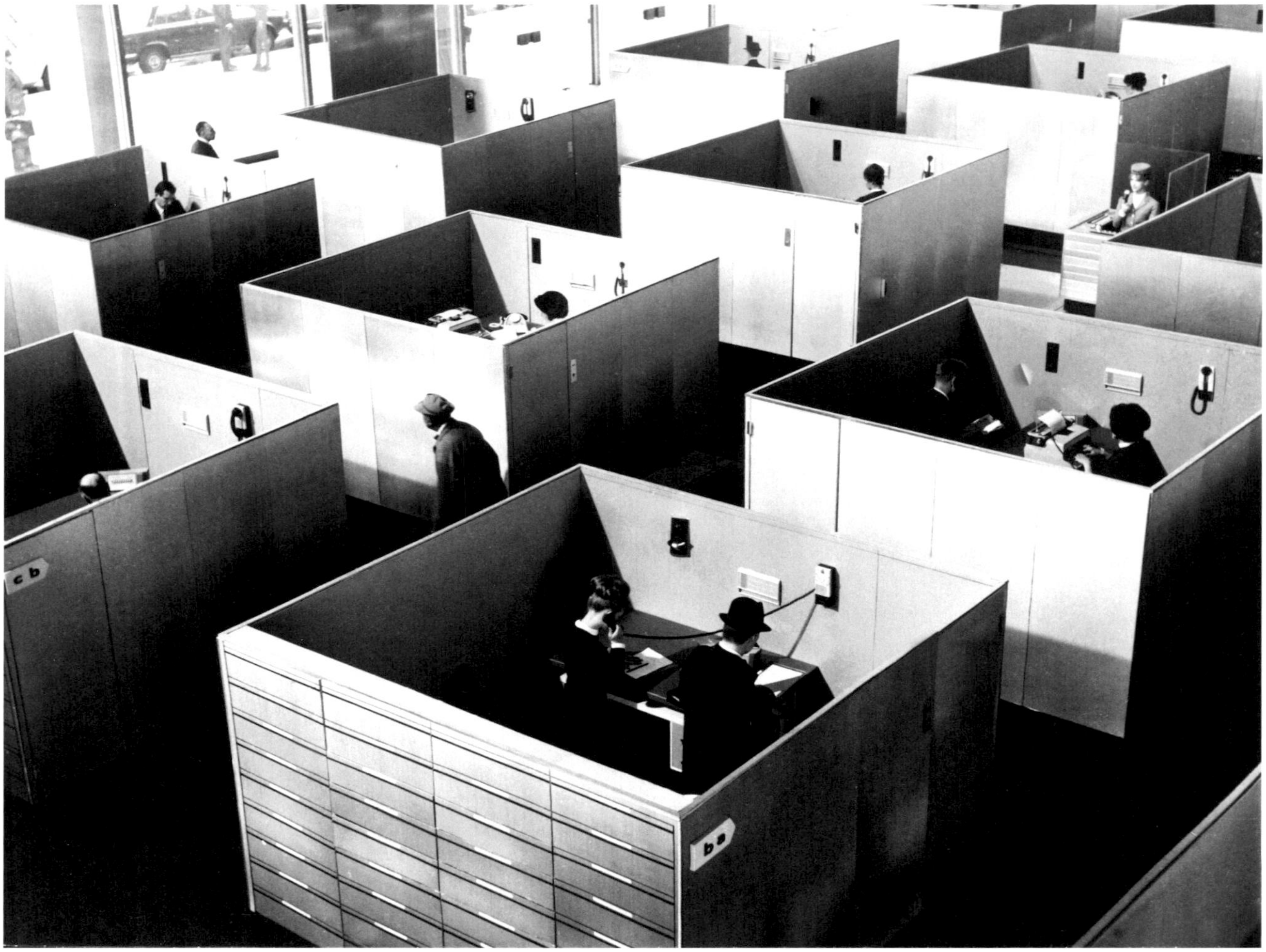

Playtime, 1967
Director: Jacques Tati
Still photographer: J. L. Castelli, André Dino
© Les Films de Mon Oncle

Arabesque, 1966
Director: Stanley Donen
In the picture: Sophia Loren
© 1966 Universal Studios

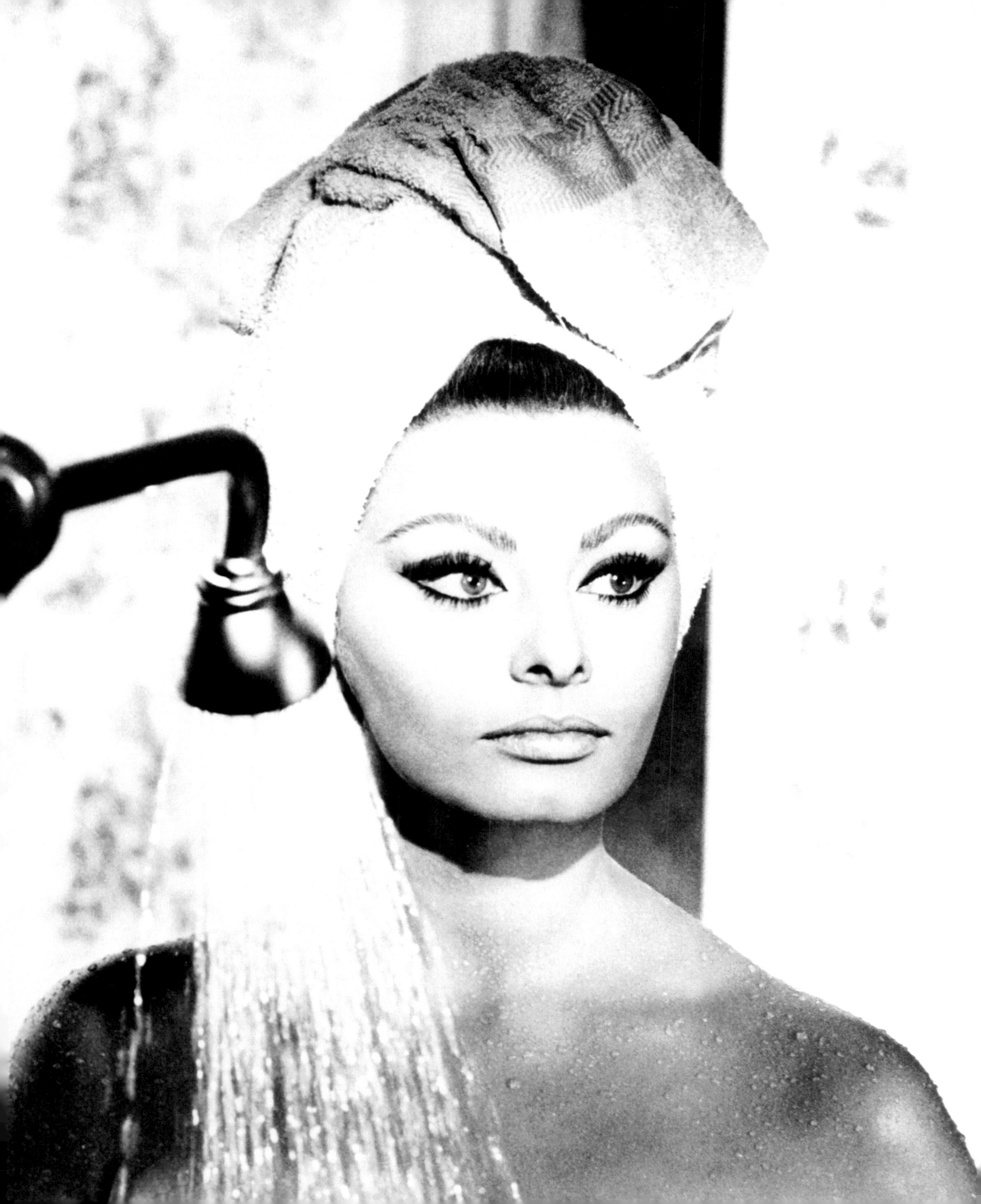

spread of the Internet, audiences now often look for their information about films in new ways – a lot of information about the film is already available before its premiere. The time has long passed when the still was a perfect print made by the photographer. A minor technical revolution in photography equipment and the whole transition from analog to digital photography has meant that all material from films is now available electronically, and stills for films are something you download from the film companies' websites – increasingly in the form of so-called *framegrabs*; pictures copied directly from the physical film. You could say that in these cases the cameraman, consciously or unconsciously, creates the still as part of his work and thus takes over the role of the still photographer. All artistic expression is of course dependent on the conditions of its time – at present we can only guess whether the fusion of the cameraman's and the still photographer's jobs is the result of a natural and inevitable development, or just a sign that the rationalization of the process has gone too far. Framegrabs can be manipulated in digital imaging programmes – in that respect their use represents technical progress and a processual simplification, but they are no longer stills in the traditional sense.

However, a proud still photography tradition continues. If we must accept on the one hand that the venerable profession of still photographer – and thus the ideas that the pictures can give us of the mysterious and inciting world of the film – has been in decline for a period, at the same time there is much to indicate that this tendency has gradually peaked, at least here where we work, in Denmark. Looking at the stills for some recent film titles, there is a clear tendency towards a renewed special emphasis on this part of production – a dawning awareness that it is the accurately observed moments or staged situations that can and must sell the film. As an example of this development I can mention Dagur Kári's film *Dark Horse* from 2005.

NEW RECOGNITION

Film stills have been able to arouse so much attention from the established art world in 2006 that Louisiana has chosen to make them the subject of a major exhibi-

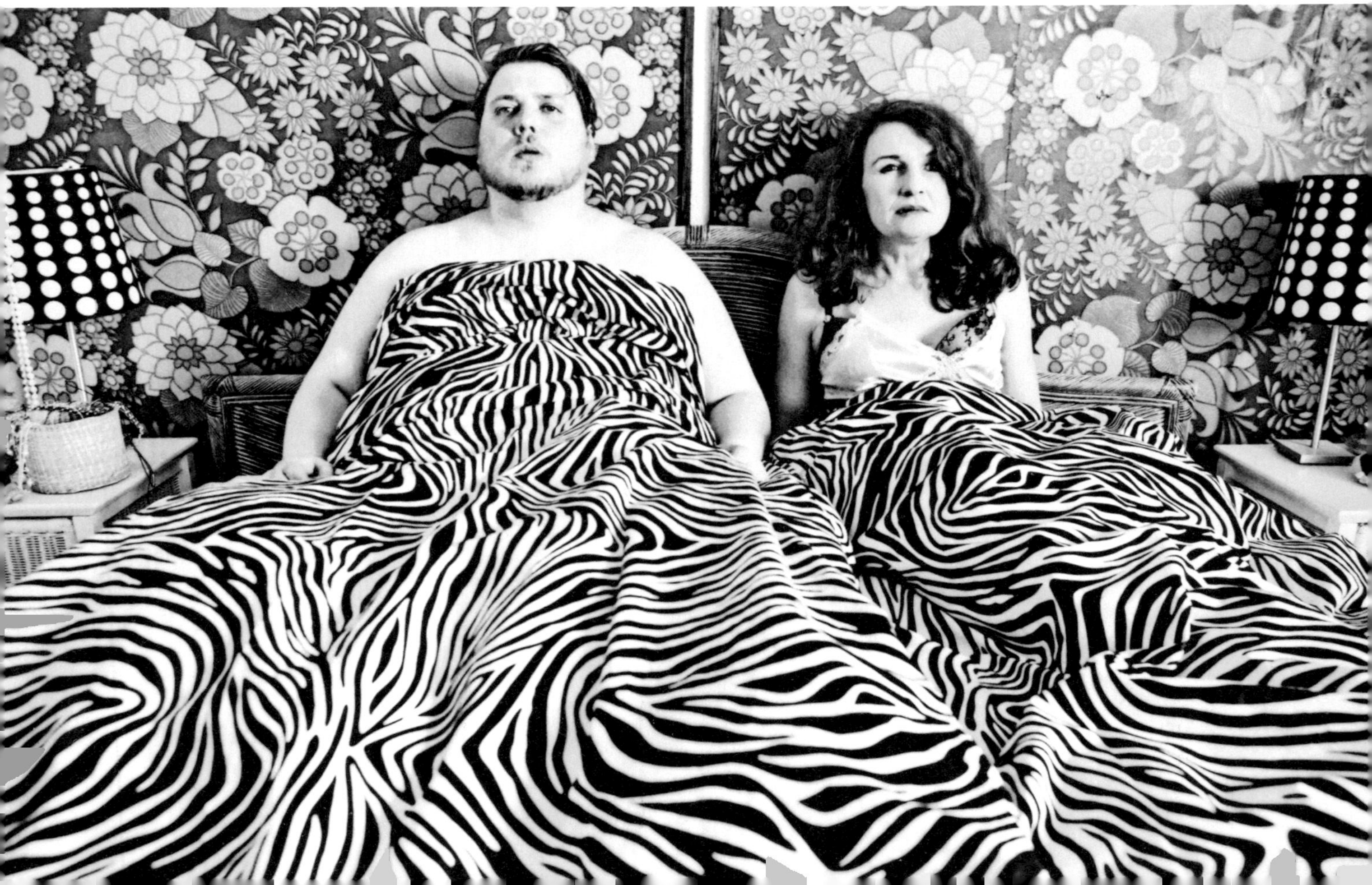

tion. This says something about the enduring power of these underappreciated visual jewels. In recent times film stills have gained a status as esteemed, valuable and not least saleable collectors' items. For years collectors and *aficionados* have collected, bought and traded original stills at prices that have in time grown relatively high, for example at websites devoted to the various big names of the glory days of Hollywood. But stills and portraits from more recent times – and from films that have been premiered this year – or yesterday for that matter – are also collectors' items. At auctions of graphic works, original stills are being offered for sale more and more often. If you are lucky enough to find an original print from a well known Hollywood film in the attic, it can be worth a lot of money. The expert collector will quickly make an offer in a net auction. In other words there is a dawning understanding that this is, if not established art, at least a *kind of* artistic expression. In this way film stills are sharing the fate of other kinds of 'anonymous' photography, which has also been drawing attention over the past few years.

The still photograph often resembles other kinds of photographic art. As viewers we may think that it sometimes *is* photographic art. Louisiana's exhibition is doing a lot to establish that film stills taken out of their original context can be experienced this way. So in many ways we are seeing a shift in the use and status of the still.

Against the background of the pictures that have been produced over the years, the film industry has been able to create a whole fan culture – just think of the classic 'glamour shots' that could be pasted into the film enthusiast's scrapbook – preferably signed. The fan culture has in turn generated a merchandise industry that no longer places as much emphasis on the still photograph. But if you ask which pictures are sold most, for example through the Internet-based sales outlet www.allposters.com, among the big hits you will find a wealth of film stills that are published as postcards, fan photos and posters. Stills from both recent and older films still have the power to fascinate us so much that we want to have them hanging in our homes – to remind us of good film experiences, and perhaps just as much to remind ourselves and others of who we are and what we stand for. After all, there is nothing coincidental about the pictures we choose to surround ourselves with in our everyday lives.

Madeleine Schlawitz, b. 1966. Head of Stills & Posters Archive, the Danish Film Institute.

1. See the website http://www.pbs.org/wnet/gperf/shows/misfits/multimedia/intro.html

Voksne mennesker, 2005
(Dark Horse)
Director: Dagur Kári
In the picture: Nicolas Bro, Bodil Jørgensen
Still photographer: Henrik Ohsten Rasmussen
© Nimbus Film 2005
DFI / Stills & Posters Archive

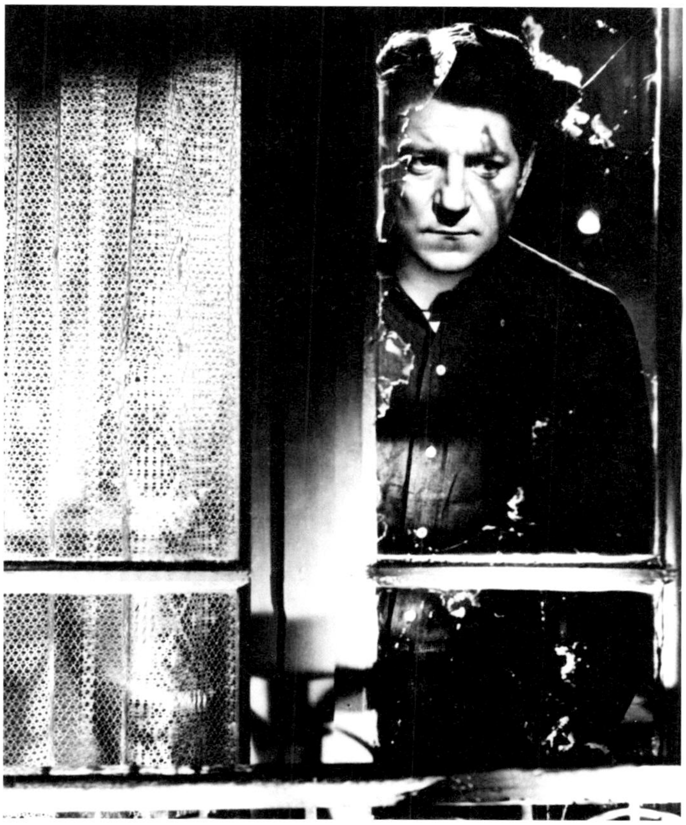

Le jour se lève, 1939
Director: Marcel Carné
In the picture: Jean Gabin
© Still photographer: Raymond Voinquel. Jeu de paume

Du rififi chez les hommes, 1955
(Rififi)
Director: Jules Dassin
In the picture: Marie Sabouret, Robert Hossein

The Encounter: The transient and the life-changing, the blissful and the final. Man is a social animal; all desire seeks out the other – only there do we truly find ourselves. Or escape from ourselves.

The Red Shoes, 1948
Director: Michael Powell, Emeric Pressburger
In the picture: Moira Shearer, Robert Helpmann
Still photographer: George Cannon, Cornel Lucas, Alistair Phillips

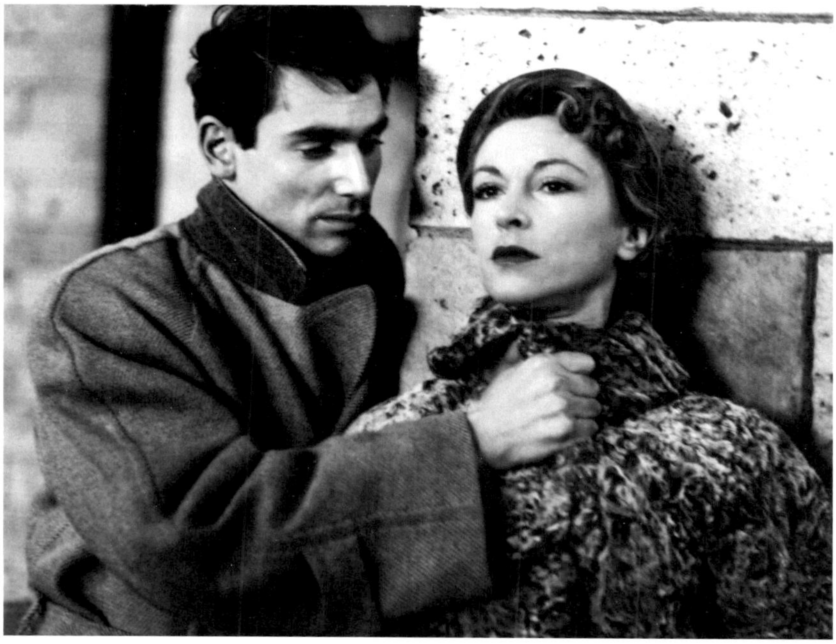

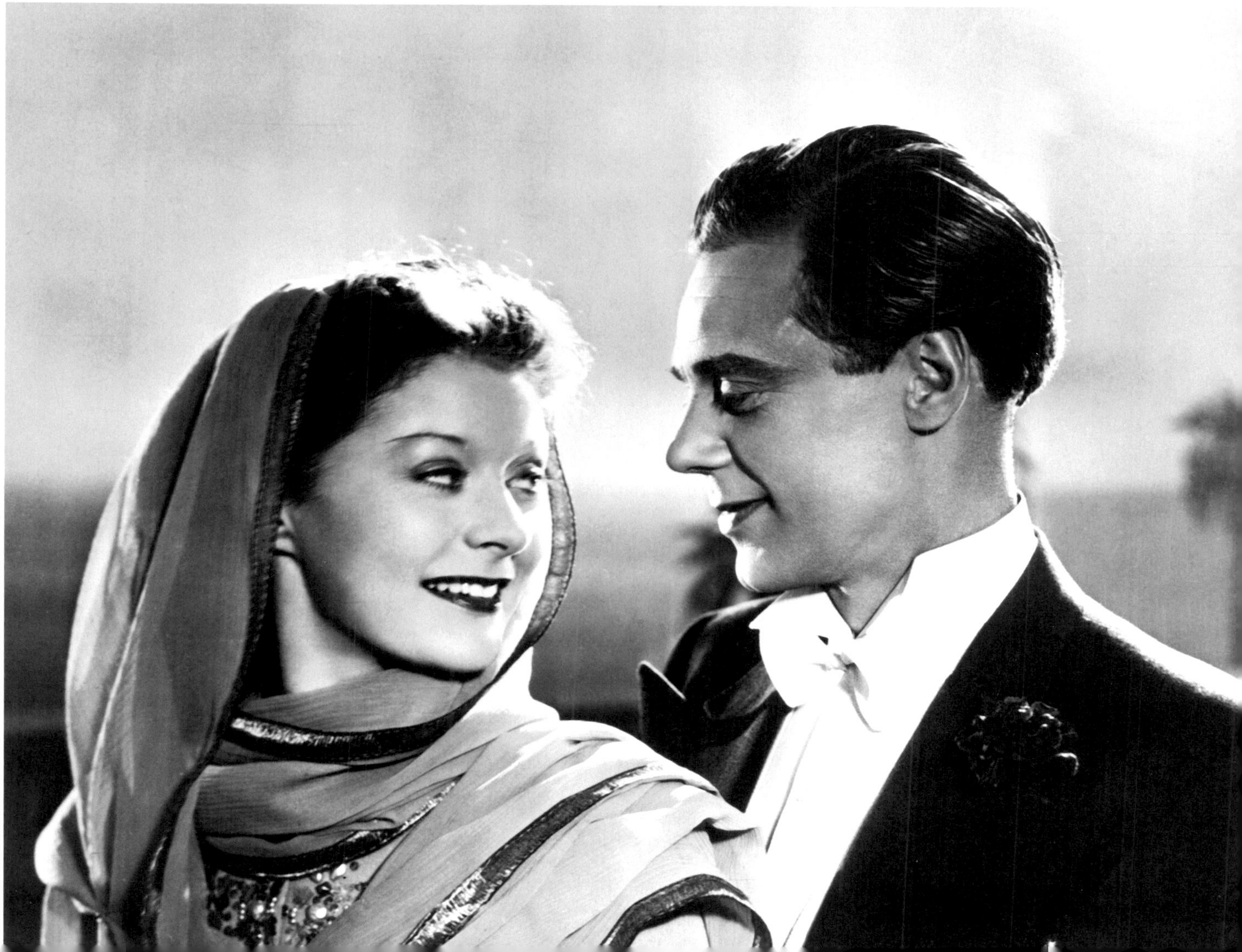

Wild at Heart, 1990
Director: David Lynch
In the picture: Nicolas Cage
Still photographer: Kimberly Wright

Nature: It isn't from films that we know nature. But maybe it's in films that we best see ourselves in it, *as* nature. And at the same time learn that it is something other than ourselves, something that overwhelms us.

Fitzcarraldo, 1981
Director: Werner Herzog
Still photographer: Beat Presser

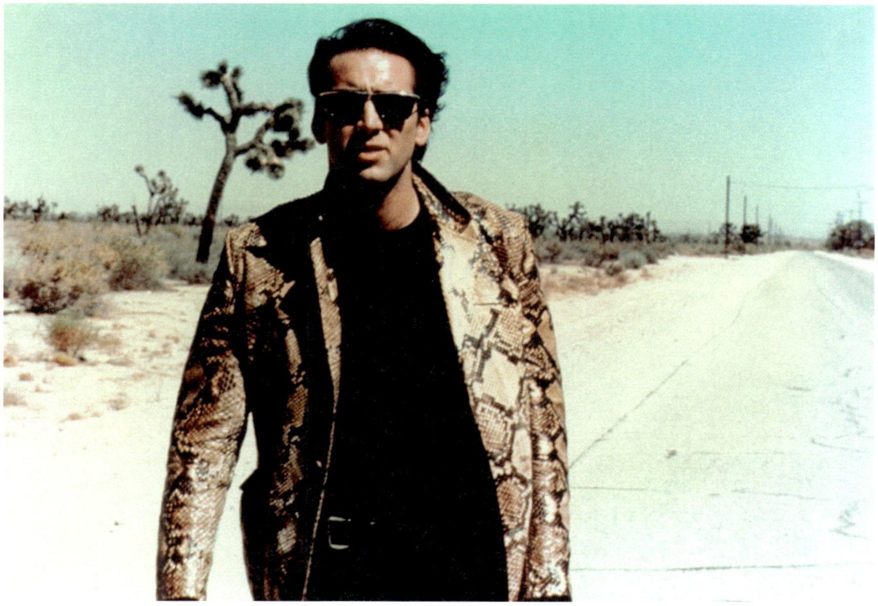

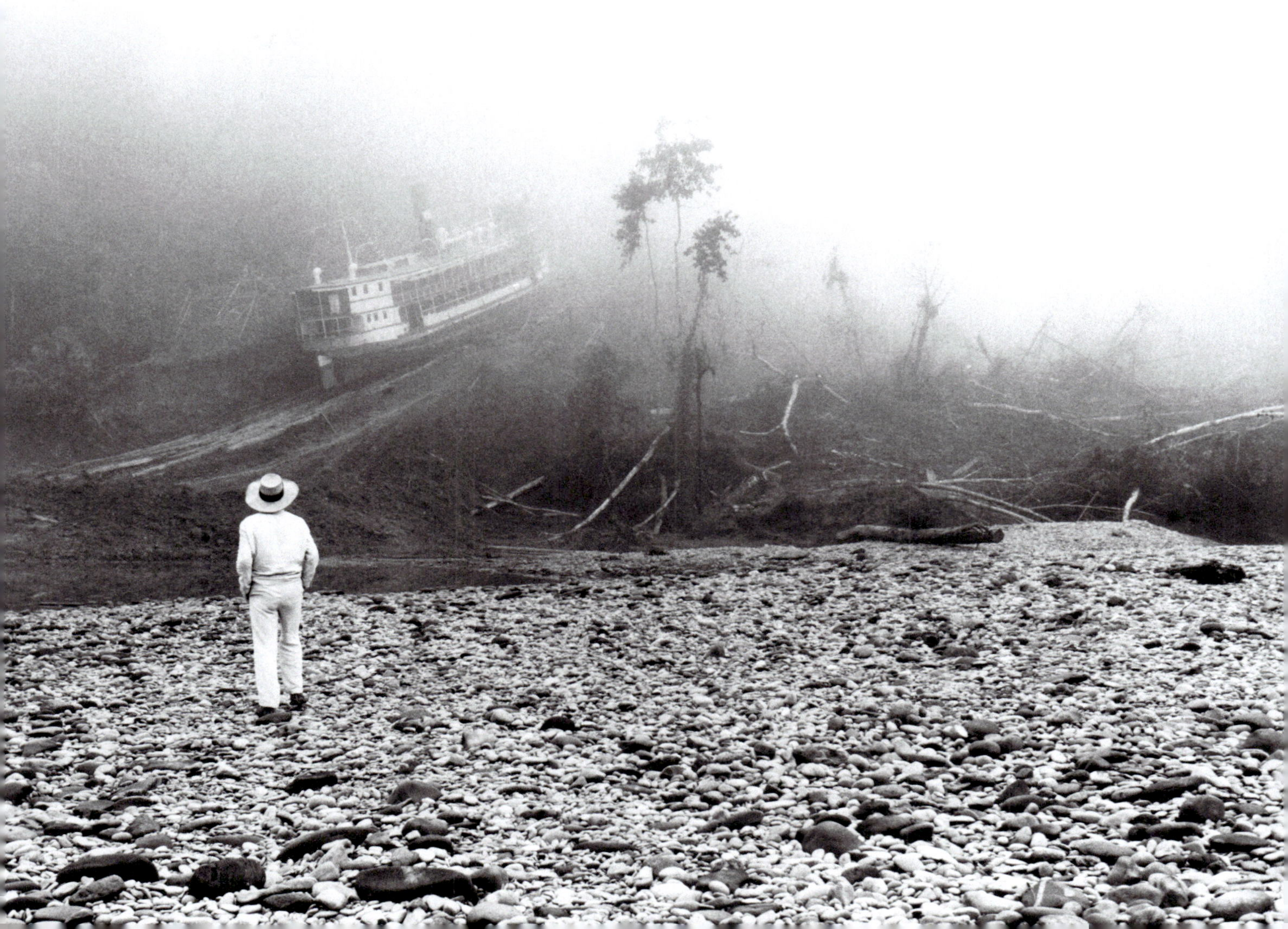

En fremmed banker på, 1959
(A Stranger Knocks)
Director: Johan Jacobsen
In the picture: Birgitte Federspiel, Preben Lerdorff Rye
Still photographer: Gergely Szabo

The Mirror: "For now we see through a glass, darkly; but then face to face" – so writes St. Paul in his First Epistle to the Corinthians about human incomprehension of the divine and the nature of love. The mirror (water surface, window ...) is an ancient symbol in our culture; in it we find an infinity of possible reflections (in all senses). And here the photographer can concentrate a dramatic sequence into one crucial moment.

Paris, Texas, 1984
Director: Wim Wenders
In the picture: Nastassja Kinski
Still photographer: Robin Holland

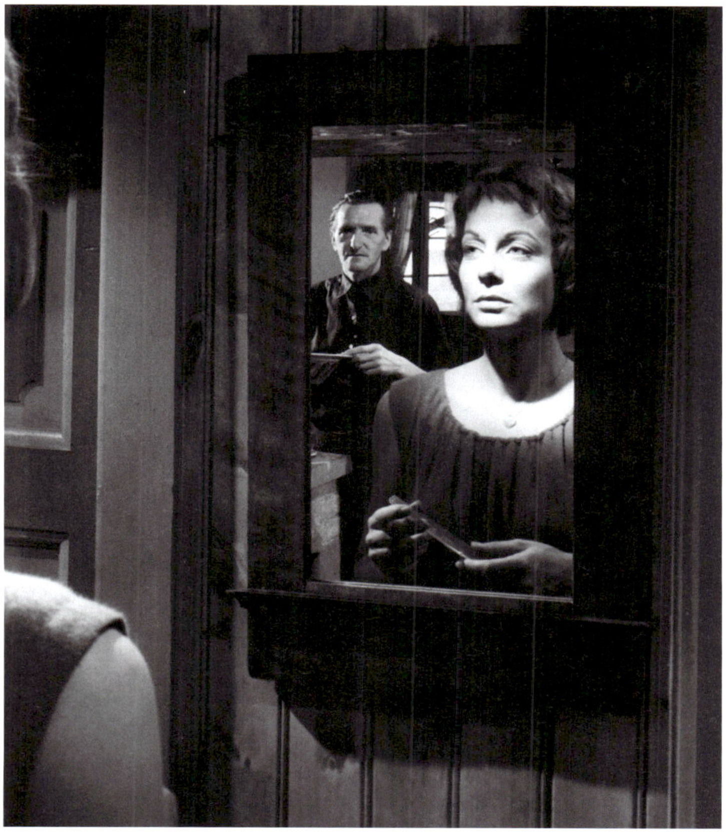

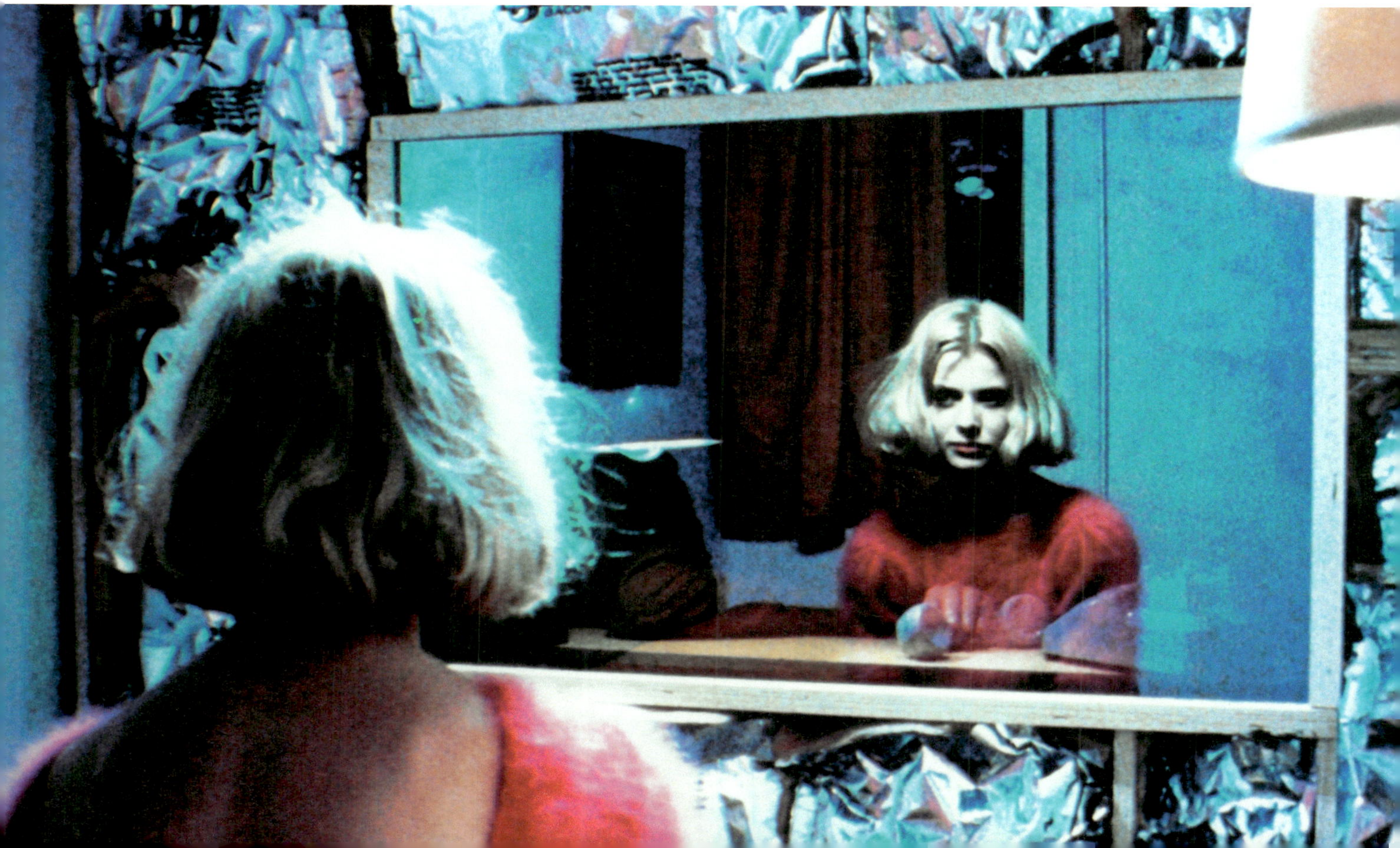

The Elephant Man, 1980
Director: David Lynch
In the picture: John Hurt
Still photographer: Frank Connor

Cityscape: A liberated zone, a continuation of the living room, but without the personal details and old hang-ups; a hiding-place; a stony landscape as alien and harsh as any wilderness; a course marked out for the everyday rat race.

American Graffiti, 1973
Director: George Lucas

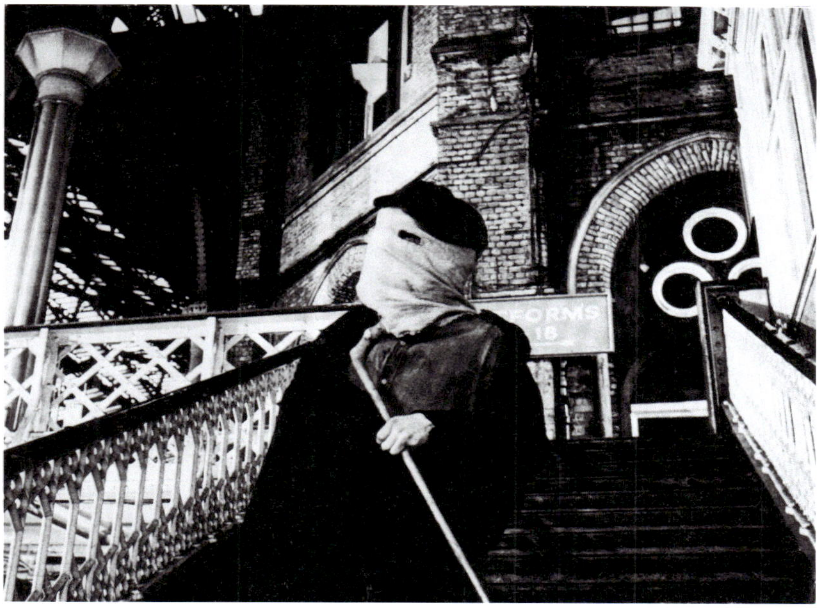

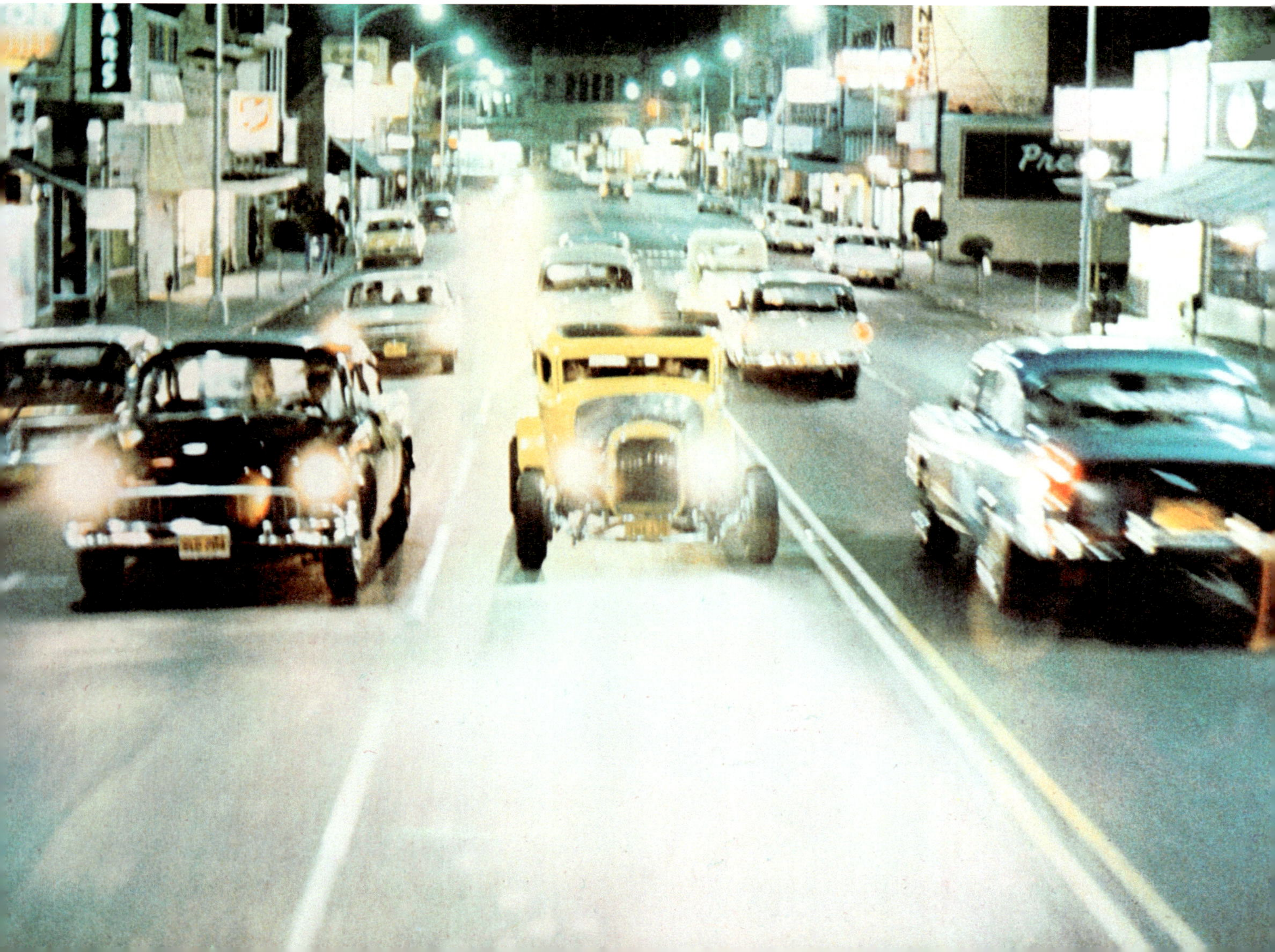

Nattevagten,1994
Director: Ole Bornedal
In the picture: Sofie Gråbøl, Nikolaj Coster-Waldau
Still photographer: Rolf Konow © Thura Film

The Kiss: How do you get something that means so much inside to look like something from the outside? Often it looks pretty awkward, but we know it's important. When the chemistry is right and the light falls as it should it's enviable – in the good sense, that is – free of true envy, just full of sighing identification.

Pierrot le Fou, 1965
Director: Jean-Luc Godard
In the picture: Anna Karina, Jean-Paul Belmondo
Still photographer: Georges Pierre ©
Société Nouvelle de la Cinématographie (SNC)

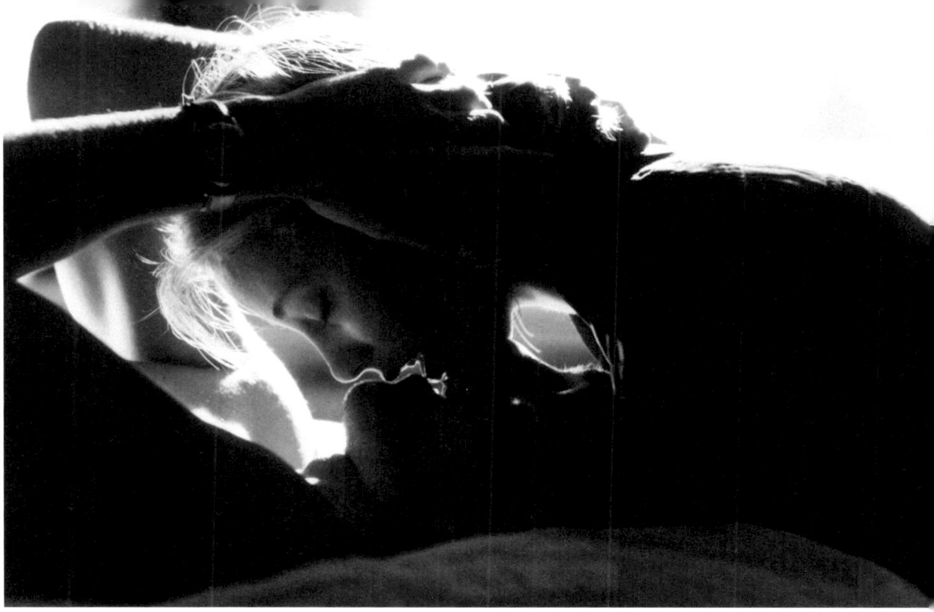

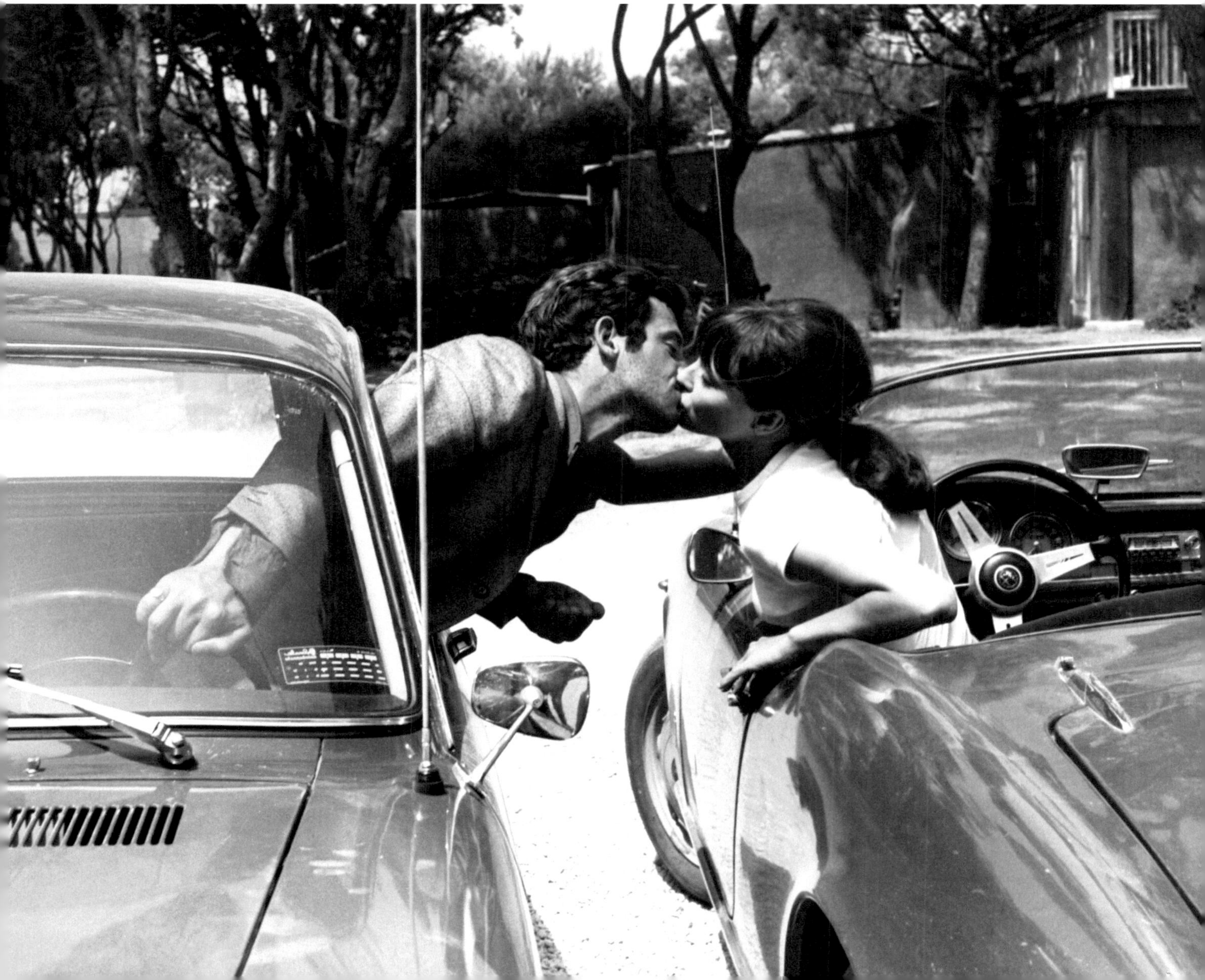

The Erotic: The French call orgasm 'the little death', and use the same phrase for abandonment and sacrifice. In the staged choreography of the still, Eros and Thanatos meet. But only rarely, for the strongest scenes are not suitable for freezing. Better to whisper about them. In the few erotic stills it is usually the face that expresses it all; sex is something that happens between the ears.

Suna No Onna, 1963
(Woman of the Dunes)
Director: Hiroshi Teshigahara
In the picture: Kyôko Kishida

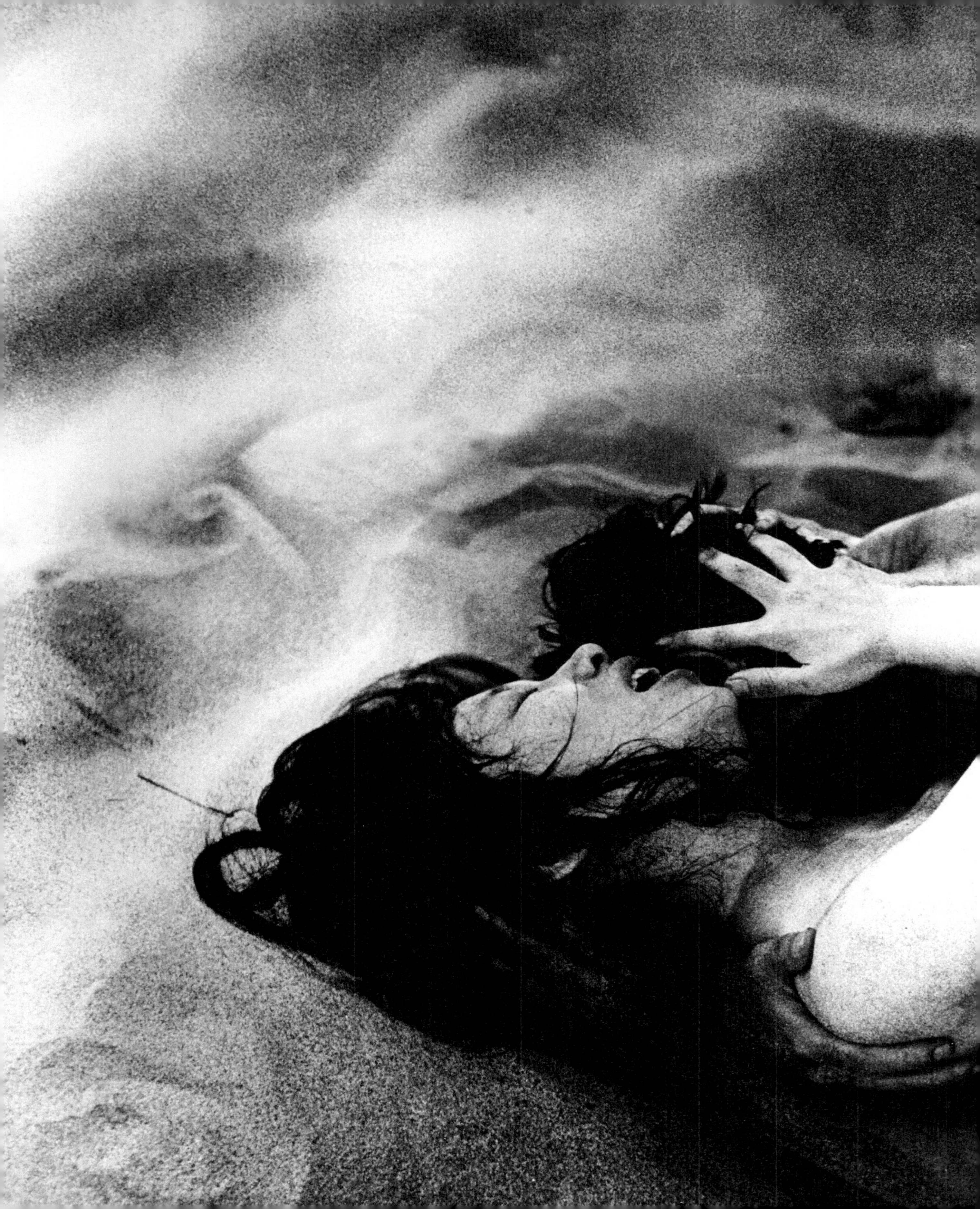

Hard Target, 1993
Director: John Woo
In the picture: Lance Henriksen

Power Play: It's nothing personal – it's much worse. It's raw power applied for a rational purpose. Or it's the realization of a secret dream of escaping all the oh-so-human reservations and considerations. The whole world reduced to a formula: my formula.

Shichinin No Samurai, 1954
(The Seven Samurai)
Director: Akira Kurosawa
In the picture: Toshirô Mifune

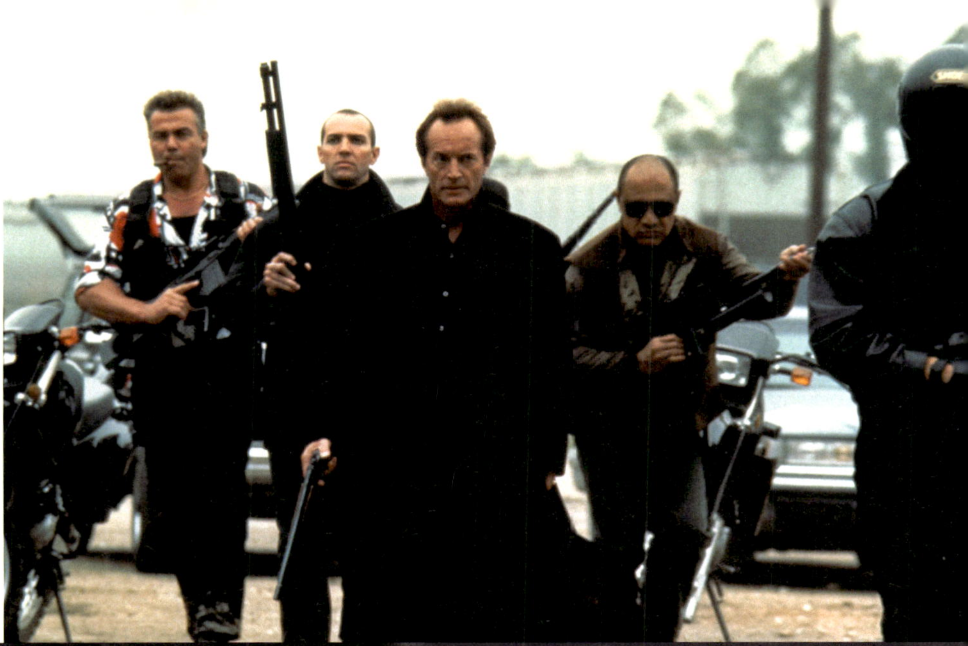

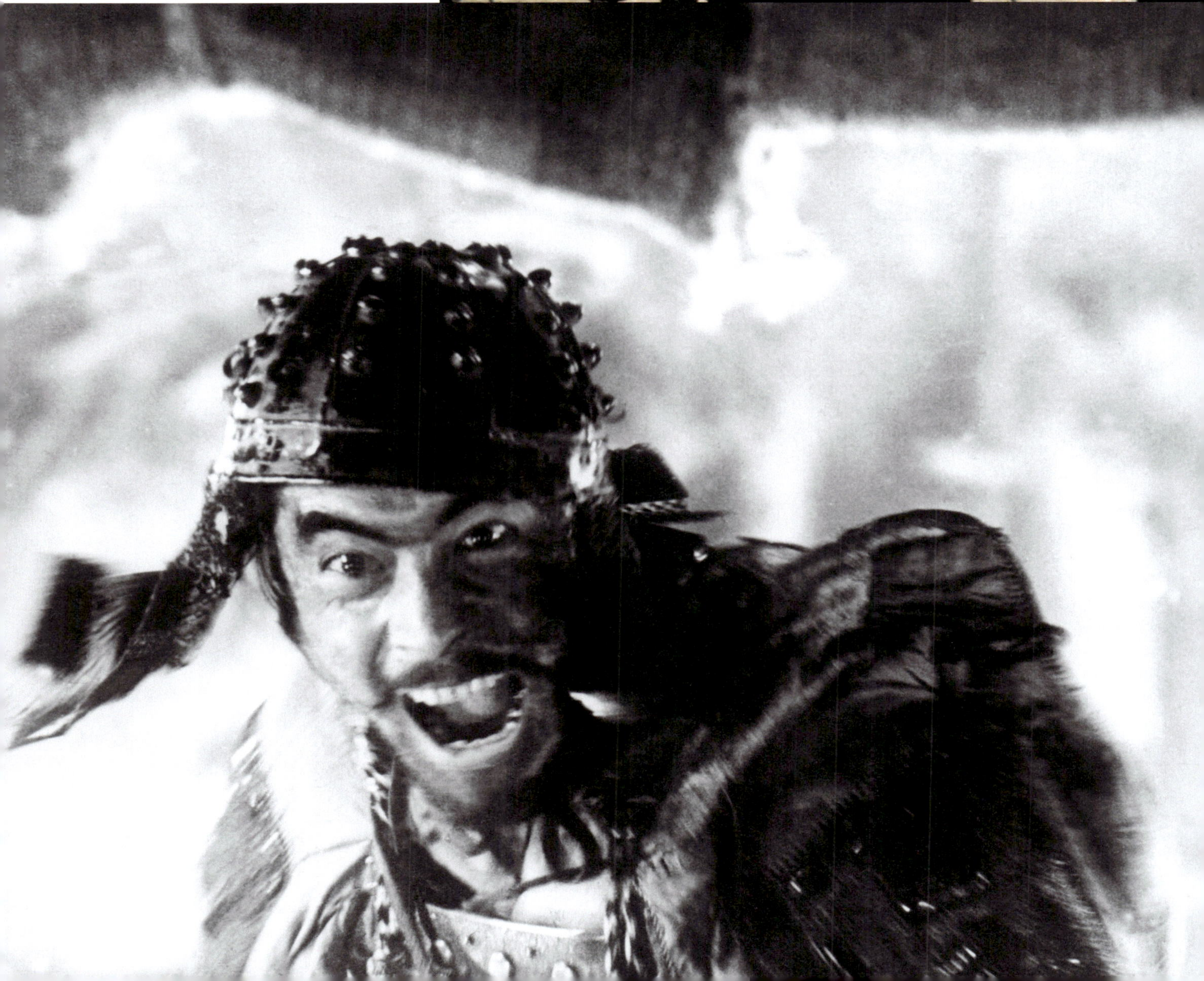

Kill Bill, 2003
Director: Quentin Tarantino
In the picture: Uma Thurman
Courtesy of Miramax Film Corp

Power Frauen: With the latest wave of films about women who refuse to turn the other cheek, the filmic killing machine has gained a refinement and elegance that the more hard-pumping male equivalents can never match; "Anything you can do; I can do better ..."

Nikita, 1990
Director: Luc Besson
In the picture: Anne Parillaud
Still photographer: Patrick Camboulieve

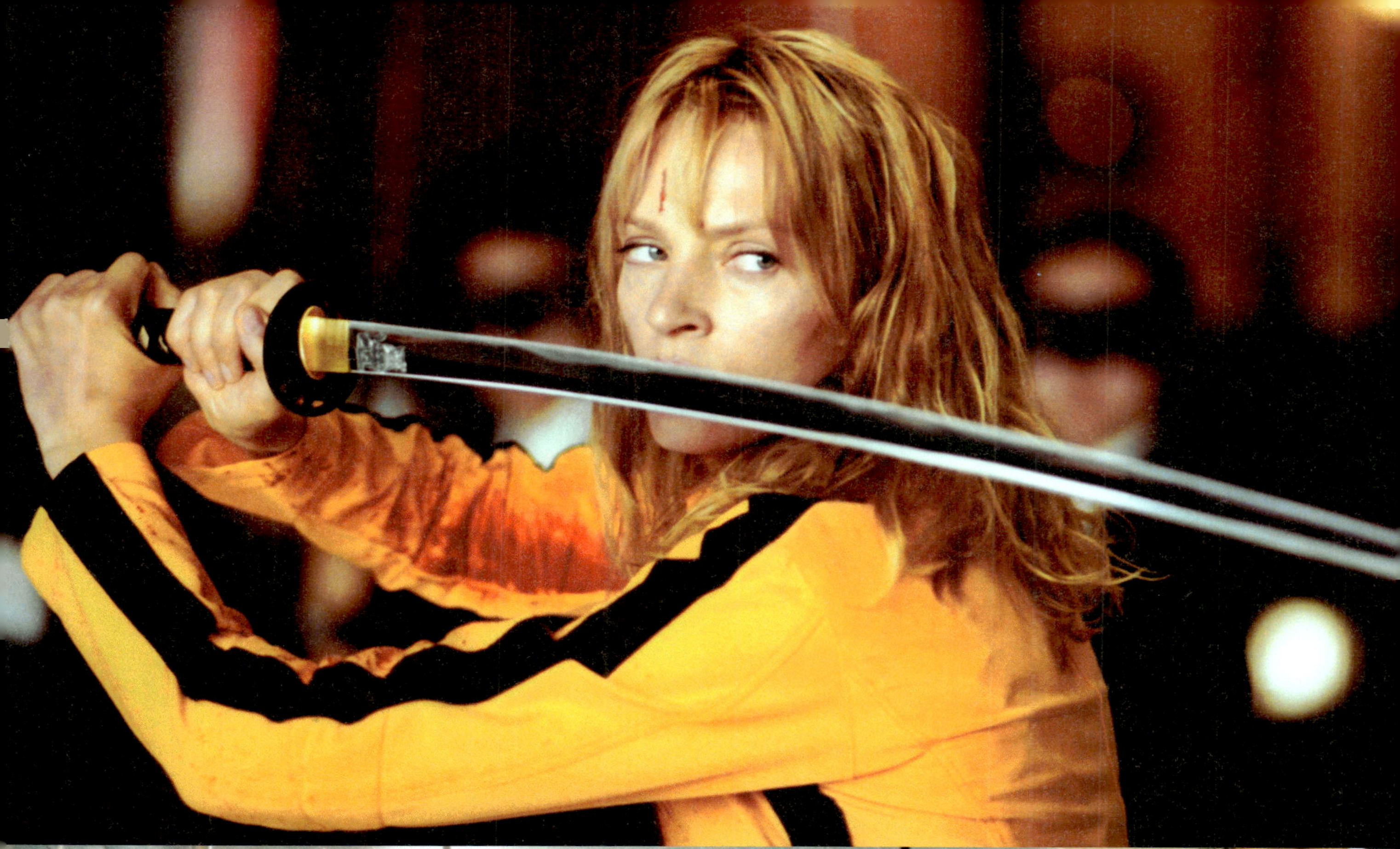

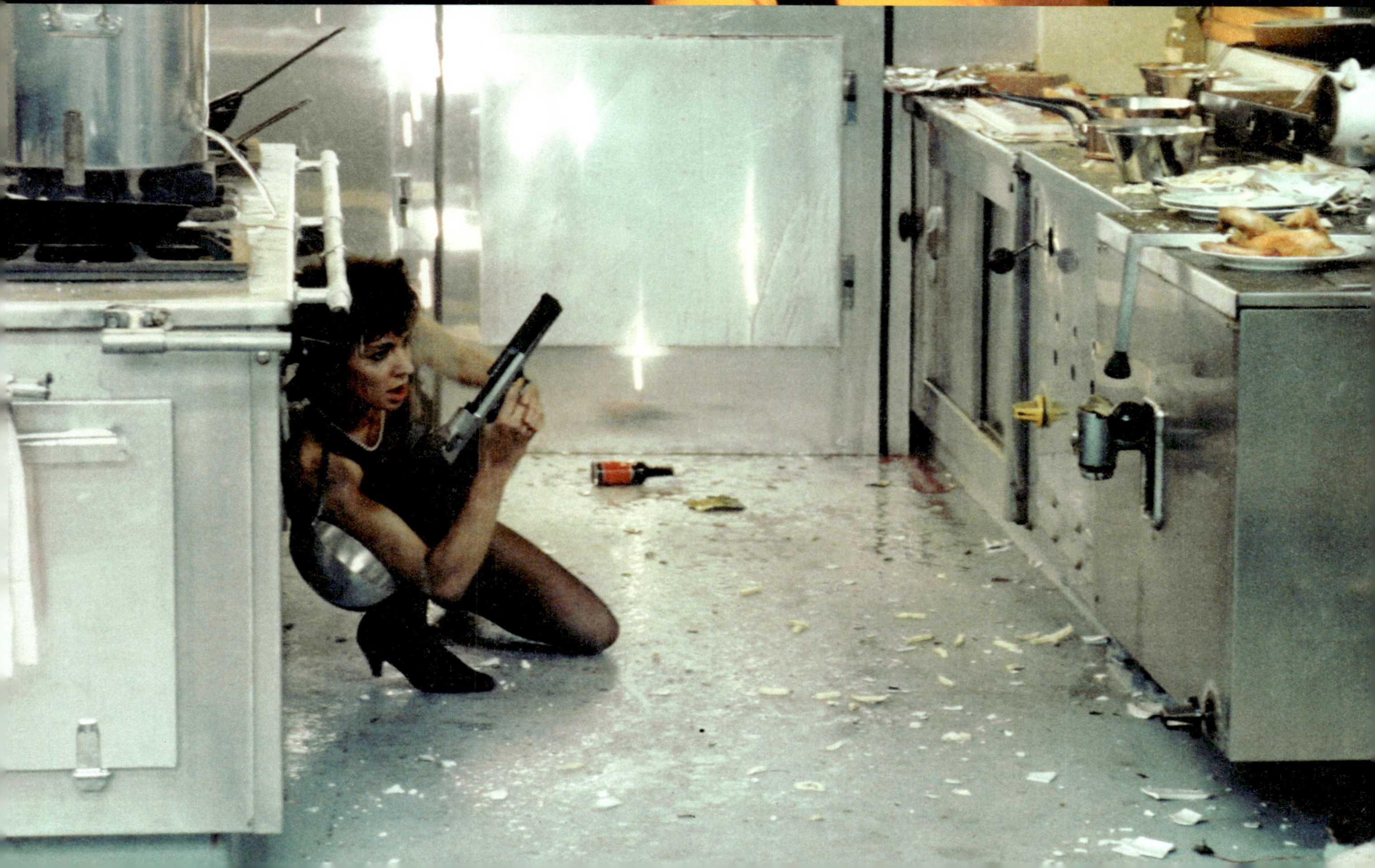

La Passion de Jeanne d'Arc, 1928
(The Passion of Joan of Arc)
Director: Carl Theodor Dreyer
In the picture: Maria Falconetti

Desolation: It isn't easy to be anyboby, but sometimes it's quite impossible to be who you are. When you can't face it any more, when all hope is lost, when the party carries on next door while you yourself stand with an unlit lamp. Or a glowing cigarette.

Festen,1998
(The Celebration)
Director: Thomas Vinterberg
In the picture: Henning Moritzen
Still photographer: Lars Høgsted

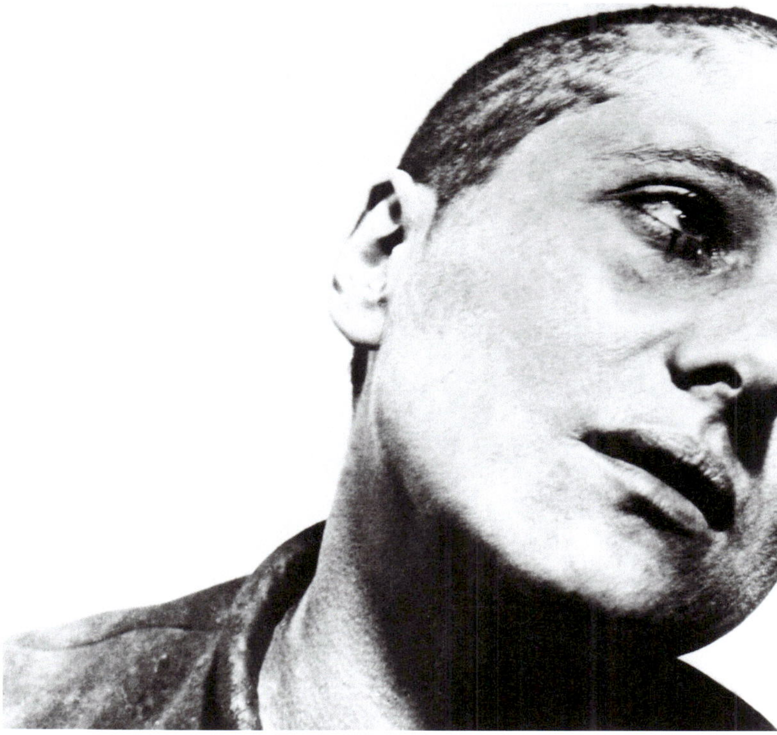

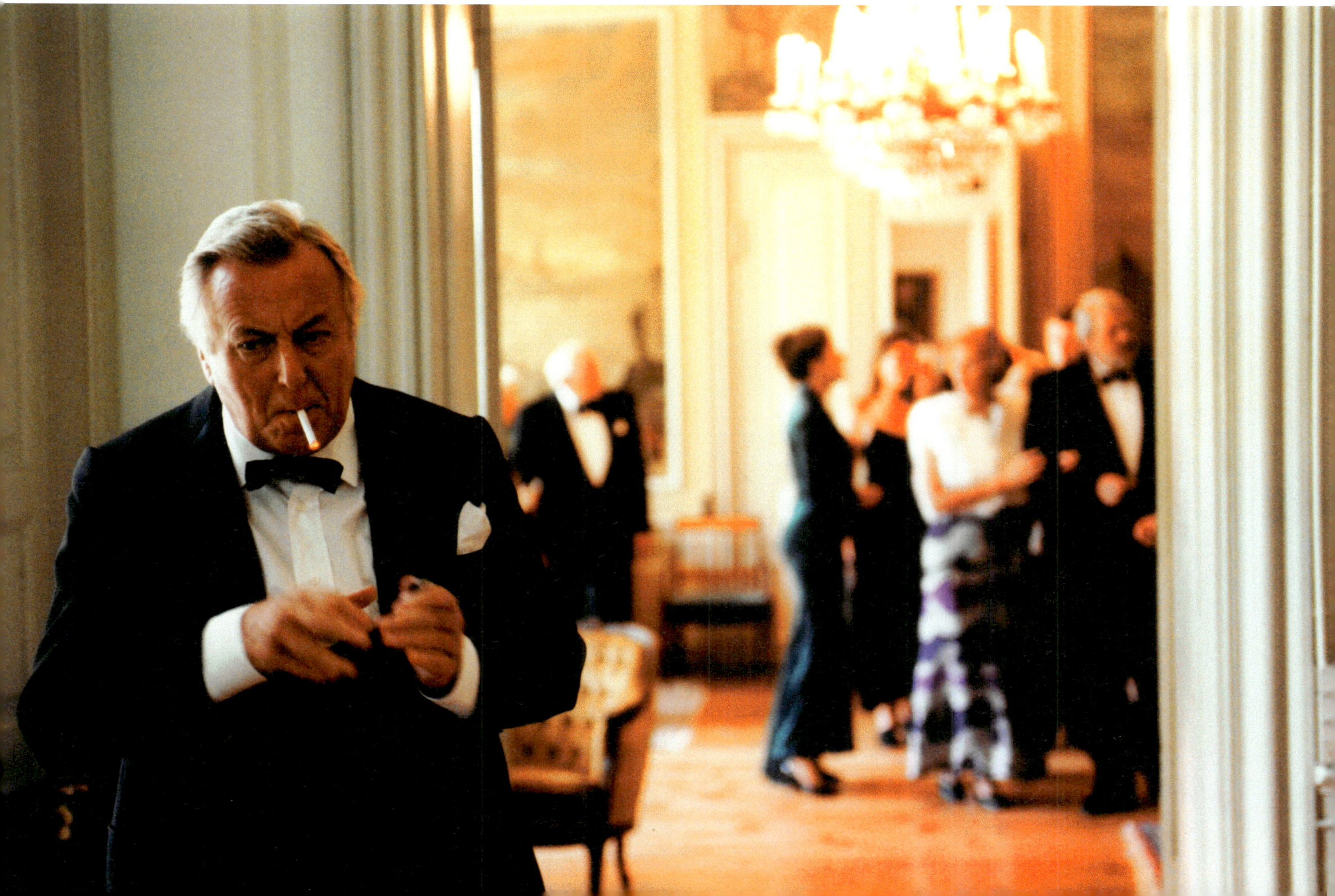

L'Homme de Rio, 1964
(That Man from Rio)
In the picture: Jean-Paul Belmondo
Director: Philippe de Broca
Still photographer: Edmond Séchan

The Escape: You only have a very small head start - IT is always just behind you, and all you know is you mustn't be caught. Not yet.

Le notti di Cabiria, 1957
(Nights of Cabiria)
Director: Federico Fellini

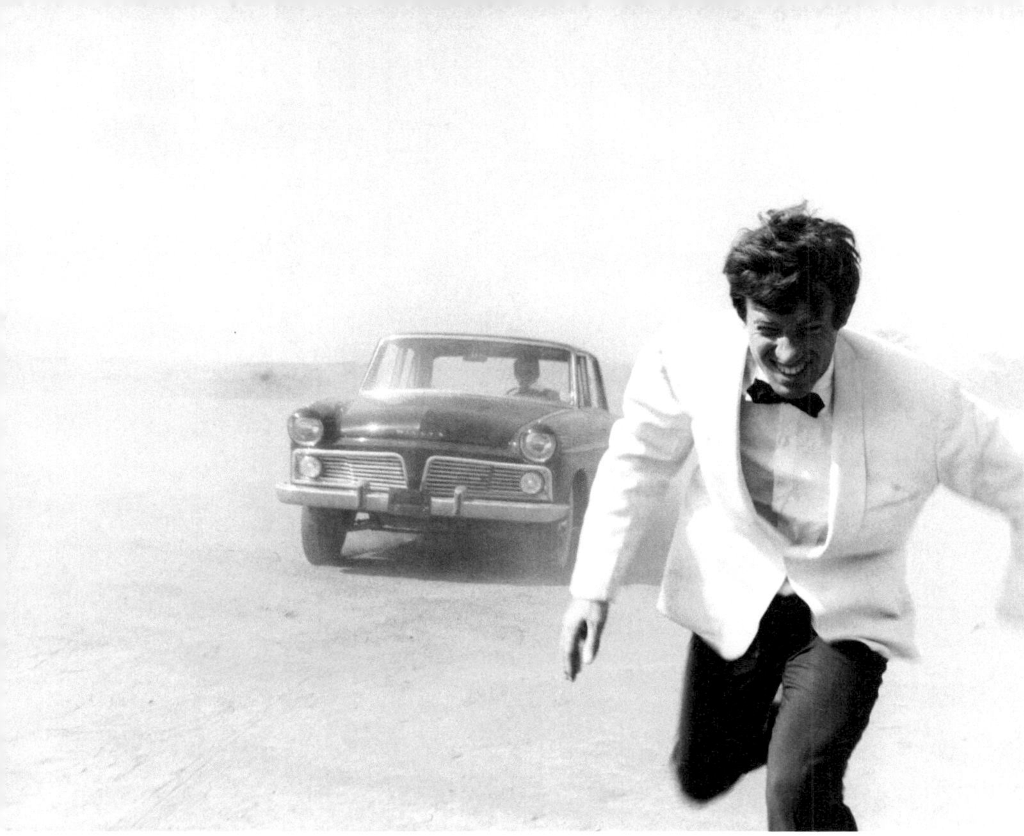

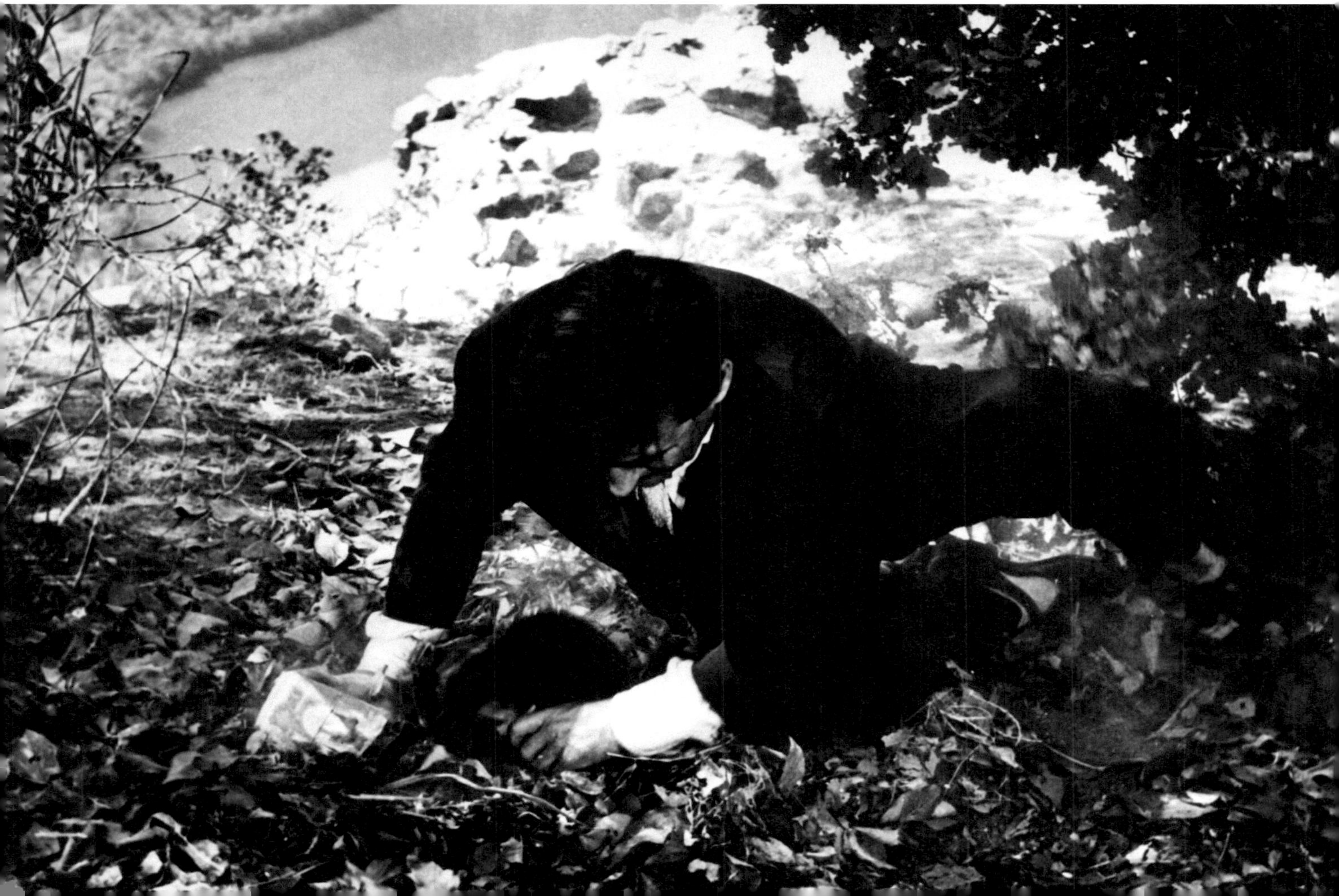

Det sjunde inseglet, 1956
Director: Ingmar Bergman
In the picture: Bengt Ekerot

Departure: We can't deal with the final farewell, but we can prepare for it in the departure scene. With its flurried haste or heart-rending adagio it also always points forward to its opposite: "We'll meet again ..."

Les parapluies de Cherbourg, 1964
Director: Jacques Demy
In the picture: Catherine Deneuve, Nino Castelnuovo

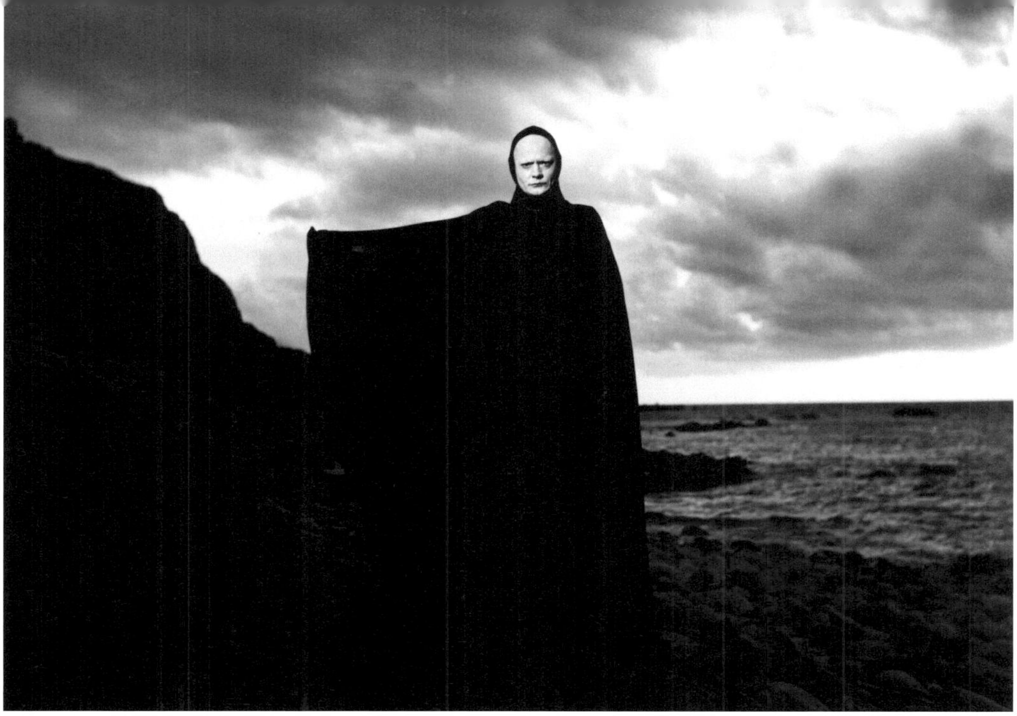

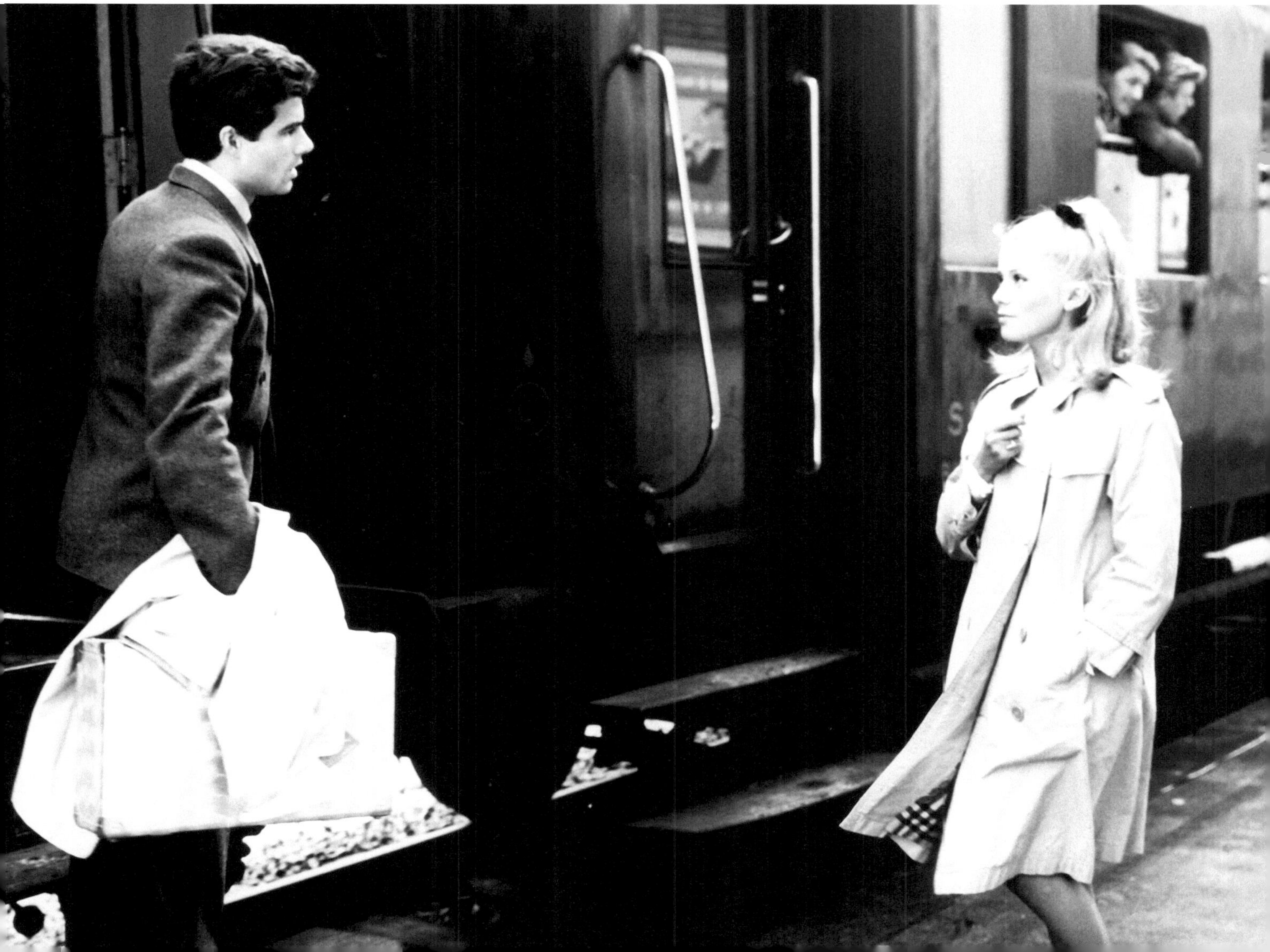

Henning Carlsen, b. 1927, is one of Denmark's most important film-makers. Since the mid-fifties he has created a succession of films whose economy of expression and psychological depth have inspired several generations of younger directors. For many years he has also functioned as the director of the Dagmar Cinema in Copenhagen and worked as a theatre director and a teacher at The National Film School of Denmark. Over the years Carlsen has been active in a number of associations of film artists, written articles and comments in the newspapers *Politiken* and *Information* and besides film scripts written the books *Mit Livs Fortrængninger* (Gyldendal, 1998) and *Flyvske Billeder* (Gyldendal, 2000). 2006 is the fortieth anniversary of the premiere of Carlsen's film of Knut Hamsun's novel *Hunger*. He is awarded a so-called Golden Swan Lifetime Achievement Award at the Copenhagen International Film Festival 2006. Right now, he is working with the producer Nina Crone and scriptwriter Jean-Claude Carrière on a film of Gabriel Garcia Marquez' novel *Memories of My Melancholy Whores*.

One spring day in 1966, while we were finishing work on *Hunger*, Jesper Høm came to my home and, on the floor of our largest room, spread out his selection from the over seven thousand black-and-white stills he had taken during the Oslo shoot in autumn 1965. I think there were about two hundred 18x24 images, so almost seven thousand had already been weeded out. We were to use at most thirty for the set of stills – that is, the pictures to be displayed in cinema showcases – and maybe fifty, including the showcase pictures, for the press. Plus about a dozen mainly working shots for special articles. And finally, we had to choose one for the poster.

It soon became evident, perhaps because it was the only portrait format picture in the selection, that this photo was the most suitable for a poster. It expressed many statements about the content of a film we had to assume people had not seen. The picture screams hunger at us; it firmly establishes that the man is 'outside', alone, and the date of the action is uncertain. We are in no doubt that he is looking at something edible. And our curiosity is piqued: what is he carrying under his arm?

That the picture later became a kind of icon for the film is another story. At the time we selected it we had no idea that Per Oscarsson would soon be a famous actor and that the character in the picture would in time be a world-famous figure. I don't think we even dreamed of it.

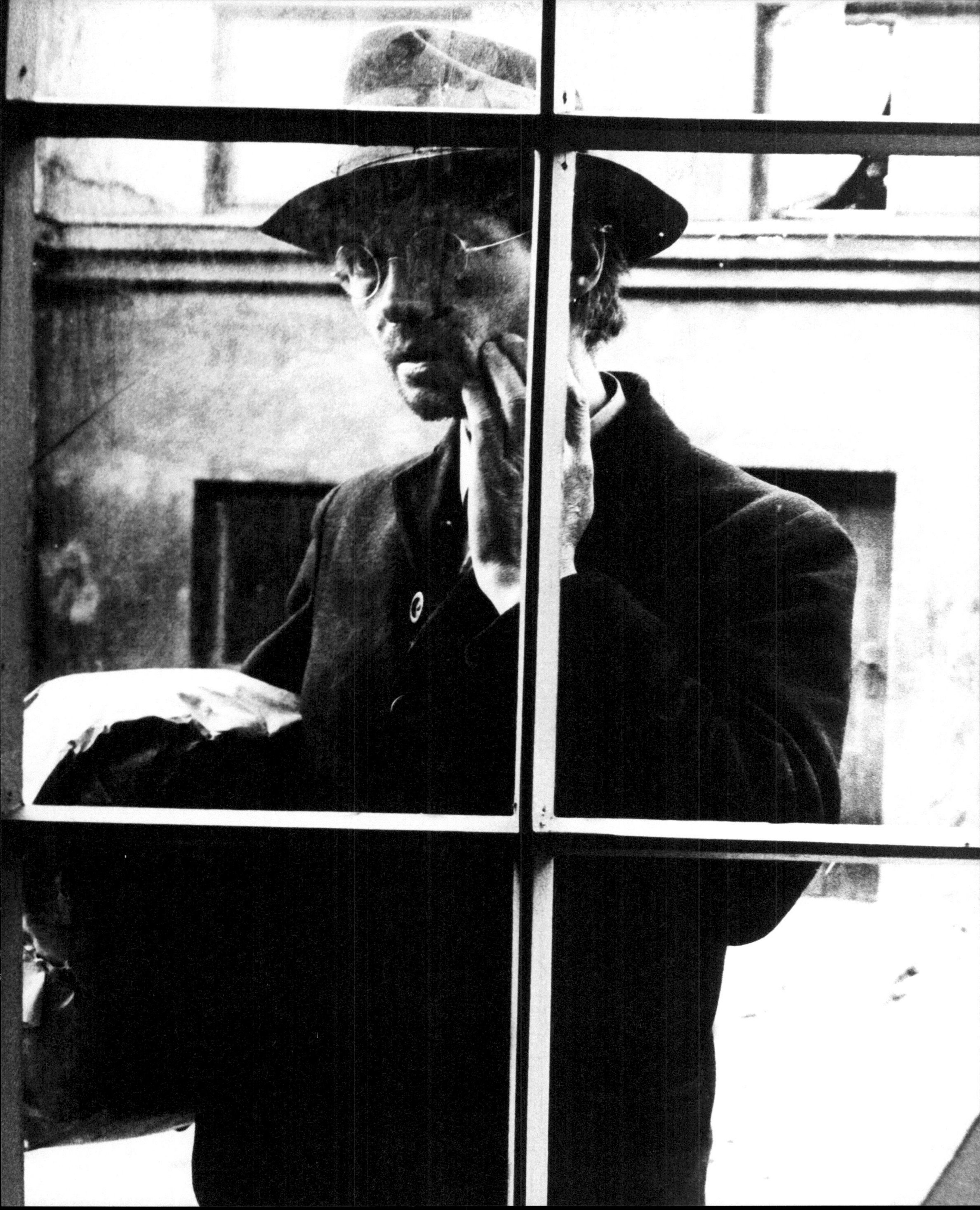

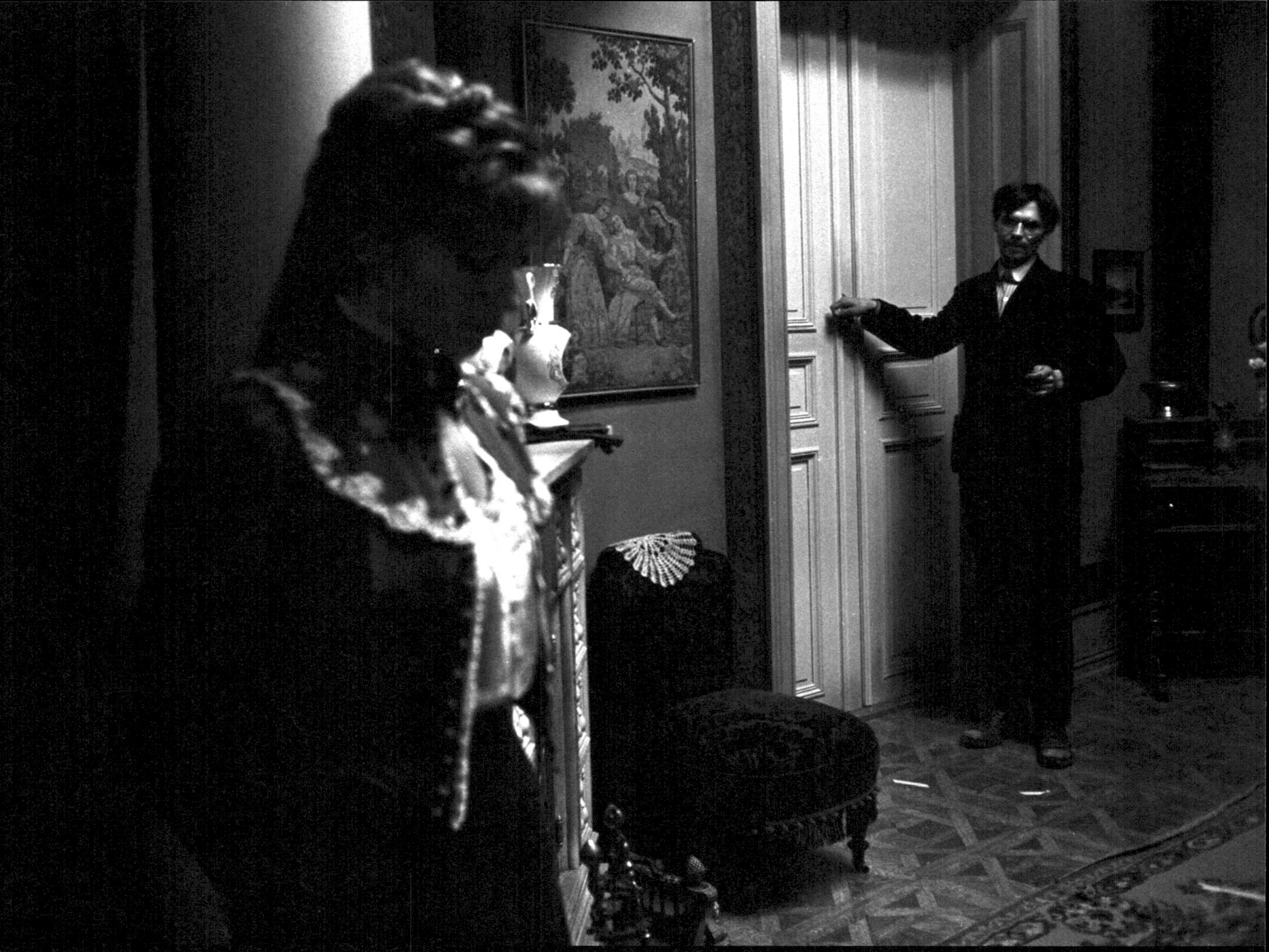

The movie still, especially the indoor shot, depends on the lighting created by the Director of Photography. So Henning Kristiansen must take the credit for the ingenious distribution of light and shadow in this picture shot in the farewell scene in Ylajali's apartment.

We sense that the relationship between the two has cooled – both from her rather guilt-ridden, downcast gaze and from his hand, which touches the door handle without turning it. The framing leaves room for the darkness at the outer edges – the emptiness into which the relationship between the two is fast disappearing. He cannot move, riveted to the spot by her look. But we also sense the mood from what he is saying, which the still picture obviously cannot convey. Since it is a key line of both novel and film, I will break out of the confi-

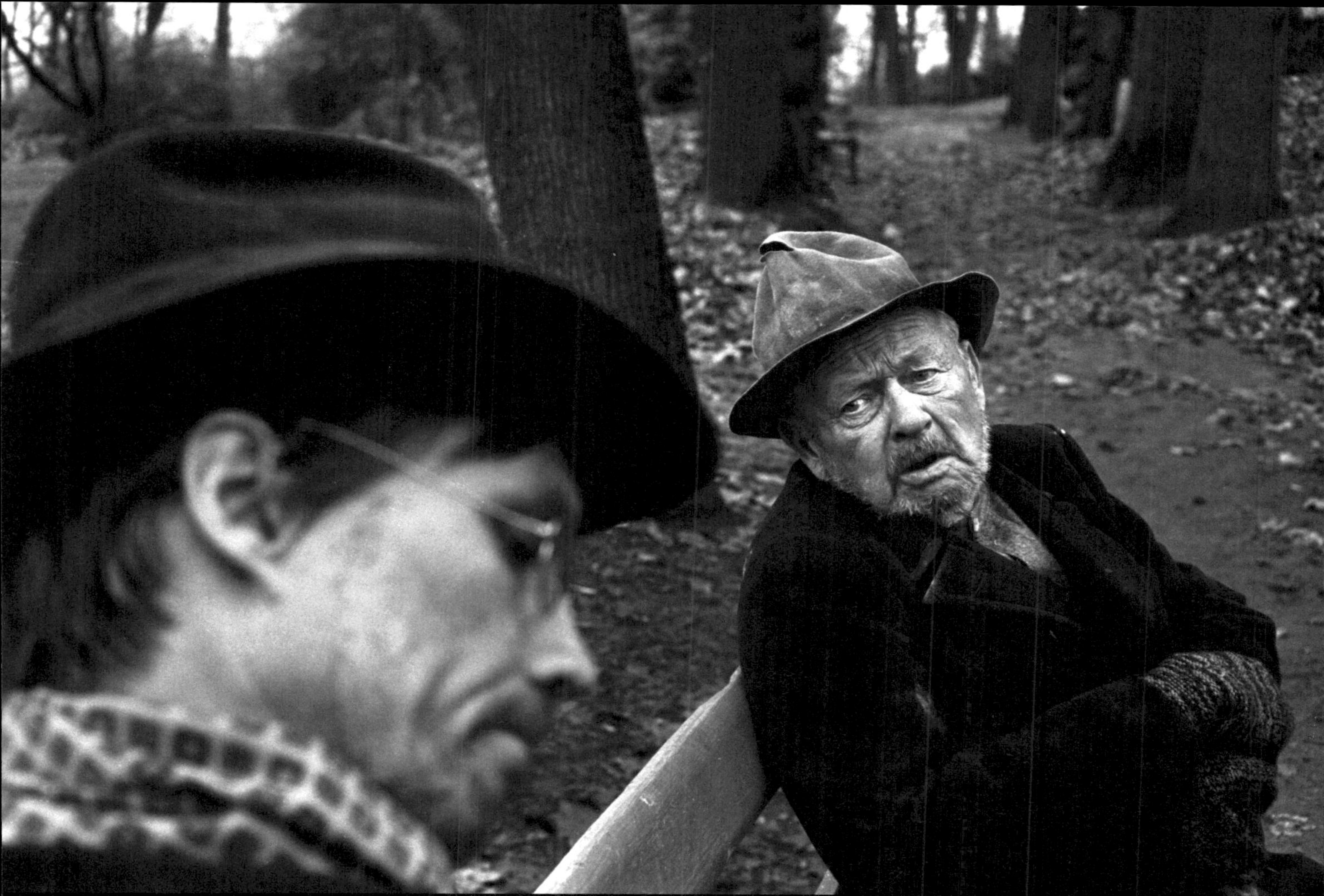

The framing is an important part of the still photograph's expressive idiom. Of course, the cinematographic camera operator has the same ability to frame his picture, but faces the additional challenge inherent in his always being able to change the framing. He can also draw on light and shadow as well as focus to express himself, not to mention those changes called camera movement. Some still photographers, whether working on films, shooting documentaries or doing art photography, already frame the image with the camera, that is at the moment of shooting. Others prefer to take shots with 'redundant content' that they can later crop. I think Jesper Høm worked in the first way, with a few exceptions of course. For when I compare his contact prints with the pictures he had chosen from all his shots, there are generally no differences in terms of framing. (I should just mention that this was back in the days of the darkroom, long before the era of digital cameras and computer-processing.)

The way this picture is framed, with Per Oscarsson's head out of focus in the left foreground in a pose worthy of an Edvard Munch, and the old man, Egil Hjorth-Jensen, in focus deep in the picture, is anything but coincidental. If you fold the picture down the middle, you will discover that the characters' right eyes are exactly the same distance from the centre line. An invisible line extending from Hjorth-Jensen's two eyes meets Oscarsson's eye at a particular point. The height of the camera at the instant of shutter release is no accident either. Had the photographer taken the shot lower down and included more of the tall trees in the background, the two people would have been portrayed without that distance between them, so clearly indicated by the small section of the bench backrest. And the distance between the two, physical as well as intellectual, is part of the story. The perspective coming from the avenue behind Hjorth-Jensen seems to suck him in. He is already fleeing from the madman in the foreground who has helplessly lost his – mental as well as physical – focus.

In my view this is the finest of both the still and the moving pictures of the film. It was shot in the Palace Park behind the palace itself, which stands at the end of Karl Johan Street in Oslo. The leaves have fallen, just a few remaining on the trees, in itself a touch of melancholy further reinforced by the overcast atmosphere. We would hardly be able to make out the gravel paths of the park if it were not for the three benches in perspective. The truth is there was no gravel path in the location the photo was shot. But that was where all the leaves were, and that was where the picture could be composed. And the benches were certainly easy to move.

The slightly shabby man in the hat turns to look at the two fine ladies, who seem to hesitate slightly before passing him by. At all events it looks as though they are drawing to the right to avoid getting too close to him. However, we sense they are moving forward and can almost hear their feet rustling through the dry leaves.

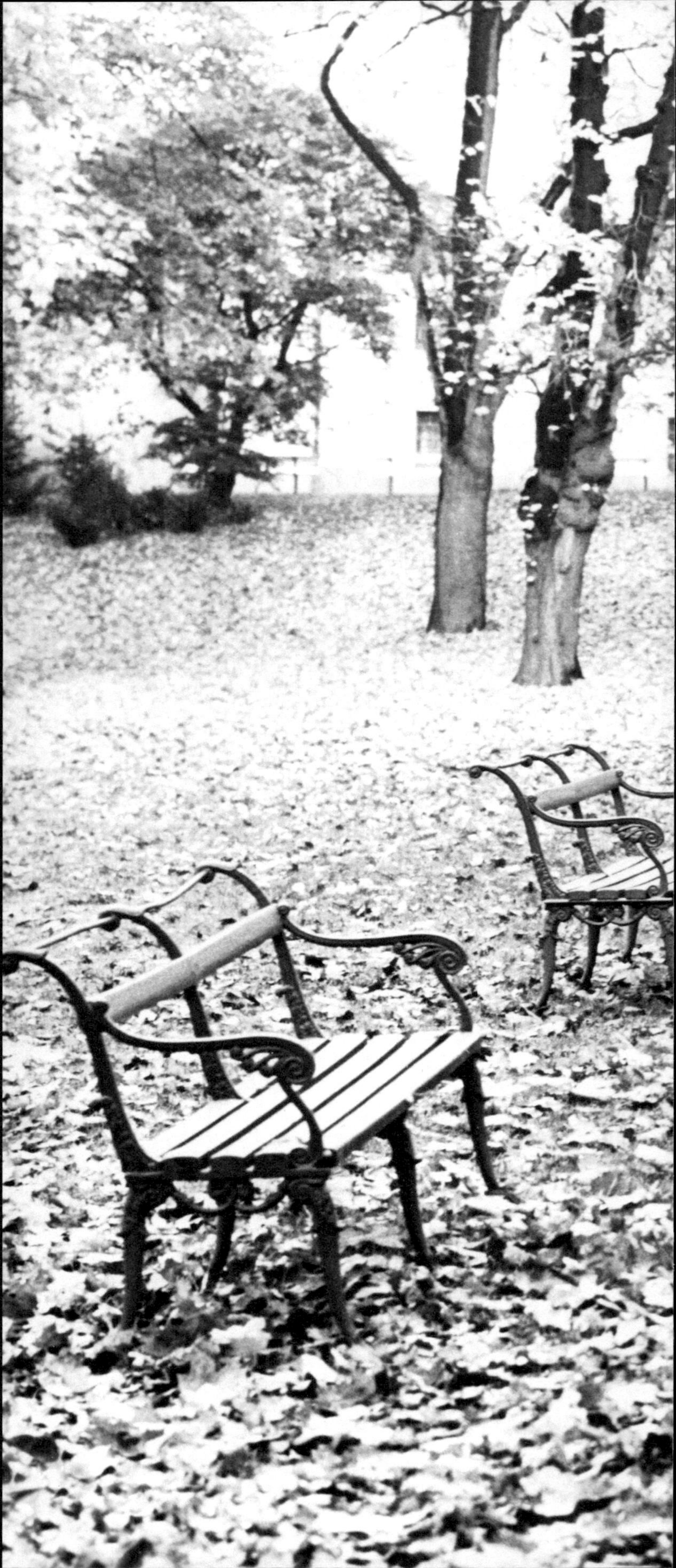

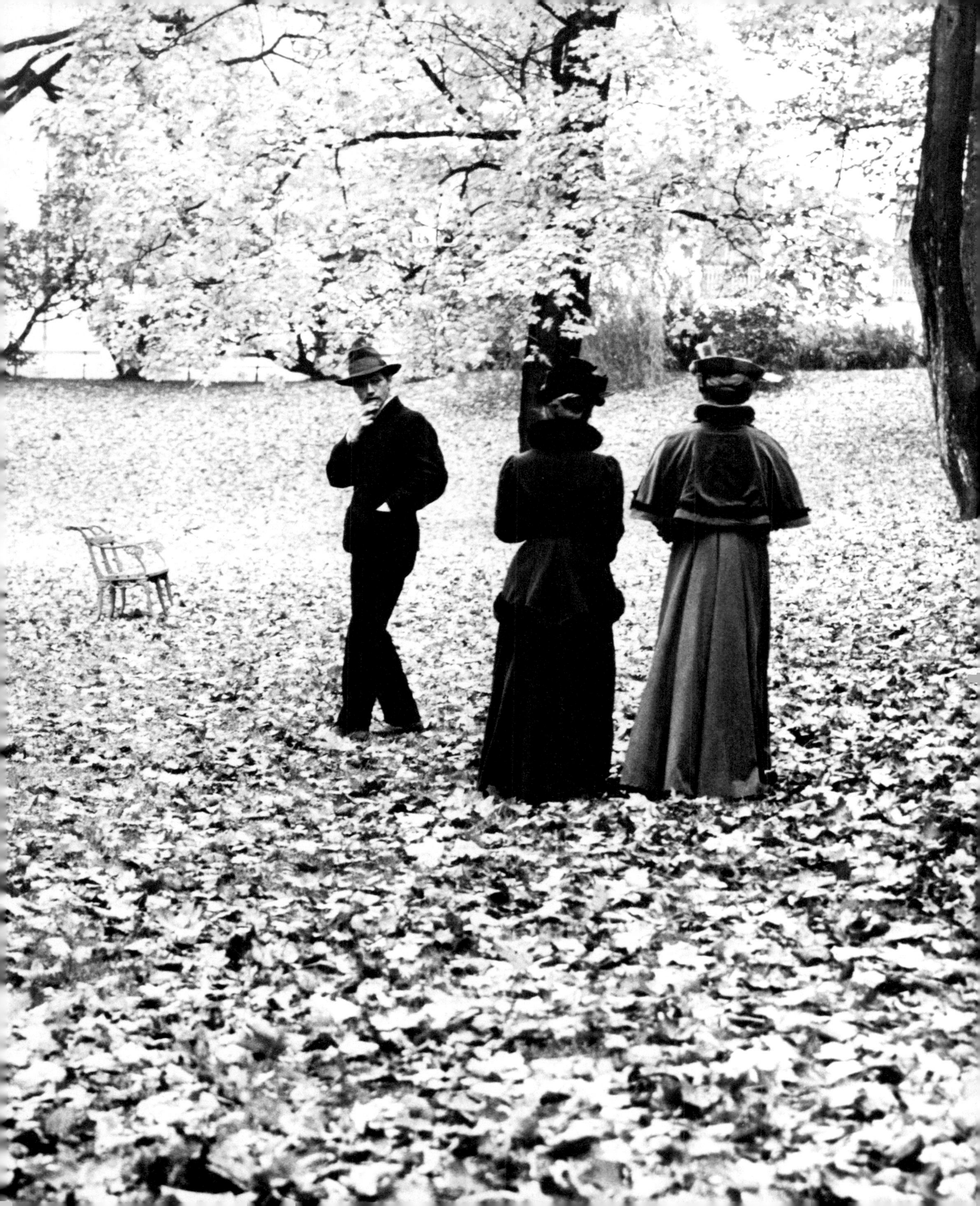

In the film itself this image precedes the one on page 57 – after passing the ladies, the man turns and looks at them. In the film sequence this demonstrates how the individual film scene experientially consists of its own content plus the scene immediately preceding it and the one following. In other words we are talking about the *flow* of the film.

The opposite is true of the stills for a film. They are rarely presented in the order in which the scenes they depict are shown in the film. On the other hand, the solitary still must illustrate the movement that the movie has 24 frames a second to depict. That is exactly what this picture does. In a moment the man will be outside the picture, and the ladies will undoubtedly stop to regain their composure after his rudeness. But if we take the corresponding *frame* out of the 24 images on the film strip, where the man by and large stays in the same position, and blow it up to a still, there is no motion, for the picture was never *intended* to perform solo.

However, we shouldn't forget in passing that it is the film and its circumstances that create the conditions for the still picture.

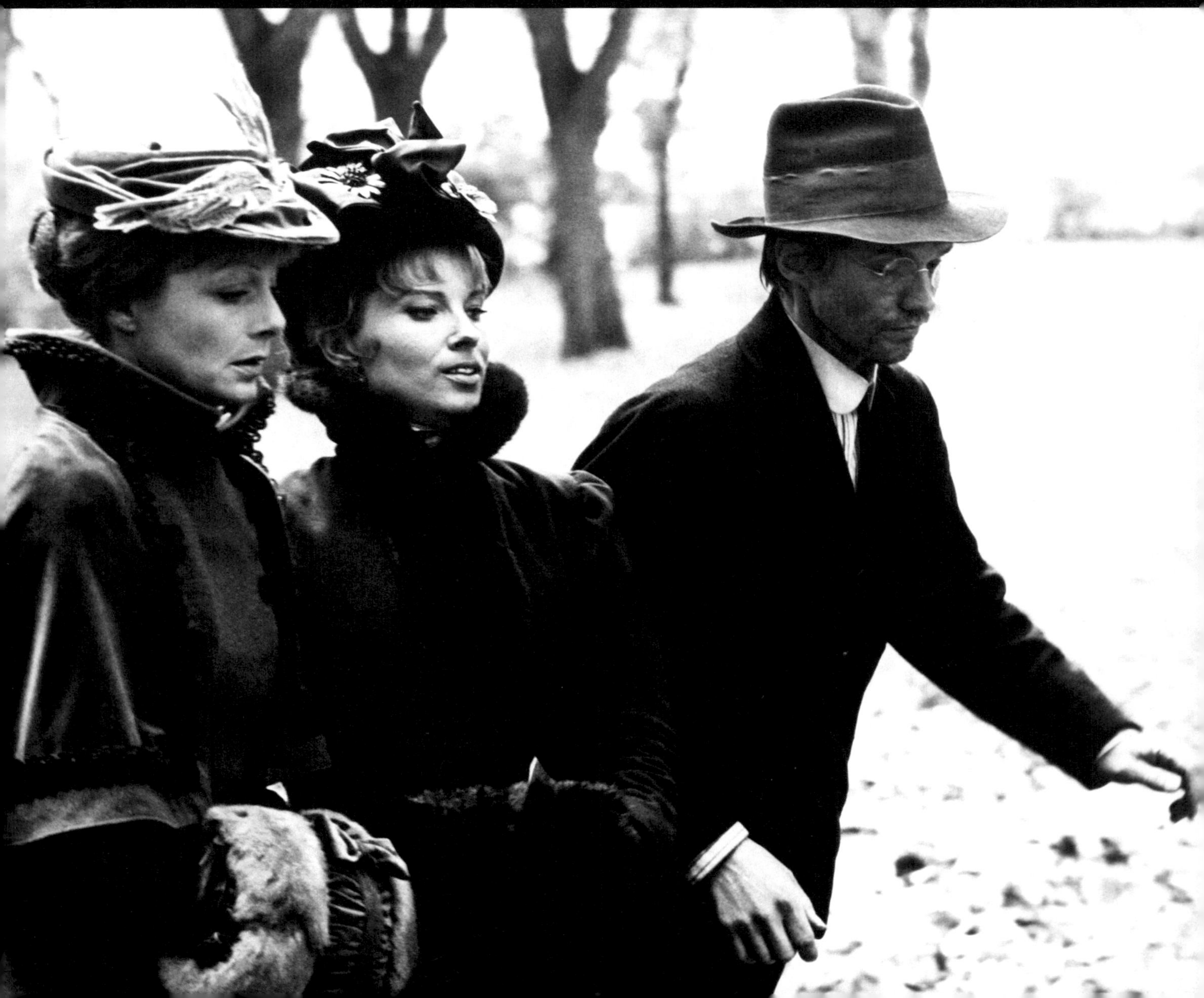

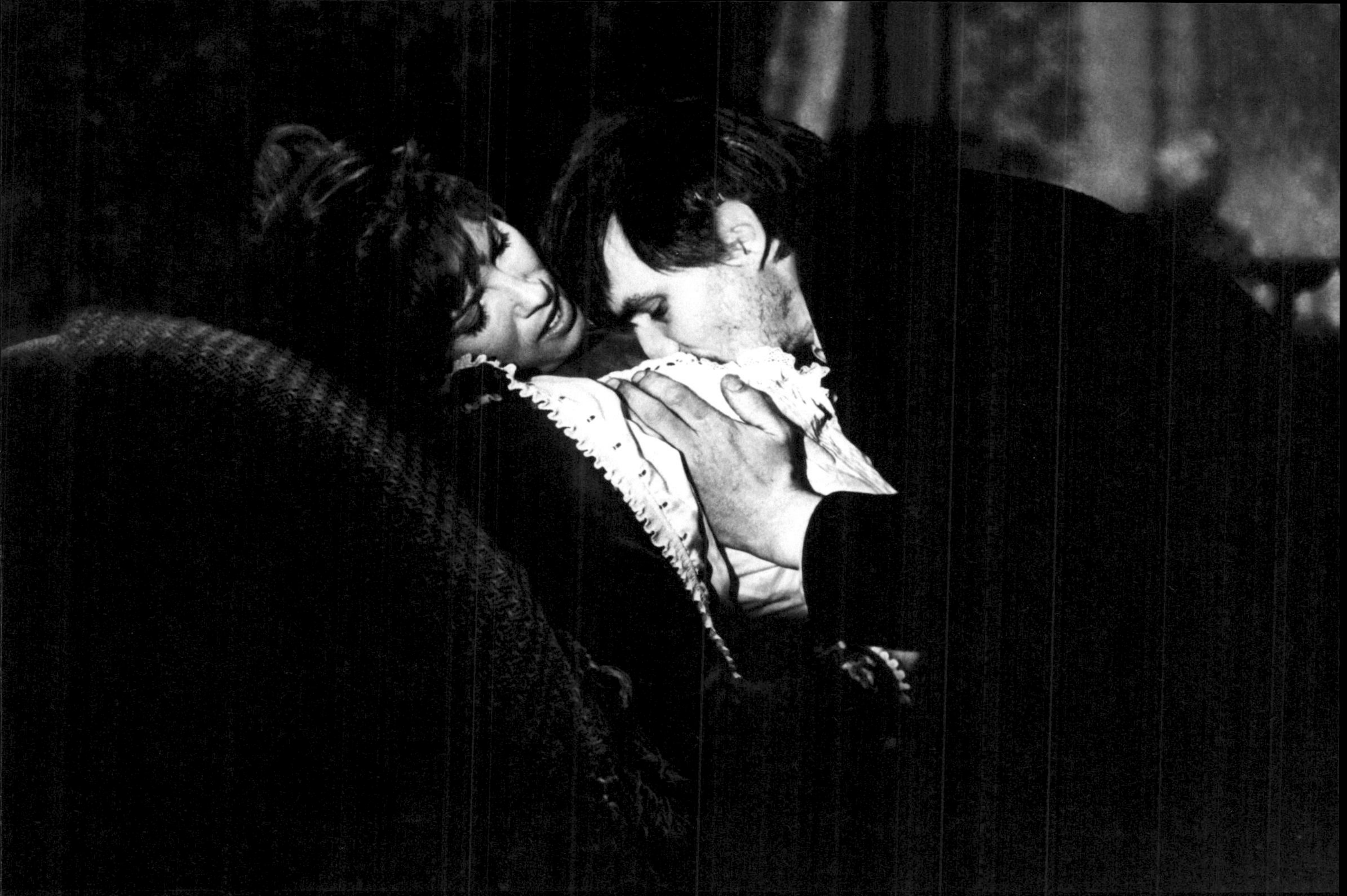

When *Hunger* had its world premiere at the film festival in Cannes in 1966, it was launched as what it is: the first Scandinavian co-production. But Scandinavia, at least Sweden and Denmark, had begun to establish a reputation for erotic emancipation in photography as well as in film and literature. Norway was still reeling from the trial of Agnar Mykle (the Norwegian equivalent of the Lady Chatterley trial). But the premiere audience's expectations of a little state-subsidized pornography had been fired up. There was no knowing what the title *Hunger* might denote!

When the first hour of the film brought nothing remotely related to 'the new erotic wave' in the North, disappointment began to spread through the cinema. So when this scene at last appeared, relieved laughter rippled through the audience: "Finally, what we've been waiting for!" But their delight was short-lived. A few minutes after the introductory manoeuvres of this erotic 'brief encounter' the scene's mood changes to embarrassment. She wants to, but doesn't want to after all. He suddenly sits up, turns his back to her and breaks out despairingly: "Oh Lord, what sort of game is this?" At that moment the cinema was so quiet you could hear a pin drop – in fact you could hear a postage stamp drop.

This image somehow contains and predicts all this. Her pent-up desire and incipient fear of where all this might lead. His total absorption in the glories before him with no particular concern for her feelings. He inhales the scent between her breasts as he squeezes them together. If he is thinking about anything, it's what to do next. And just as he makes the attempt, she cuts him off. She is already preparing to do this as she watches him.

What does a film still have to do besides capture movement and freeze it? It has to sell. Arouse the potential viewer's curiosity. Perhaps occasionally it has to appeal to the beast within. What do I know?

You could accuse this picture of a slight degree of overkill, in that it probably promises the unprepared viewer more suspense than the film actually offers. But unfulfilled promise doesn't make this a bad picture. It does signal the presence of a certain mystique, and *that* at least isn't false advertising. The eerie atmosphere between the two women is also underscored by the contrast with the coachman's blurred and almost indolent presence. Of the two women in the carriage, Birgitte Federspiel (on the left) is obviously the more horror-struck, while Gunnel Lindblom is more puzzled and curious. This picture does not appear in the film at all – for narrative reasons the same message is stretched over several shots. But it refers to a sequence in which the two women experience the mystique created by a random incident whose significance has faded into blurred obscurity like the expression on the driver's face.

So there is a meaning after all.

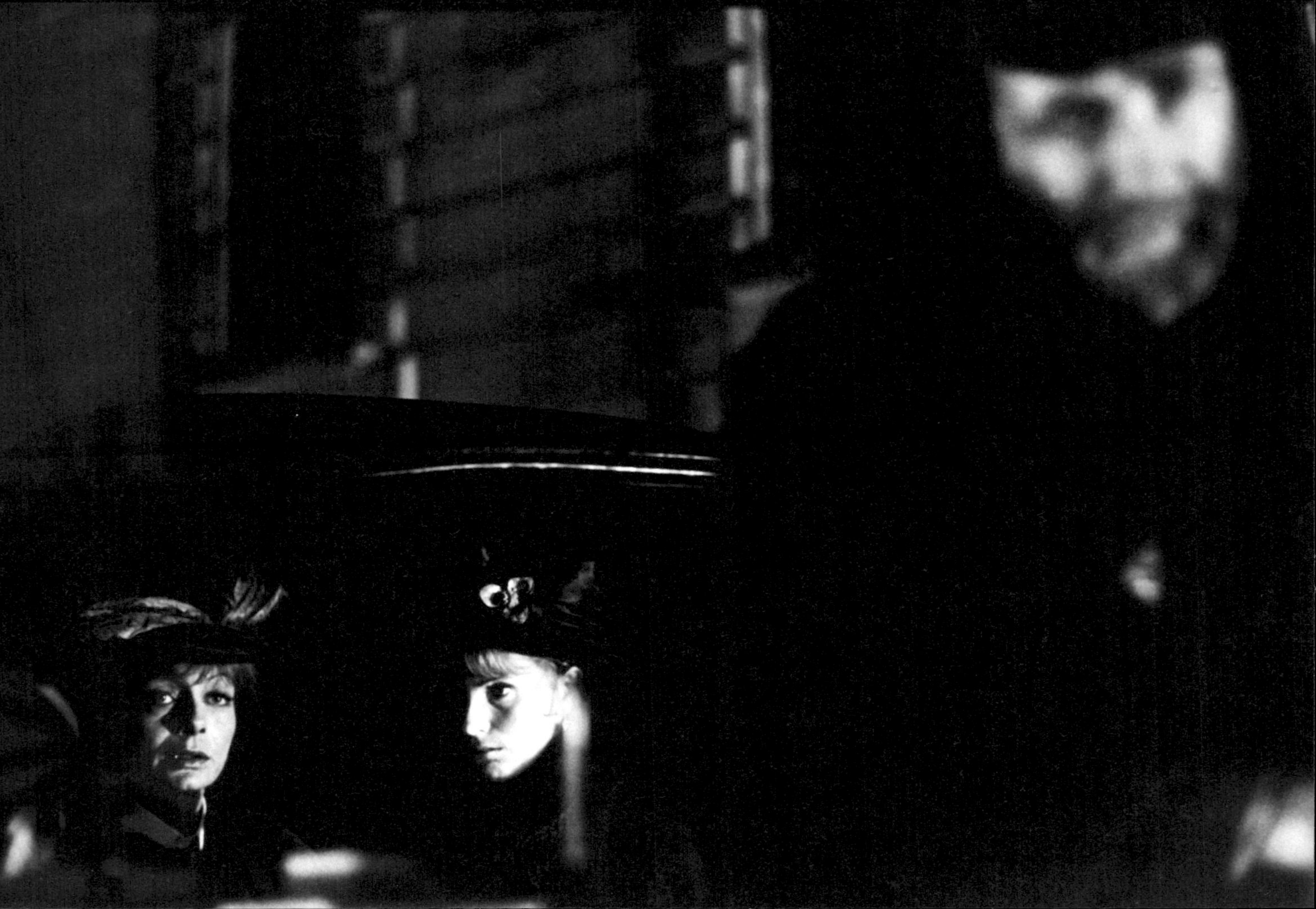

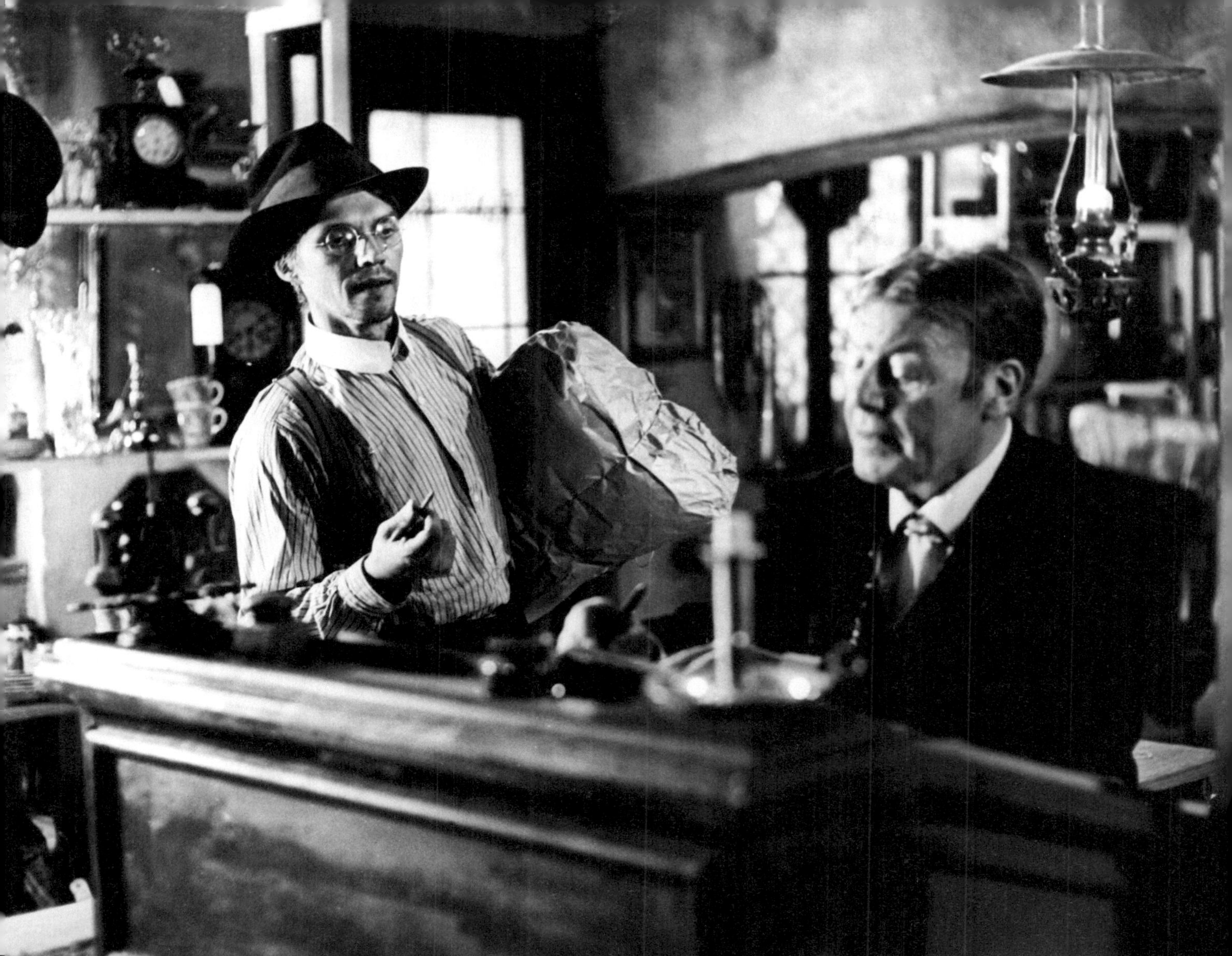

The pawnbroker was Danish actor Osvald Helmuth's last film role and one of the first stills Jesper Høm shot for *Hunger*. Throughout his long acting career Osvald Helmuth had performed solo infinitely more times than together with other actors. Now he had to work with Per Oscarsson and respond to his lines. But we had a double problem: Osvald had difficulties with Per's Swedish, and Per had difficulty sticking to the script. Osvald would prepare to react to a particular cue from Per. But during the shoot, Per would quickly rearrange the sentence, leaving Osvald waiting for an agreed cue word that had long since been engulfed somewhere in the middle of the sentence. The torments of illness and age did not improve matters. Osvald himself was in despair over it. So I asked if he would agree to an experiment. "Yes, let's try it then," he said. The experiment was that we tied a string to one of his ankles. I held the other end of the string and, when the camera was rolling and Per was in full flight, I jerked the string just before Osvald was supposed to react. Then he took over and managed everything with the precision and timing of which only truly great artists are capable.

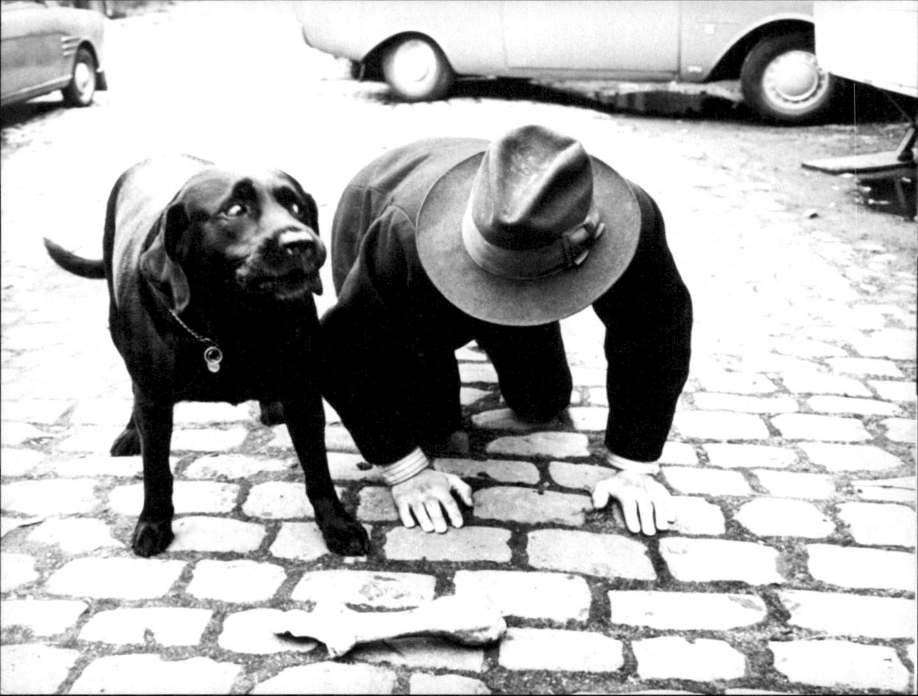

This is from a dream sequence in the film, but it is what I would call a 'borderline' working picture. It could have been cropped to get rid of the cars in the background (an anachronism given the date of the action). The white cobblestones underscore the sequence's dream-like mood, as does Henning Kristiansen's deliberately exaggerated bright lighting. For some reason Jesper Høm had difficulty dealing with these dream images, for none of the stills from the dream sequences captures the film's moods, actions and movements with the same quality as the others.

Comparing the still and the film shot to decide which is best is as ridiculous as discussing whether the film is better than the book or vice versa. Just as book and film are two different media, the film shot and the still are two very different forms of expression. Of course you could claim that the film shot comes first. For without a film shot, the still photographer must find another motif for his camera.

Greed, a film made by (not with!) Erich von Stroheim from 1925 illustrates the close relationship possible between moving pictures and stills from the same film. Von Stroheim had made a version of *Greed* lasting three or four hours, which so alarmed the producer that he cut it down to ninety minutes and, to von Stroheim's horror, burned the surplus negatives. But recently a young American film student came across the original manuscript with all the original lines. More than that, he also found a complete set of stills representing all the scenes von Stroheim had shot – in other words also those for which the producer had burnt the film negatives. So the young man spliced the stills from the missing scenes and the related silent film captions into the abridged version of *Greed* wherever the script said they were supposed to be, and thus a full-length version was born as von Stroheim had intended. A few of us saw that version (in a special showing at the Cinemateque). Discussing it the next day no one could say with certainty which scenes had been shown with moving pictures and which were represented by stills.

But one thing is certain: the long version is a far greater experience than the ninety-minute one, which has always been slightly incomprehensible and therefore rather boring.

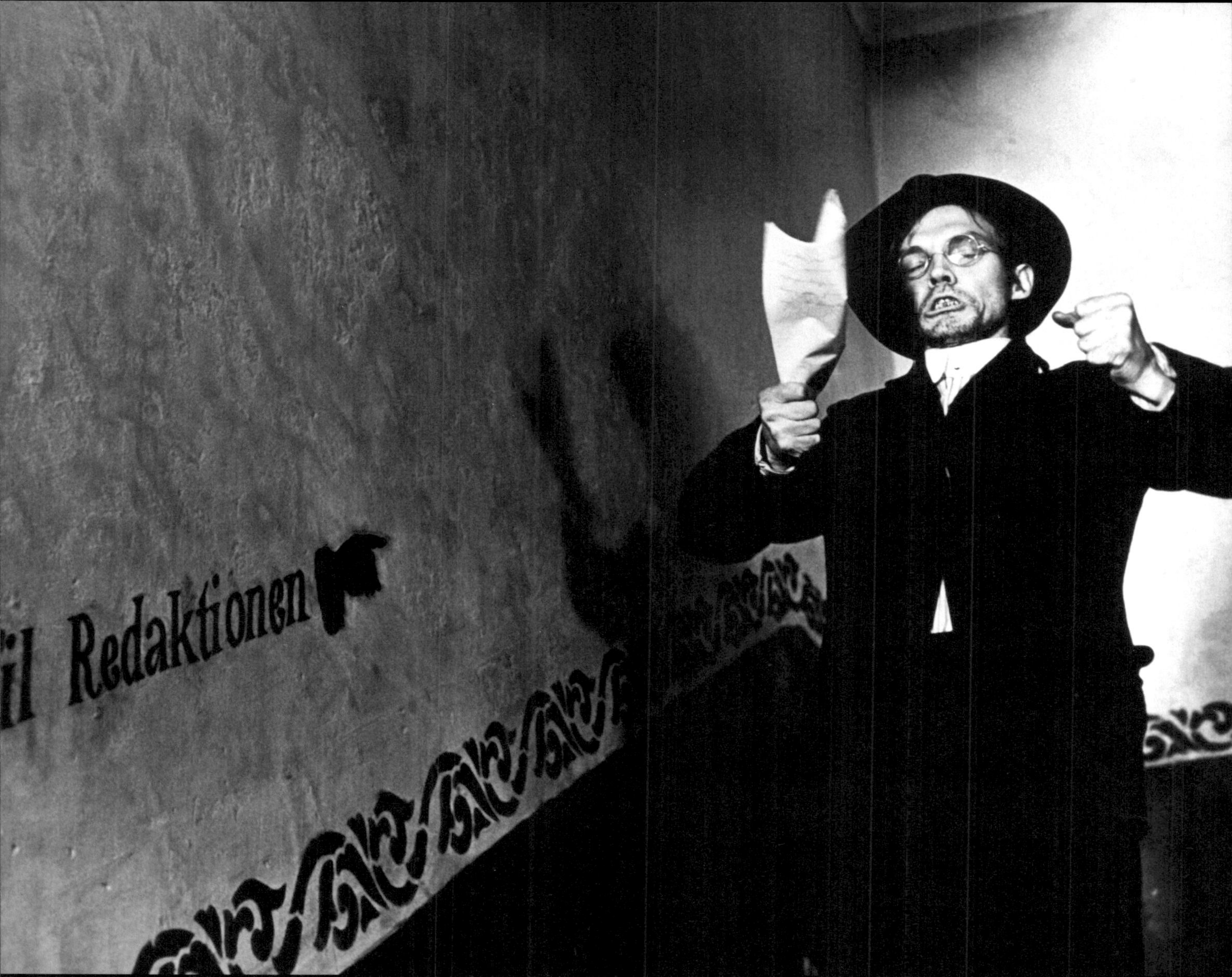

It is hard to tell whether this man is bursting with rage or enthusiasm. He is leaving an editor's office, that's obvious from the sign painted on the wall. The few pieces of paper in his hand hint that it is probably a newspaper editor's office. And we know that whatever is going on matters to him. Knowing whether the news he got was good or bad makes no difference to the effect of the still. It may help to pique our curiosity that the man

That he is about to explode over something or other and oversteps the bounds of good behaviour is emphasized by his left elbow, which the framing allows to project out of the picture.

For anyone who has seen the film, this picture is also a reminder of Per Oscarsson's astounding performances.

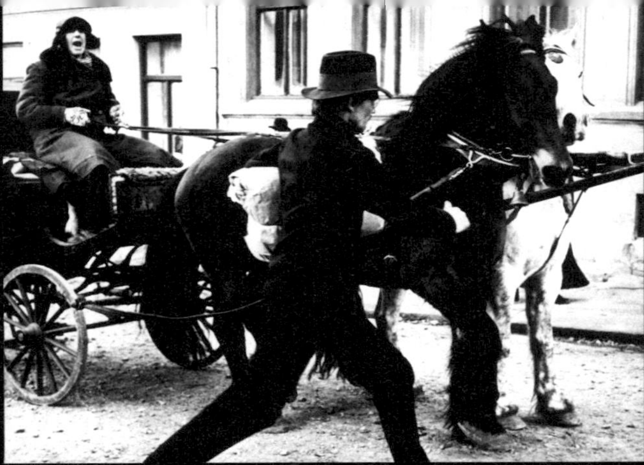

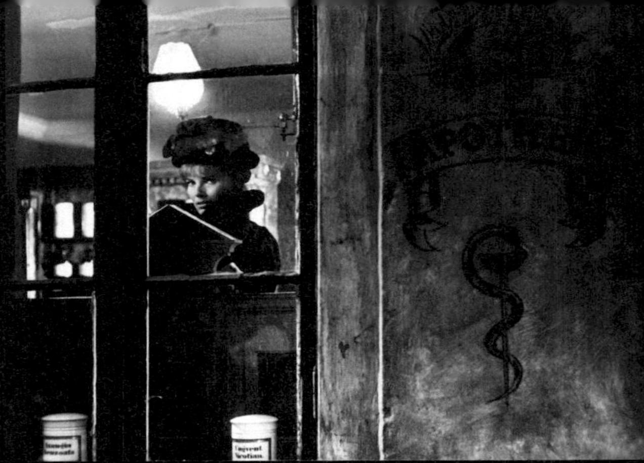

Capturing movement in a fixed image is one thing; reproducing movement in a way that lets us sense separate motions are simultaneously stopping and going – as in this shot – is quite another.

Yet another challenge is explaining how this mechanism works.

No one can doubt that everything that can move in this frame is hurtling towards the right edge of the picture. First and foremost Per Oscarsson. But the carriage is moving too, although the driver is his utmost to brake it. Even the two half-concealed people glimpsed behind the horses are headed towards the right.

I conducted an experiment. I drew three lines: one from the hole in the driver's white face – his mouth, which is more conspicuous than his eyes, but with which he tries to hail Per Oscarsson – and from there on through Oscarsson's right eye and glasses and, finally, out into a white frame I had placed around the picture. Another line from the coachman's right hand, following the tight reins almost horizontally through the black horse's halter and out into the same white frame. And, lastly, a third line from the right wheel hub flush with the lower edge of the carriage pole (that is what catches the eye, rather than the upper edge) and onward into the white frame.

The three lines converge at a single point outside the picture, a point which (because of the way the image is framed) must be presumed to lie slightly in front of the end of the pole. This is the point Oscarsson is trying to reach before the pole does, so he can safely cross the street. To everyone's relief, he did so, thanks to the driver's efforts.

Herein lies the explanation of the dynamics in this still. It remains true to the cinematic original, without in any way detracting from it – not that it should.

From one pole to another, so to speak.

You could call it a frame within a frame.

Using large surfaces that on the face of it tell us nothing, Jesper Høm exploits the window's framing of Gunnel Lindblom. A wide shot is thus turned into a close-up; distance and proximity are held in a state of mutual tension; I feel as though I am both inside and outside, literally and metaphorically. I am also forced to look up at the person who conversely is looking down at me – right into my eyes.

There you go, that put me in my place.

It makes a big difference whether a film shot or a still is the medium from which a person looks the observer in the eye. In a film sequence that cuts between close-ups of two people looking straight at each other and talking, the people are reciprocal observers. The camera typically shows them close up, one on each side of the camera lens. That is how the third party – the viewer experiences the contact between them. However, if the actors have to gaze straight right into the camera to look each other in the eye, the audience will feel excluded, an effect rarely intended.

In the still, on the other hand, the observer is an anonymous partner who never participates in way other than by looking at the picture. So to make contact with her 'partner' – the anonymous viewer of the still – Gunnel Lindblom looks at us directly, rivets us to the spot outside the picture, while yet inviting us in.

If a film still does not portray the performers' body language, a dramatic action or something mysterious, but simply shows a person – or several for that matter – without giving us the feeling that something is going on, I think we have to be able see the eyes of the person or persons whose faces are visible. Otherwise, the picture will fail to capture our interest. Faces without eyes are rarely interesting in pictures unless something is happening.

Two pictures – two actions – that combine to convey one and the same message.

This is a faithful and credible reference, similar to the movie original. There is an obvious contrast between the two well-dressed, wealthy gentlemen taking time out for a chat in the gateway, and the tramp in close-up who has nothing but time, as long as he can manage to find the means of staying alive.

Once again, the framing produces the effect of a wide shot that becomes a kind of close-up of the two gentlemen by the gate. Coupled with the true close-up of Oscarsson, this 'close-up' helps add depth to the overall structure, emphasizing the distance between him and them. That the two men and the dog are also out of focus only heightens our awareness that they belong to a world that looks a little blurred – at least to our protagonist. Moreover, the wide black space to the right of the gate graphically separates them from the tramp, Per Oscarsson, whose significance as the central figure is further emphasized by the black space on the far right.

We do not miss motion here, for there is no need for it. The reason Oscarsson is holding the bone still in the picture may be because he is considering whether he should really bite it. It is no coincidence that he is holding it at a level with the dog out in the gateway. This reinforces our expectation that the dog's owner or both men could at any moment turn and see "him in there", whereupon he will meet their gaze – but we do not know with what.

In reality a pictorial commentary on the haves and have-nots.

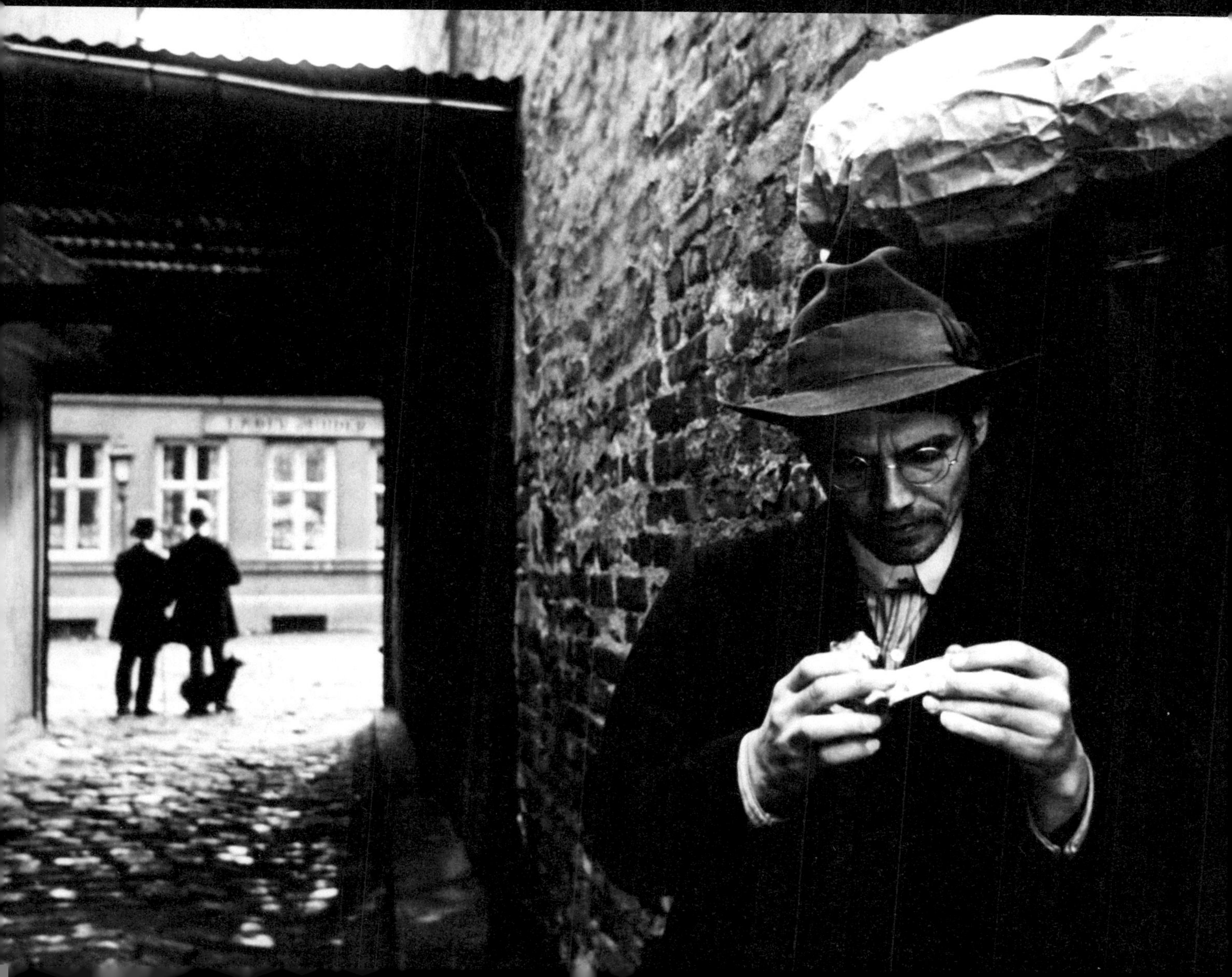

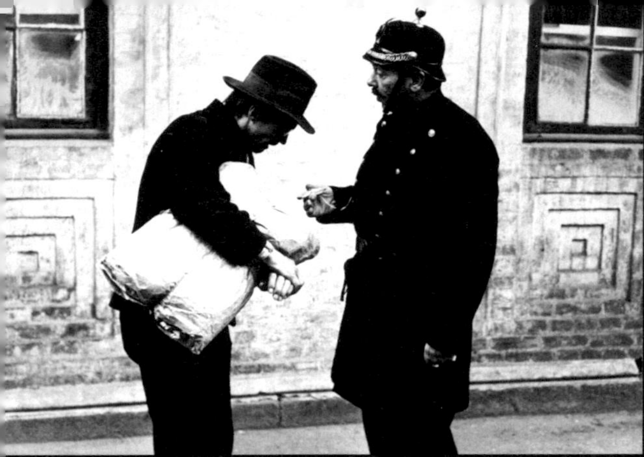

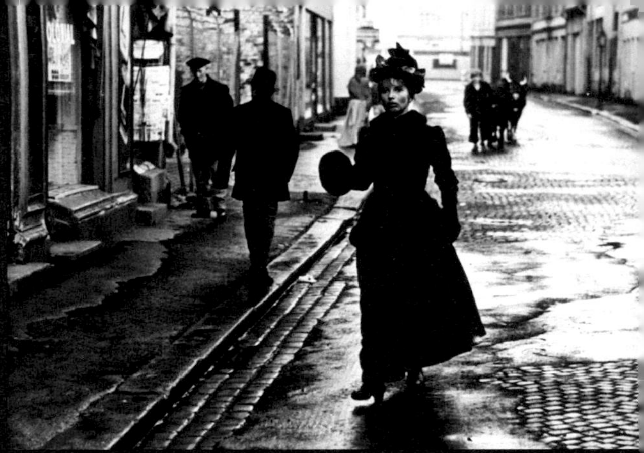

"What's the time?" is a recurrent theme for the principal character in *Hunger*. Sometimes he poses the question to put a quick end to his accidental meetings with policemen, a frequent experience for someone who spends most of his time in the public space of the city. On several occasions, time actually plays a role that almost takes him by surprise. For example, when he has a rendezvous with Ylajali at eight in the evening outside Saint Olav Square No. 2, but has forgotten it until, glancing in a watchmaker's shop, he realizes it is almost eight o'clock and is reminded of his appointment; or when he has been asked to visit the editor "tomorrow at ten", another forgotten appointment. He is snapped out of his befuddlement when the constable takes his question at face value and tells him the time is in fact 10 o'clock, and it is in fact "tomorrow".

In the film this scene has a mood of nervousness and restlessness, but also a certain humor, reminiscent of Buster Keaton, evoked by Oscarsson's body language when he dances around the constable.

The still retains some of Oscarsson's nervousness. It is no accident that the two actors are standing clear of the windows behind them, appearing almost as silhouettes against the white wall. This makes us realize that the apparent symmetry of the building wall is non-existent. While the left window is strictly parallel with the left edge of the picture, the right one is quite skewed. This is because Jesper Høm did not take the picture at a right angle to the wall. We can see that the base of the building meets the pavement below right, while the pavement ceases to exist on the left behind Oscarsson. Neither are the two (also apparently parallel) vertical strips in the back wall parallel; the right strip leans outward to the right.

All this provides the restlessness in the still that convinces us Per Oscarsson will not study the constable's pocket watch for very long; as soon as he can, he will tear himself away and dance off to his meeting.

This is – or rather was – the street in Kristiania (Oslo) in which Knut Hamsun chose to have the protagonist in *Hunger* live for a while, walking around starving in "the city that no one leaves without bearing the marks of it." Called Tomtegaten, the street no longer exists. And in any case Hamsun actually wrote most of the novel *Hunger* in Sankt Hans Gade in Copenhagen, for publication in June 1890 by P.G. Philipsens Forlag, also in Copenhagen.

So this picture is not only an example of the urban space where we worked in the autumn of 1965, when we shot the film. It also represents a kind of 'survival' – or at least a revival. This is how it looked on a cold autumn day with the night's snowfall not yet quite melted from the cobblestones, cattle being transported through the city, pedestrians walking briskly along, their hands thrust in pockets, for there is no reason to hang around.

So again there is motion in the still. Perspective almost always helps to create the sense that things are not standing still – here manifested by the kerbstone on the left and the pavement and house wall on the right. The fact that the street is a little crooked enhances the effect. And three elements help prevent this from being a 'still life'. First, the figure of Gunnel Lindblom already breaks up the lower edge of the picture. Second, her right arm is clearly swinging, usually something we do when walking briskly. Third, her right hand swings her muff across the picture's centre line, pointing in the direction in which she is walking.

Our interest also focuses on Ylajali, because she is clearly not only on her way, but also on her way *towards* someone ahead of her (on the left behind us, the viewers) on the pavement, which she is very deliberately walking beside. Perhaps she has just crossed the street to get behind her 'prey'. Perhaps she stepped out onto the road, having just foreseen that the two men whose paths will shortly cross will block the pavement and hide the person she is watching and pursuing from view.

It's hard to know what women are thinking

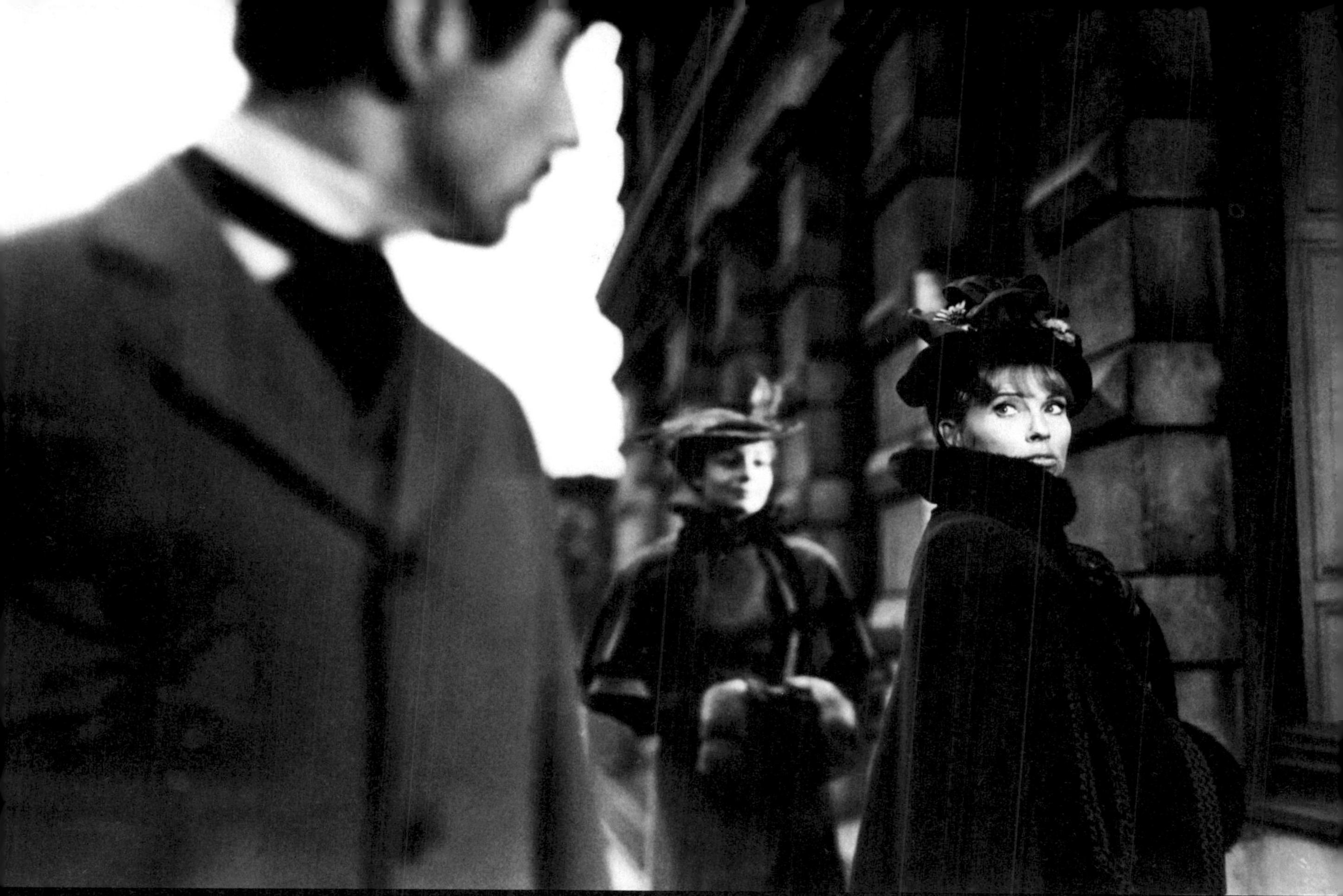

-lere Jesper Høm has partly broken free of the film since, although *Hunger* features both the characters and the locality in the picture, they do not appear in a situation like this. The extra in the left foreground has nothing to do with the scene, and the look he exchanges with Gunnel Lindblom is entirely Jesper's invention, while Birgitte Federspiel's withdrawn, worried expression could be in perfect keeping with the character she plays in the film, but never in connection with this extra.

All the same, at the time, we must have fallen for the picture's general atmosphere. Here we have a hint of the city space in which the story unfolds. The people's dress tells us it is set in a different time, a concept the film itself tries to play down. We sense a sexual undertone undeniably linked to Gunnel Lindblom's Ylajali figure.

But the picture also has a remarkable composition. The male figure is lifted slightly out of his anonymity, placed against the backdrop of a white sky without quite becoming a silhouette. With the man in this position the picture's focus shifts to Gunnel Lindblom, while Birgitte Federspiel's only half-lit face emphasizes her withdrawn presence.

This was well spotted by an observant Jesper Høm, a discreet background figure who seized every opportunity throughout the filming to 'shoot' whenever he saw a tempting motif. There was plenty to tempt him, as his enormous consumption of negatives in 35mm Leica format amply shows. As I have said, there were over seven thousand individual pictures, the contacts for which I have recently perused for other reasons. On-set pictures of the film crew during shooting make up about a third of the complete collection of negatives. And I must say there are few duds in the heap. In fact, I don't remember a single one.

So we kept this picture in the set of stills, maybe because we saw it as expressing an unfailing power of observation and initiative that we, too, wished to emulate.

A decision we still don't regret today.

BLIMP!

ROLF KONOW INTERVIEWED BY MICHAEL JUUL HOLM 17TH AUGUST 2006

MJH: Rolf Konow, you've been a professional still photographer on film productions for more than 35 years, in Denmark and in recent years abroad too. How did you actually get started with this highly specialized job?
RK: I trained as an advertising photographer, but originally I actually wanted to be a film cameraman. Then when I was at boarding school I met Ole Lütken, who was a cameraman at Saga Film, and he said, "You should try being a still photographer first; that'll give you a sense of what it means, and then at any rate you'll have some sort of training. So I became a trainee for four years with the commercial photographer Guldbrandsen. One of my good friends, Jan Lehmann, was at that time a production assistant at Nordisk Film. He told me that they needed a new still photographer. *Ballade på Christianshavn* ('Trouble in Christianshavn') was the first feature film I worked on – I began on 1st December 1970. At that time you still quite anachronistically used the expression a fixed plate for a still, but in fact you worked with a Hasselblad or Rolleiflex camera. Erik Balling was directing, and the work of the still photographer consisted of getting the actors lined up after the filming, and then Balling would say "Hup!". That was the signal for the actors to take up the positions they were supposed to be in. Then I had to take the picture. He said "Hup!" three times. If I hadn't got the picture by then, that was my problem. But it seems to have gone very well, because I carried on at Nordisk Film as a permanent freelance photographer; I was involved in twelve of the *Olsen Gang* films, 72 episodes of *The House in Christianshavn and six episodes of Matador ...*

The method you've just described was very common in the past – that is, the actors posed specially for the still photographer. The director von Sternberg was notorious for making an incredibly big thing out of stills; he did the lighting himself, the whole situation was directed, and at the right moment he said NOW and NOW. In that sense the still photographer was more or less the tool of the director. But what has happened since then, how do you work today?
– At the time when I started at Nordisk Film, it was with actors who were posed, but then I met a cameraman who had been in Hollywood, and asked him how they did it over there. He told me that they used a soundproofed box there, a so-called 'blimp' – and that meant you could take pictures during the filming without bothering the actors and the sound people. The pictures are not so frozen, not so posed; you get closer to what the film camera sees – what the audience at the film also sees. Very often it can be hard to get the actors up to scratch again after they've played a scene; they're so happy that it's all over, even the most professional actors start to fool around. When the clapper board sounds, there's an intensity and a magic that can't be recreated, so for me it's obviously best to get the pictures during the process. So I bought one of those blimps in Hollywood, and I already began using it on one of the Olsen Gang films.

How do you capture the essence of a process or the point in a film, how do you find the exact point where the drama unfolds – can you say something about concentrating things?
– Well, sometimes you actually 'cheat' as a still photographer. You change things around a bit in terms of the way a situation is experienced in the film. When you shoot a film, maybe you'll cut between two actors – but you can't use two portrait stills; you have to narrate the whole sequence in one picture. In those cases I try to get a picture where, instead of getting the back of one actor's neck and the front of another, I get them together from the front, and the story is told in a better way so everyone understands it. In the classic Hollywood stills, for example, you often find three people posed in the set so that the drama and the conflicts or

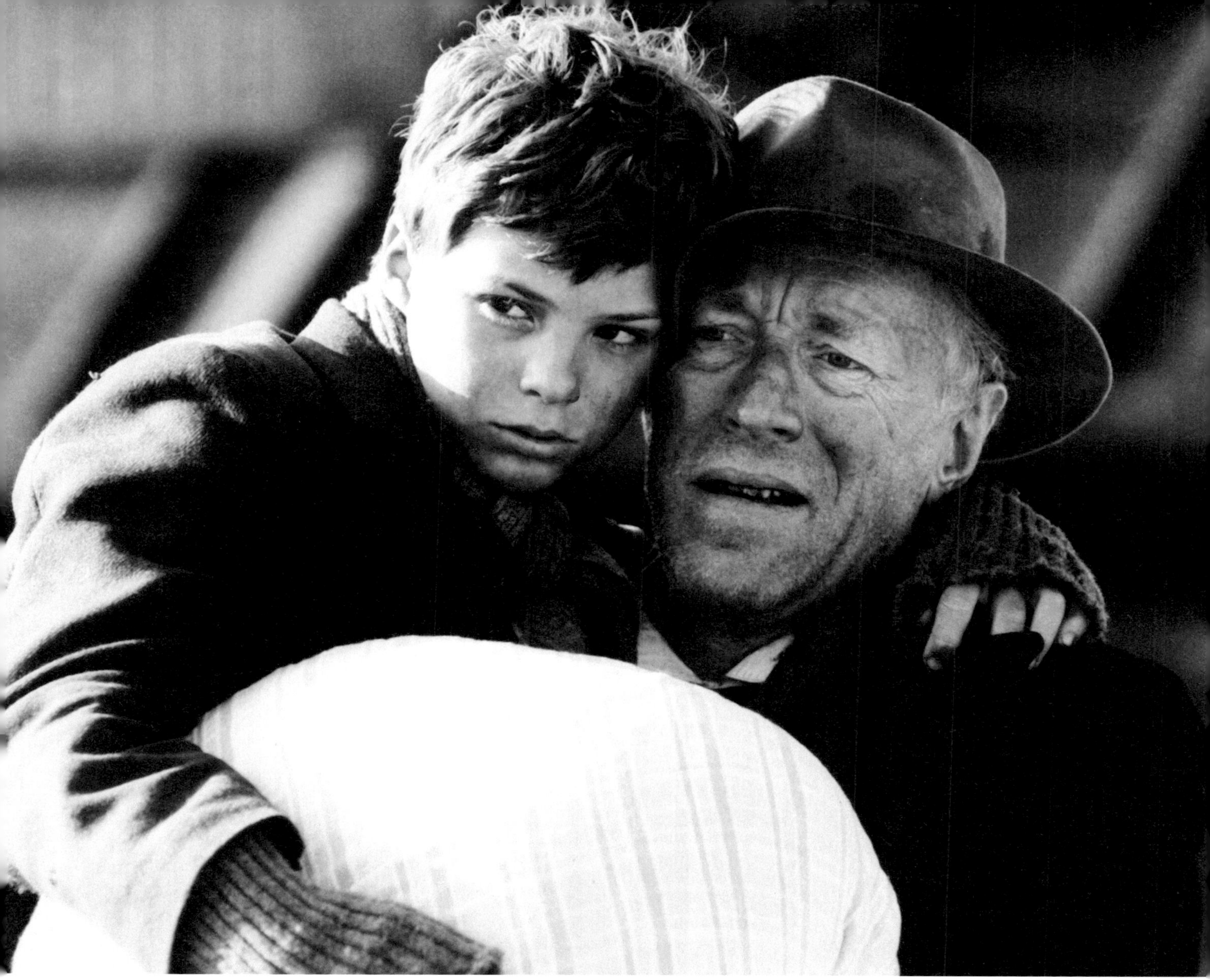

Pelle the Conqueror, 1987. Director: Bille August. In the picture: Pelle Hvenegaard, Max von Sydow
Still photographer: Rolf Konow © Nordisk Film

relations among them are clear. There's no guarantee they stand that way when the film is being shot, but to get the essence of the scene they've been posed that way. In *The Lost Treasure of the Knights Templar*, which I worked on last year, there's a scene where Kurt Ravn, in the role of Erik Isaksen, is standing with the Ark in the foreground, and the kids who actually play the main role are standing in the room behind. When we were about to take the picture I thought, let's get those children out so they're standing beside Isaksen and the Ark, that tells the story betters. But it's cheating, for in reality they were out in the back room... But it's all about telling the story, what is going on. And there are other important images, for example one from *Breaking the Waves* and another from *Othello* with Laurence Fishburne and Kenneth Branagh, also taken after the actual shooting. Sometimes, you see, I discover along the way that I won't get the picture with my blimp. You can't avoid that working with Lars von Trier, since he often is the cameraman on his own films – he rushes around with his camera, and sometimes you simply can't get in there while it's happening. So I ask them to line up again, and it works too. In that case at least it's OK.

Why do you have a still photographer along with the film at all – why not just print a blown-up frame from the actual film?
– Actually they often do that now: they're called framegrabs ... but the quality of framegrabs isn't particularly good. A film frame runs through the camera in a fiftieth of a second and if the actors move around, the picture will be blurred. And the picture is quite small, so if it has to be blown up for example for a centre page in a magazine or for a poster, it just can't be used.

What else are the still photographer's pictures used for?
– The long and short of it is that it's about getting people into the cinema. If it costs 20 million dollars to produce a film, another 20 million are set aside for promotion – trailers, TV spots, posters, publicity pictures, anything. The stills form part of the overall marketing on posters, in display cases, as press photos, for books – very often a book is made when the film is finished. It's all about selling the film. In Denmark there are film companies that would like to save on the costs of a still photographer: after all, we can use framegrabs, they say, can't you just come now and then and take a few pictures? But then, where are all the production stills,

Ballade på Christianshavn, 1971. Director: Erik Balling. In the picture: Poul Bundgaard, Kirsten Walther
Still photographer: Rolf Konow © Nordisk Film

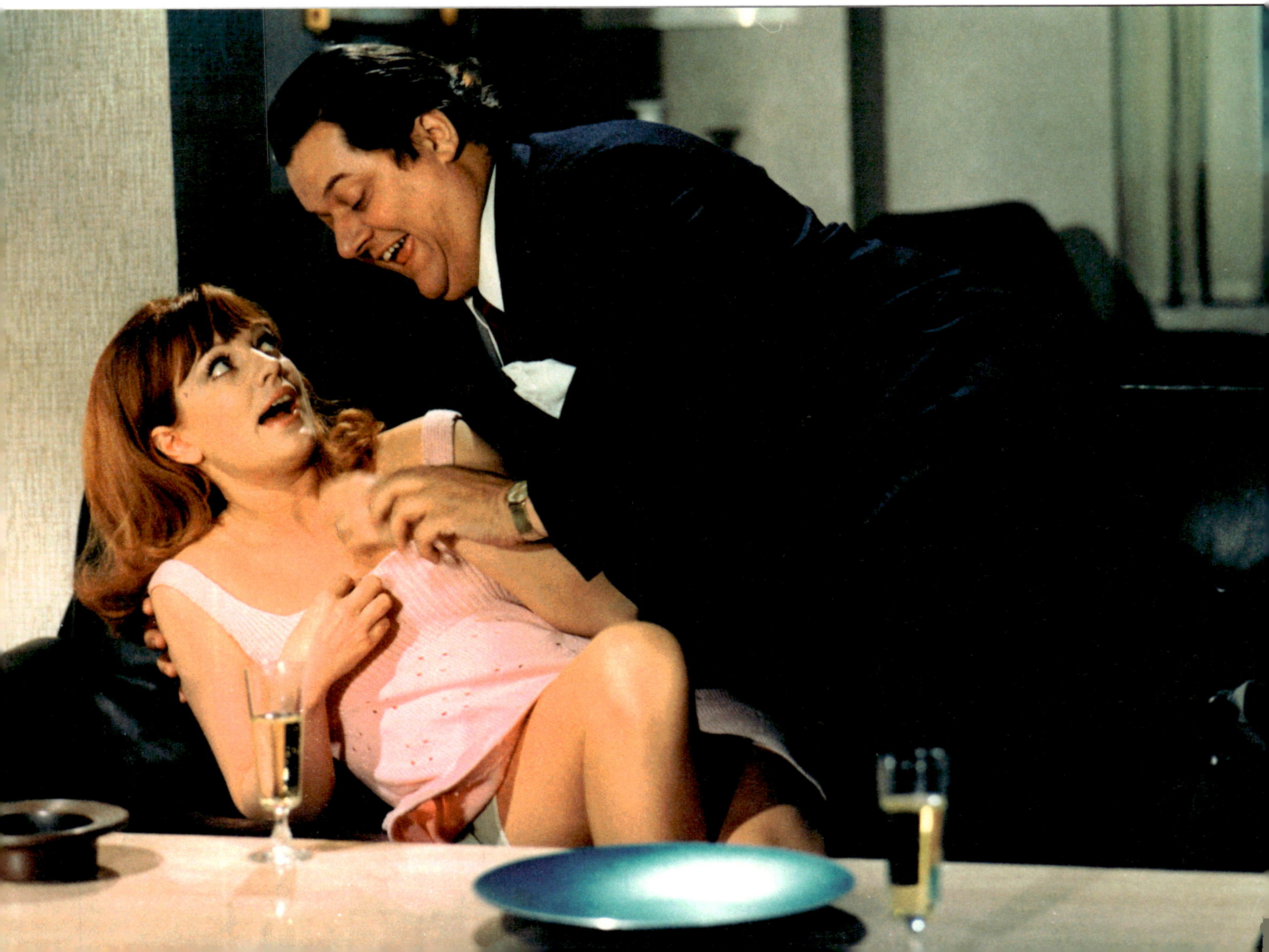

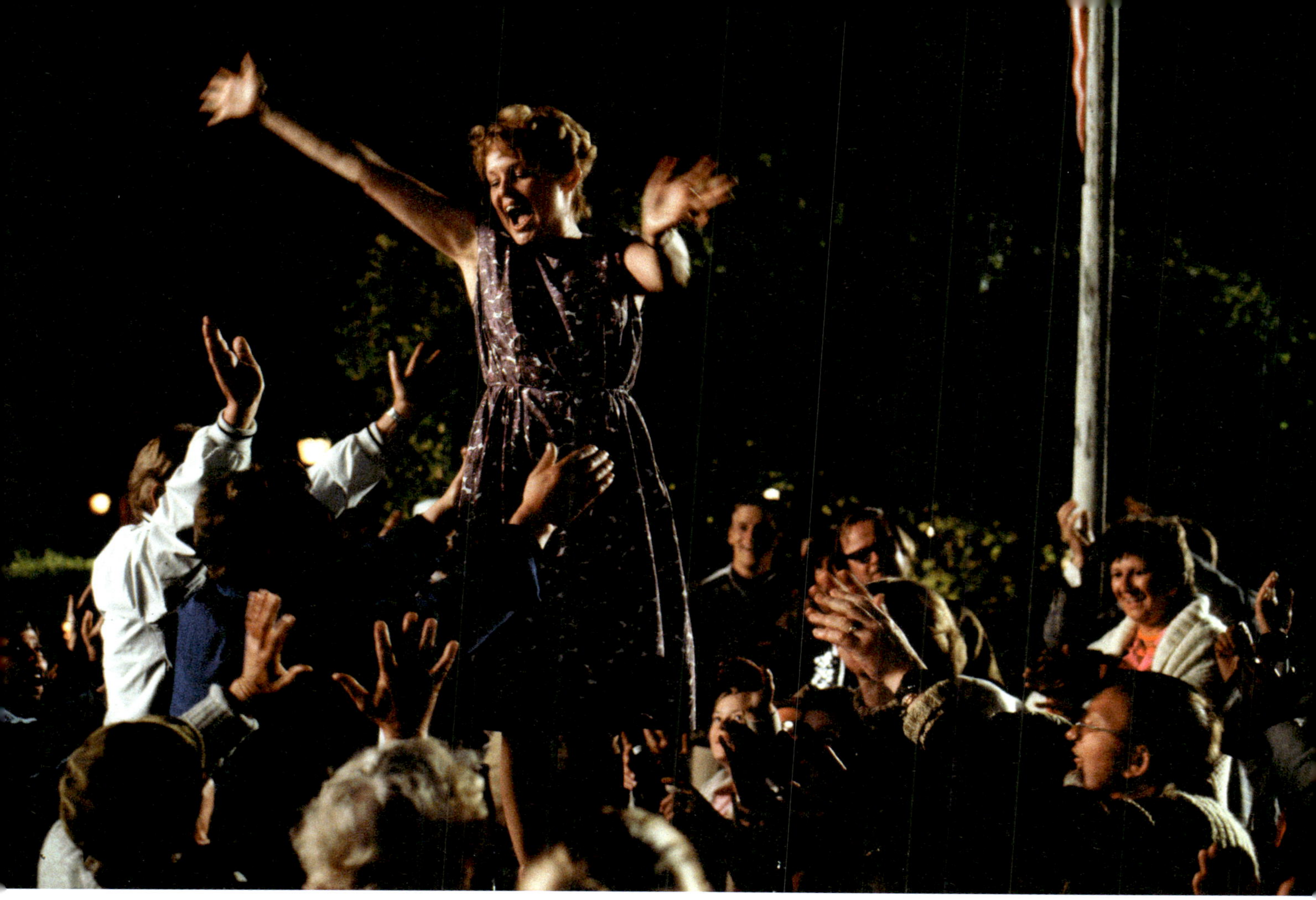

Waltzing Regitze, 1989. Director: Kaspar Rostrup. In the picture: Ghita Nørby . Still photographer: Rolf Konow © Nordisk Film

where are all the pictures where the director is standing with the film actors? Where are all the photos that will be used in the film magazines, where are all the documentation pictures when a book is to be written about the director? The production stills are almost as important as the actual film pictures – the "set stills". Many film magazines are wild about showing behind-the-scenes pictures. That's why it's really important to have those pictures too. There's a magazine, *American Cinematographer*, which only works behind the scenes, where you see the photographer with the director and the actors – that's a very important part of it: Getting the pictures that are to be used in newspapers, magazines and books in the box. When a film like *Batman* is released, at the same time they make a Batman book with the script and a whole lot of production and set stills.

Often, too, you take portraits: you build a little studio and then you take the actors in and photograph them for poster pictures and other promotion. In Denmark you typically post 8-9 stills on the Internet, and then you can use the ones you want, but abroad they work much more deliberately to coddle the various media. *Vanity Fair*, for example, gets a few exclusive stills – no other magazine gets *those* particular pictures. That way, I believe, you get more press coverage than if you just post eight pictures on the Internet. A magazine will be much more interested in giving you coverage if it gets exclusives than they will if anyone can download them to their computer.

Some stills have become so iconic of a particular film that people actually remember them better than the film itself. Your picture from Pelle the Conqueror, I think, has that quality, and it's also an important picture for you perso-

nally, because that was the film that was really the start of your international career ... how did that photo arise?
– While the film *Pelle the Conqueror* was being shot we stayed for a while on the island of Bornholm, and we had the idea of making a poster picture with Max von Sydow and Pelle on the boat with the people who came from Sweden. I also took some pictures when he got off the boat with Pelle in his arms. But I could sense that I hadn't got what I wanted, so after the filming I asked Max von Sydow to lift Pelle up on his arm again, and then I got what I thought was the best one. Later I took some stills with me to America to show to various people, and I went to see an American publicity lady. About the picture we took during the filming she said: "Oh no, don't use that. It's far too sad, it looks like a refugee camp, that would scare people right off." But the other one – that had something, it had life, much more intensity. So that's what was chosen for the poster picture, and that's the picture everyone associates with the film *Pelle the Conqueror.*

Two other pictures that have similarly become iconic are the one of the Olsen Gang where they're walking single-file out by the water – that motif is almost as well known here as the Beatles on their way to Apple Studios – and then there's the picture of Ghita Nørby in the role of Regitze, dancing on the table at a summer party ...
– I wasn't involved in the first two Olsen Gang films, as I was still a photography trainee with Guldbrandsen then, but even back then the silhouette march was used, the black on the white background, and for all the Olsen Gang films since then they've had the three men in a row down at the harbour in front of the old Soya Bean Cake Factory. It's also been repeated in other places, for example in Paris in *Olsen Banden over alle bjerge* (The Olsen Gang Over the Hills and Away) – for that they made a silhouette march too. It was quite obvious that all the Olsen Gang films had to have a silhouette march – with Bent Fabricius's wonderful music. The picture for *Waltzing Regitze* is one of those I could see immediately was just right, and I told the film company that I thought it was the picture that should be used as the poster, and that's what happened. But you never know whether it'll be used, the picture you've taken. I've just been working on *The Magic Flute* in

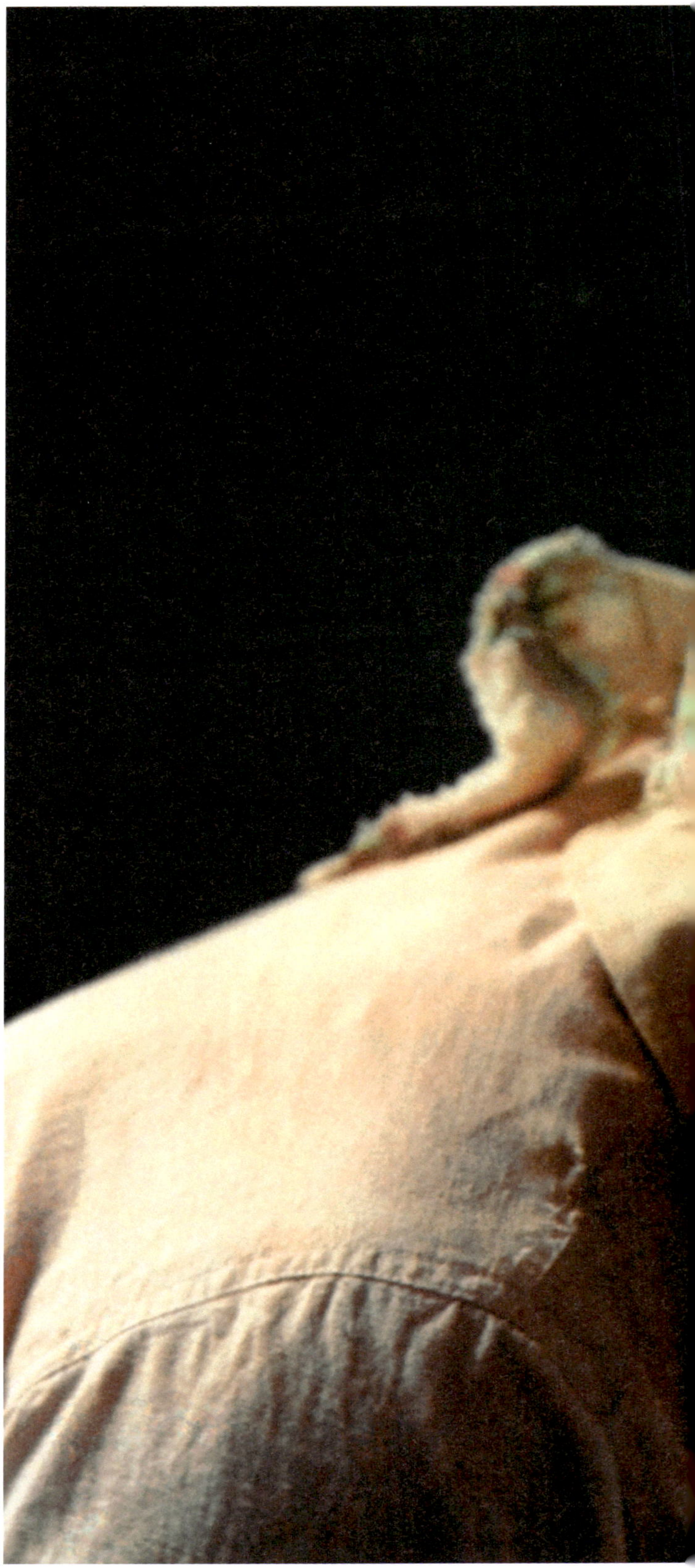

Dogville, 2003. Director: Lars von Trier
In the picture: Nicole Kidman
Still photographer: Rolf Konow © Zentropa Entertainments

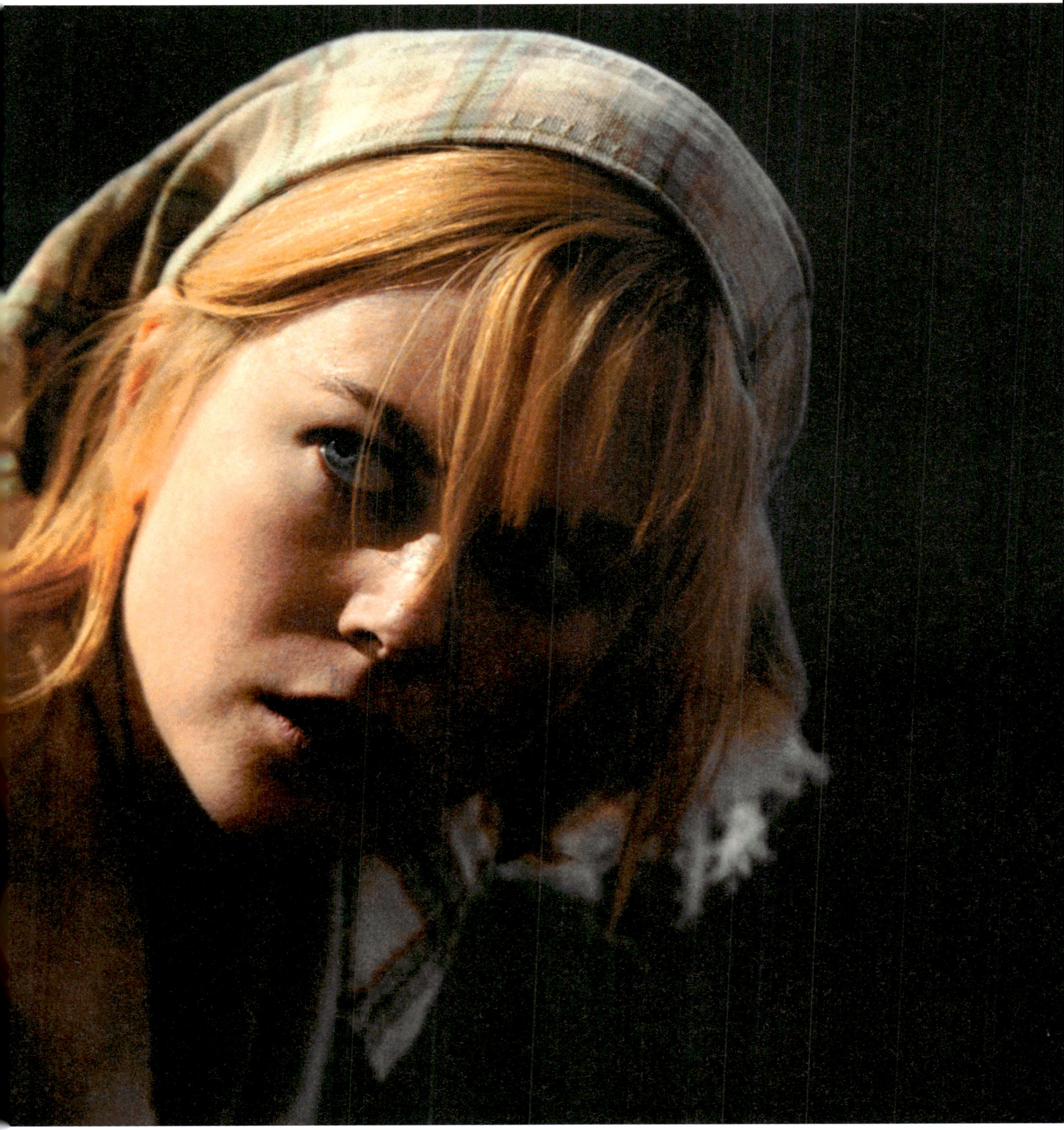

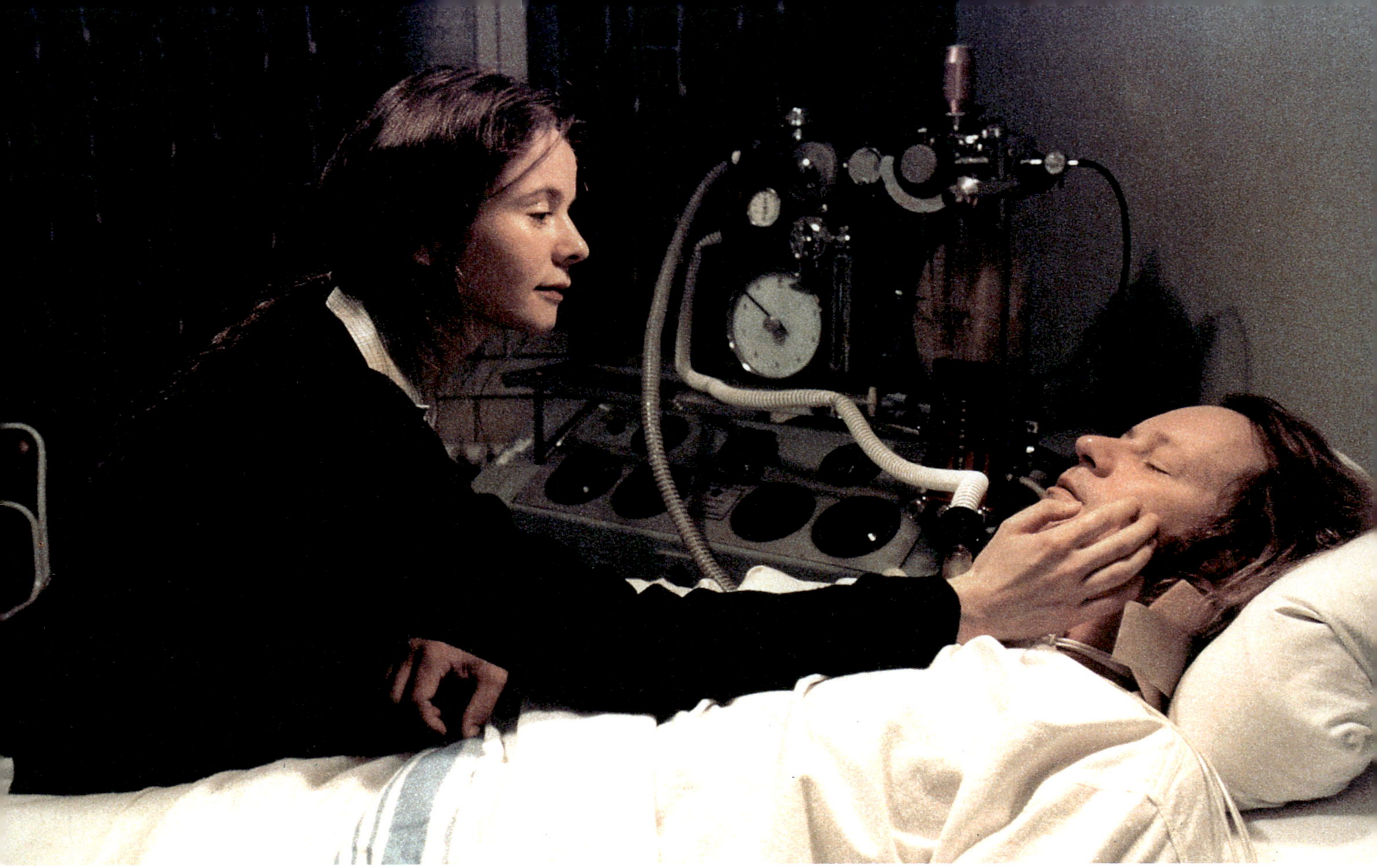

Breaking The Waves, 1996. Director: Lars von Trier. In the picture: Emily Watson, Stellan Skarsgård.
Still photographer: Rolf Konow © Zentropa Entertainments

England, where I took 10,000 pictures. You can feel it when you take the kind of picture that will be good, but basically it isn't up to me to make the choice. My job on a film begins with me getting an assignment, a piece of paper that says what I have to do, what kind of pictures are to be taken, and it also says that when the film is finished there should be 250-300 pictures that have been approved by the actors. I deliver a product to a film company which then has to choose which of many pictures they want to use. I may well feel that I've taken a good picture, but there's no guarantee that it will be used.

Ghita Nørby is just one of the grand female stars you've worked with – offhand I can mention Kate Winslet, Meryl Streep, Agneta Ekmanner, Irene Jacob, Milla Jovovich ... Throughout the history of film we have had a long line of divas, from Asta Nielsen, Ava Gardner and Lillian Gish through Dietrich, Garbo and Marilyn Monroe to female actors like Michelle Pfeiffer and Nicole Kidman – women who besides being good actresses have a special aura and have become brands in their own right. Some of your diva portraits stay very close to the tradition, while for example the picture of Nicole Kidman from "Dogville" shows a whole new interpretation of the diva as a little fragile – a wisp of hair hanging down over one eye, and you've let whites of the eyes stay pink. Can you say something about your work with these actresses?

– It's true whether you work with men or women: trust is something you build up over time and it's quite crucial to how close you can get, in several senses. I also worked on Henning Carlsen's *Oviri* with Donald Sutherland, who played Gauguin the painter, but he had this little touch of vanity: *"Rolf, look here at this wrinkle – I really don't like this wrinkle, so could you please avoid it?"* So although he had to show us the worn-out painter, he mustn't have that wrinkle on his neck, and I think that's quite OK, I accept that. The great stars have the privilege that they get to approve all the pictures. I can sit with a picture that I think is quite wonderful and nevertheless there's something about it an actor doesn't like, and so it's scrapped. Or there may be two actors in a picture where one of them doesn't care for the image of himself or herself – or thinks the other one looks too good, I don't know. When I worked on *Hamlet* with Julie Christie, she said: *"Rolf, it's not your photos, I don't like – it's me I don't like"*. It was kind of her to say that after she had rejected the pictures I thought were marvellous.

In Louisiana's exhibition we've set up a small cabinet of erotic stills. Not pornographic – it would be a quite different exhibition if we were to talk about what pornography has meant to modern man – but all the same, pictures that are a bit more than just suggestive. They're very rare – after going through more than 120,000 stills we've actually been able to find little more than a handful, which is also something to do with the fact that those scenes are best left as something people tell one another about instead of something they can check out in advance. But pictures like that must also require a quite special relationship with those involved to succeed?

– That's another reason it's important to be involved in a film right from the start: you develop a relationship of trust with the actors; you don't do that if you just come in now and then. Then they think, "Now he's just coming because there are sexy scenes". American actors are often almost paranoid about these things, maybe because they have in fact experienced being exploited. For them a so-called closed set is very often used, and you can't get in. When we did the rape scene in *Dogville* it was a completely closed set; no one was allowed in. European actors work with a different kind of trust in you. They know you won't exploit them. I worked on the film *Per*, which Hans Christensen directed, where Ole Ernst acted with Agneta Ekmanner in some nude scenes. I made an agreement with Agneta that she would be allowed to look through all the pictures, but when it came to the crunch she didn't reject a single one. This picture from *Othello* – you see some naked bodies, but you don't really see anything... Before we started, the actress – Irene Jacob, who was also in Kieslowski's *Red* – said *"Rolf, not too much nudity!"* You try to create some pictures that don't betray the actors and that way you build up a relationship of trust with them; you also have the chance to create the *right* pictures. On the poster for Susanne Bier's *Open Hearts*, for example, we have some intimate pictures of the two actors Mads Mikkelsen and Sonja Richter. If you don't have a good relationship with the actors that kind of picture just can't be done.

Can you tell me a little about how it was for you to go from being a Danish still photographer to an international still photographer?

– It's always a great challenge to go abroad and do something different, and when you've made twelve Olsen Gang films, you want to.... It was Bille August who made it possible with *Pelle the Conqueror*, where we won an Oscar. The film company, Constantin Film, which made *House of the Spirits* and *Smilla's Sense of Snow* afterwards, had other films where they engaged me – and it is a big thing that you start with one film company, and if they like what you do you're allowed to do some more for them. It's exciting to get out and do something bigger. In Denmark we use film crews of 30-40 people – in the big international productions they work with two film crews: the first unit with 150 people, and second unit similarly of 150. The fact that it's big doesn't necessarily mean it's better, but it gives you greater filmic potential – for the stills too. On action films there are explosions and people shooting, it's a lot of fun and very exciting for a still photographer

You've worked for example on the two "Resident Evil" films, which is quite different from something like "Waltzing Regitze" ...

– Actually I've worked on three Resident Evil films. The first one was made in Berlin, the second in Toronto – and I've just come home from Mexico after the production of number three. They're films with a plot and some figures adopted from a very popular computer game, so you know in advance that there's a big – in fact a huge – audience. They're real action films where there isn't very much talking, but an awful lot of action. And pictorially it's been incredibly exciting to do, because something is going on in the pictures. In a way it isn't so far from the *Olsen Gang* films – after all, they're comic-strip figures with hats on – and the same goes for *Resident Evil*, where the goodies and baddies step right out of a computer game. It means a lot to the people who see the films that they look like the figures they know from the computer game – the production company and actors will certainly hear about it from the audience if they do something that doesn't come up to their expectations!

I suppose it also poses some technical challenges for the photographer to know that the stunt to be photographed

now can't be repeated, that it costs millions to set it all up and that it'll only happen now, this once?

– For that kind of film I sometimes set up three cameras and give a fourth camera to someone from public relations, and say, "Shoot just from that angle". And then I have some remote-release shutters; I stand there with two or three remote releases to be sure there'll be something there afterwards. I need to get it from all angles, I can't risk being left with no pictures!

You trained as a still photographer in the advertising business and learned all the basic techniques there, but you learned all the stuff related specifically to the film business simply by doing it. Later you've become very aware of your own trade – how much of an interest have you taken in your predecessors in the trade – do you look at other photographers' stills, are you inspired by them and by the tradition you're part of in one way or another?
– I've always been interested in pictures. There is a still photographer, Bob Willoughby, who published some books about still photography, which I've read and looked at a lot. I also visited him last year in Vence – I'm a member of the Society of Motion Picture Still Photographers in Los Angeles, and Bob Willoughby is one of the honorary members – and it was a fantastic experience to meet him. I very much admire Kjeld Helmer-Petersen, who's a wonderful Danish photographer. He's more than 80 years old now and has had exhibitions all over the world. I go to exhibitions everywhere I visit and look at pictures; you just can't help it as a photographer. Exhibitions, photo magazines; pictures, pictures, pictures – everywhere.

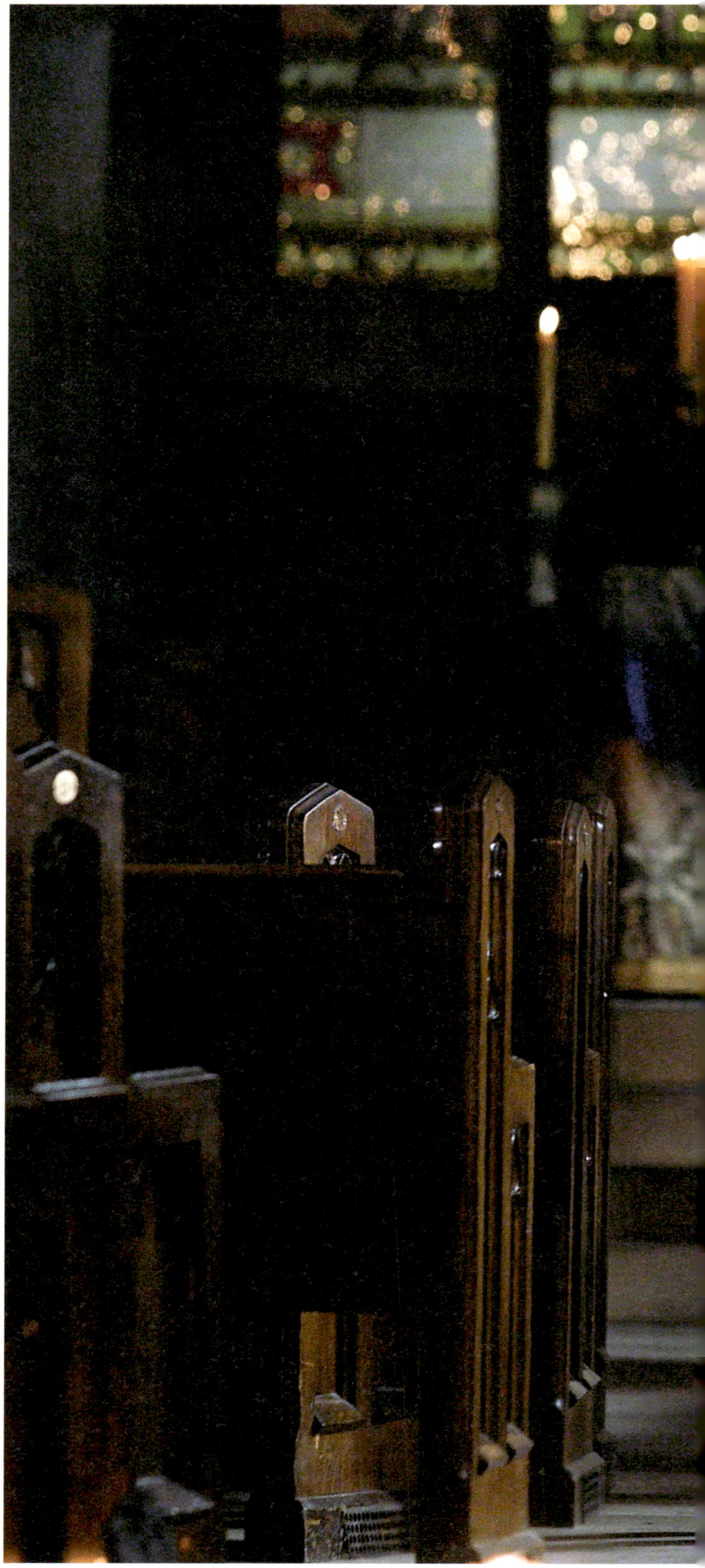

Resident Evil: Apocalypse, 2004
Director: Alexander Witt
In the picture: Milla Jovovich
Still photographer: Rolf Konow © Constantin Film

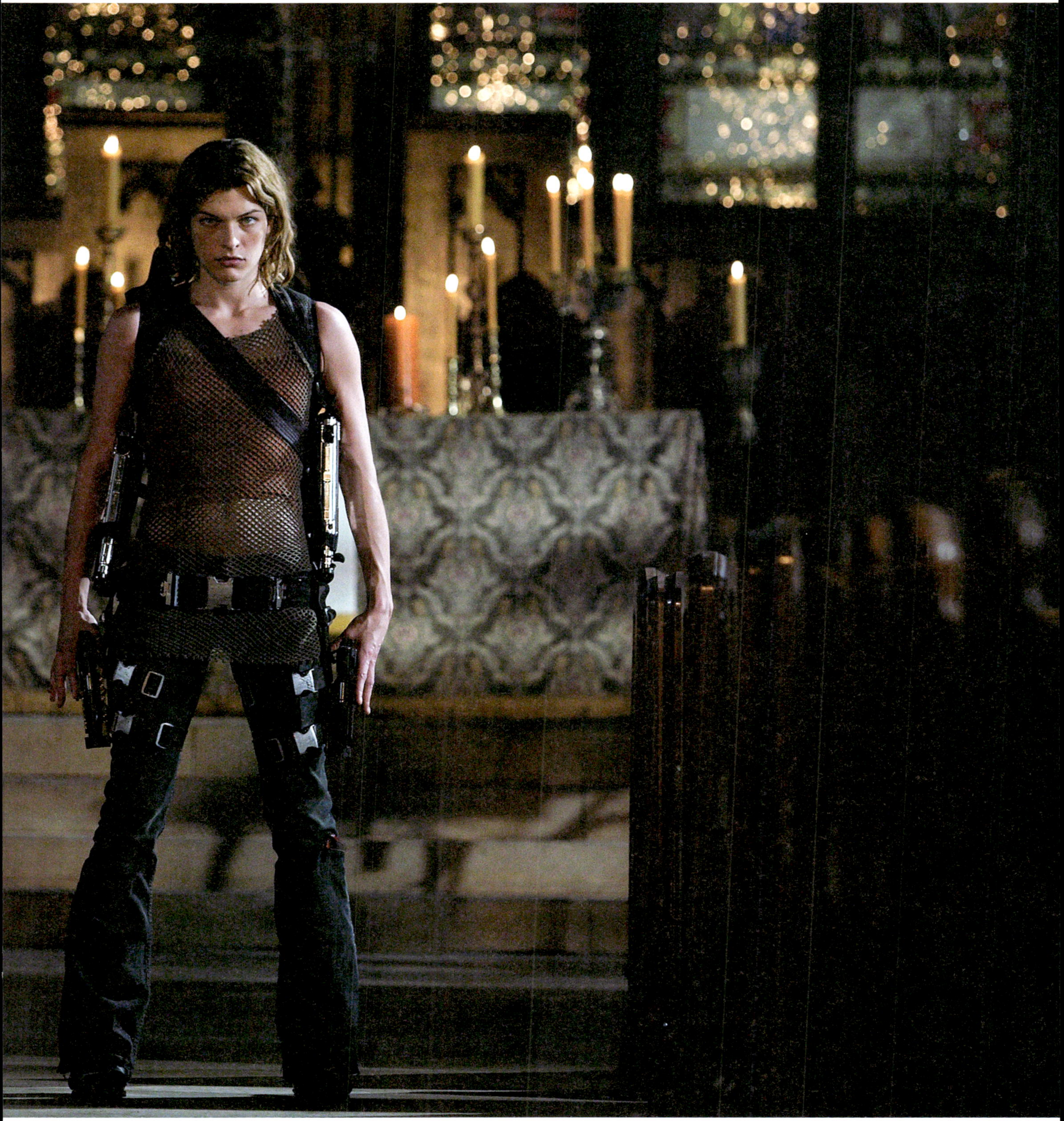

THE ETERNAL THREAT

By **Mette Kia Krabbe Meyer**

When *Jaws* (Steven Spielberg, USA, 1975) was premiered I was four years old and quite definitely too young to watch horror films. Nor did I see it later as a teenager, when you could rent it on video, and I've never sat glued to the screen when it has been shown on TV. Nevertheless I've had a clear impression of *Jaws* and the white shark, and probably I'm not the only one who has – without actually having seen the film. There is no doubt that this is partly due to the film poster and the many stills. They have left me and many others with an unpleasant impression of a faceless mass, a nose-like, corpse-pale lump of flesh with a horrifying slit full of razor-sharp teeth. They have led to innumerable imaginings and nightmares about the ravages of the shark, and they have created a feeling of knowing the film.

And now I have finally managed to see *Jaws*. To tell the truth I used this article, which is about disaster films and stills, as a pretext to rent it, and besides the satisfaction of finally meeting the white shark, the film also gave rise to a number of reflections on the relationship between film and film still. I found out that the feeling of familiarity with a film I'd never seen was determined partly by seeing the images from it, but even more so because the posters and stills express exactly what I look for in the disaster films – that is, dramatic moments.

By disaster films I mean a wide range of films which, since early in the history of the film medium, have exploited the way one can stage-manage destruction and ruin dramatically[1]. You can show nature going amok, microorganisms that spread uncontrollably, invasions by aliens, human destruction. Like all genres, the disaster film is not clearly demarcated from other genres, but one criterion for calling something a disaster film, apart from the fact that the film will in all probability be American, is that it shows an often sudden, destructive intervention in an existing order. The disaster films therefore satisfy a need for excitement, and appeal to a fearful and pleasurable expectation of destruction with both psychological and culture-historical dimensions, and it is precisely this need that the film still satisfies – in a way that is related to the appeal of the film, but at the same time different in its presentational form.

KEPT IN SUSPENSE

One might well imagine that *Jaws* would have disappointed me. If I hadn't seen that particular disaster film within the past few years, I'd seen a number of others – from *Independence Day* (Roland Emmerich, USA, 1996) to *Volcano* (Mick Jackson, USA, 1997), Armageddon (Michael Bay, USA, 1998) and *The Day After Tomorrow* (Roland Emmerich, USA, 2004). These are films in a quite different financial and technical league, and as far as special effects are concerned, the animations of attacks from outer space, asteroid showers and towering tidal waves can easily outstrip a single cardboard shark. However, *Jaws* has something else that only a minority of the more recent disaster films have: it dramatizes fear and the anticipation of disaster in a long, nerve-rackingly suspenseful process. In the film we are taken into the life of a small town on the coast, where the recently-arrived police chief and his family are looking forward to a cushy job and a beautiful summer. Carefree relaxation is the order of the day when the shark claims its first victim from among some teenagers who have been spending the night on the beach. The police chief, who is a responsible man, wants to close off the whole beach, but the mayor won't give up the earnings that come from the holidaymakers, so he ignores all warnings of the disaster. In other words the film effectively cultivates the viewer's fearful anticipation of the attack. This sets the carefree life of the small town in relief. We see everyday normality presented as a picture postcard that is about to be torn up.

This presentation of life as a vulnerable construct that risks destruction by dangers from the outside can be found not only in *Jaws*, but also in a number of older and more recent disaster films. *Volcano* and *Earthquake*

Jaws, 1975. Director: Steven Spielberg.
© 1975 Universal Pictures

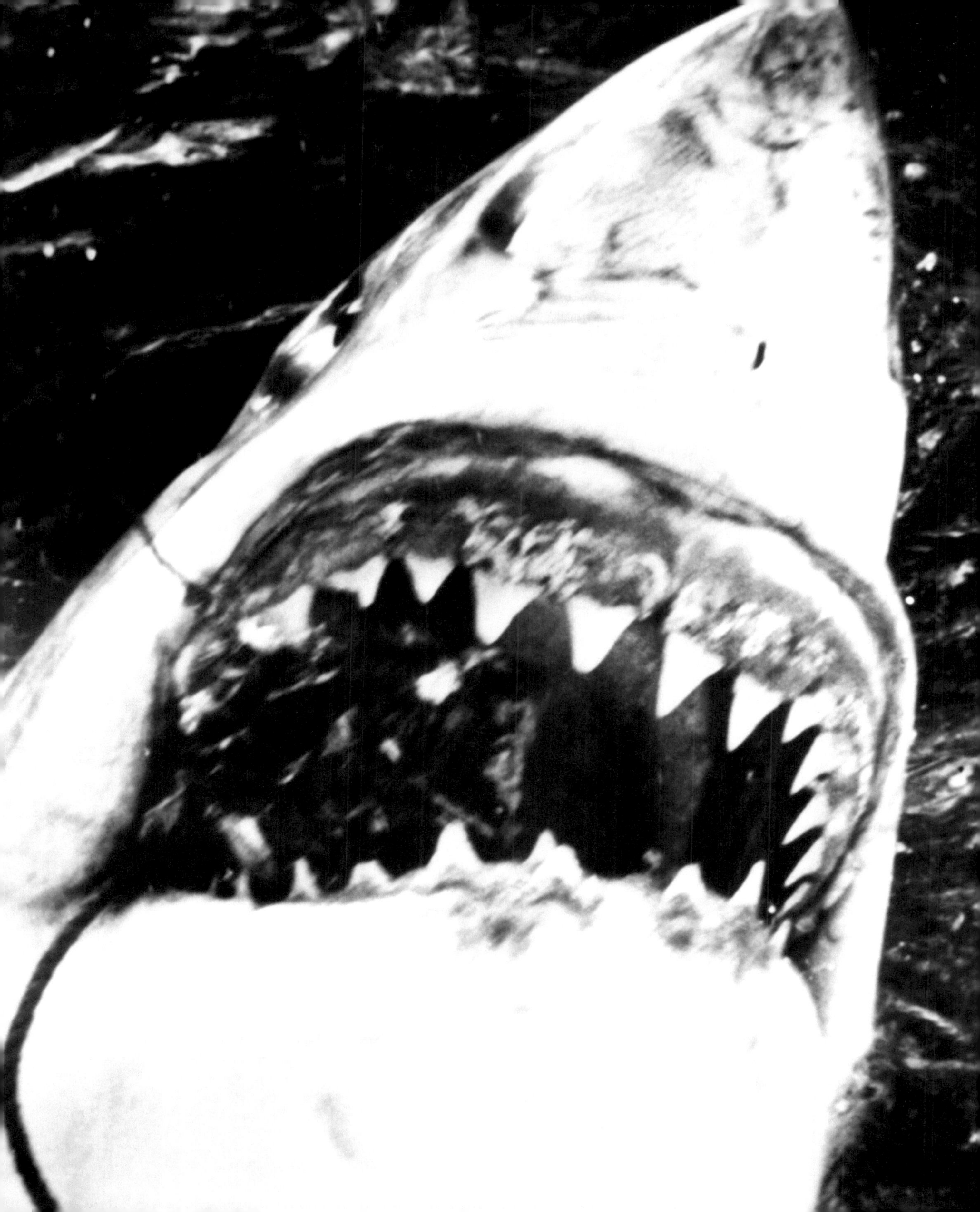

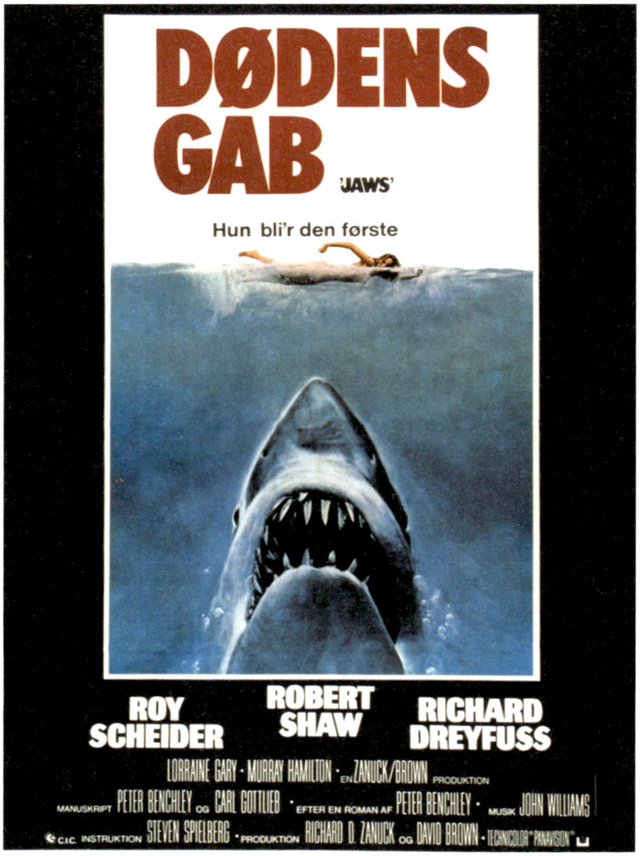

Jaws, 1975. Director: Steven Spielberg.
© 1975 Universal Pictures

(Mark Robson, USA, 1974), both of which take place in LA, tell stories of human struggle against destructive nature. Both films begin with a sequence where the camera moves over a bird's-eye view of the thronging city with its tangled network of freeways and skyscrapers. It is early morning, and the film cuts to a series of everyday scenes. In *Volcano* we see tradesmen and hotel staff opening shops and hotels. We watch people working out, demonstrating against subway construction etc. and are even introduced to Lake La Brea, the city's geological tourist attraction which, with its methane emissions, testifies to tireless activity just under the feet of the city-dwellers. In *Earthquake* the main character jogs and then quarrels with his alcoholic wife, while two policemen chase a speeding motorist and children are sent to school. In both films there are hints of the danger. In *Volcano* there is a cut to close-ups of molten lava in narrow cavities, and in *Earthquake* a small quake makes the alcoholic wife wake up suddenly from her fake pill-suicide attempt, while a dam superintendent is killed.

In all the films we are aware of what is about to happen; after all, the disaster films are cut from the familiar cloth of the fairytales. In *Little Red Riding-Hood* we know, for example, that Riding-Hood will be swallowed by the wolf and saved by the hunter; but also that the tale is just as much about all that comes before her being eaten. First she has to be led astray by the wolf, which lures her into the forest to pick flowers; and when she comes to the house we have to shudder when she asks the wolf in Grandma's clothing: "Why have you got such big ears, Grandmother? Why have you got such

The Day After Tomorrow, 2004. Director: Roland Emmerich.
© Twentieth Century Fox Film Corporation

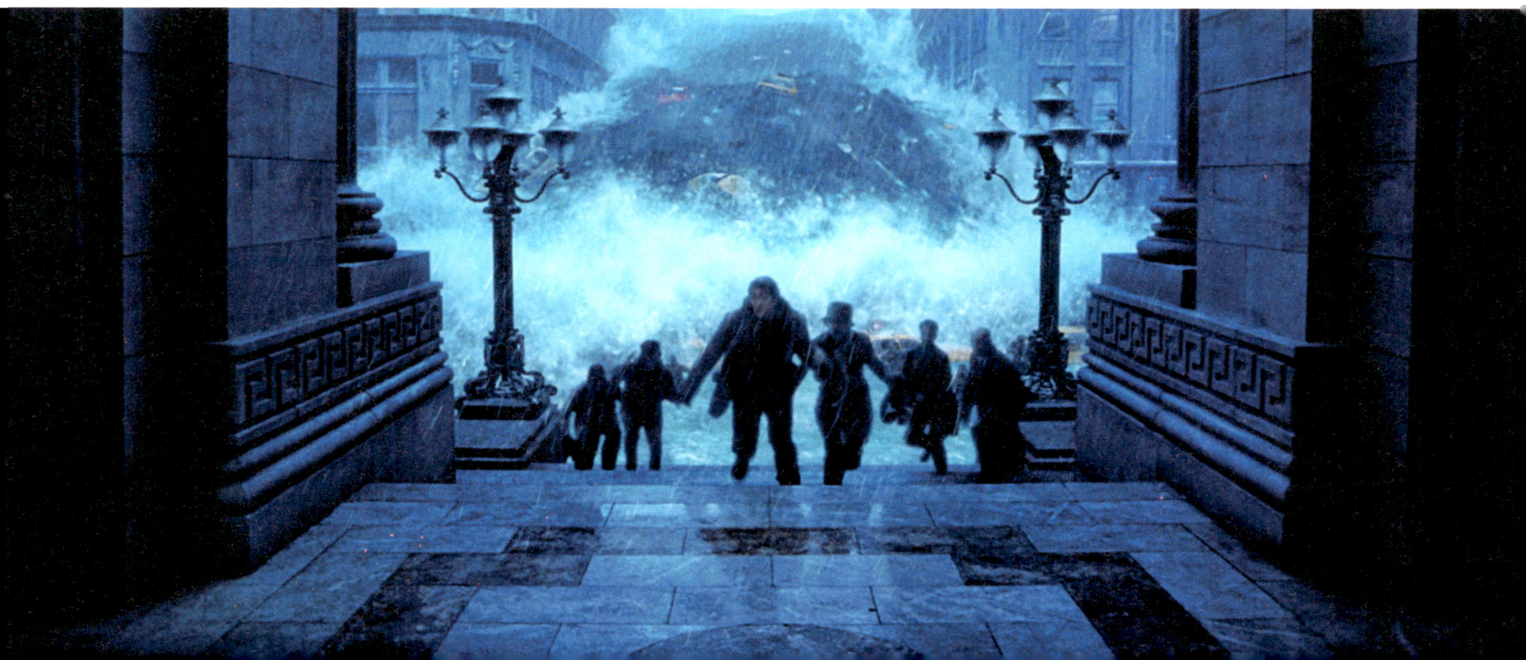

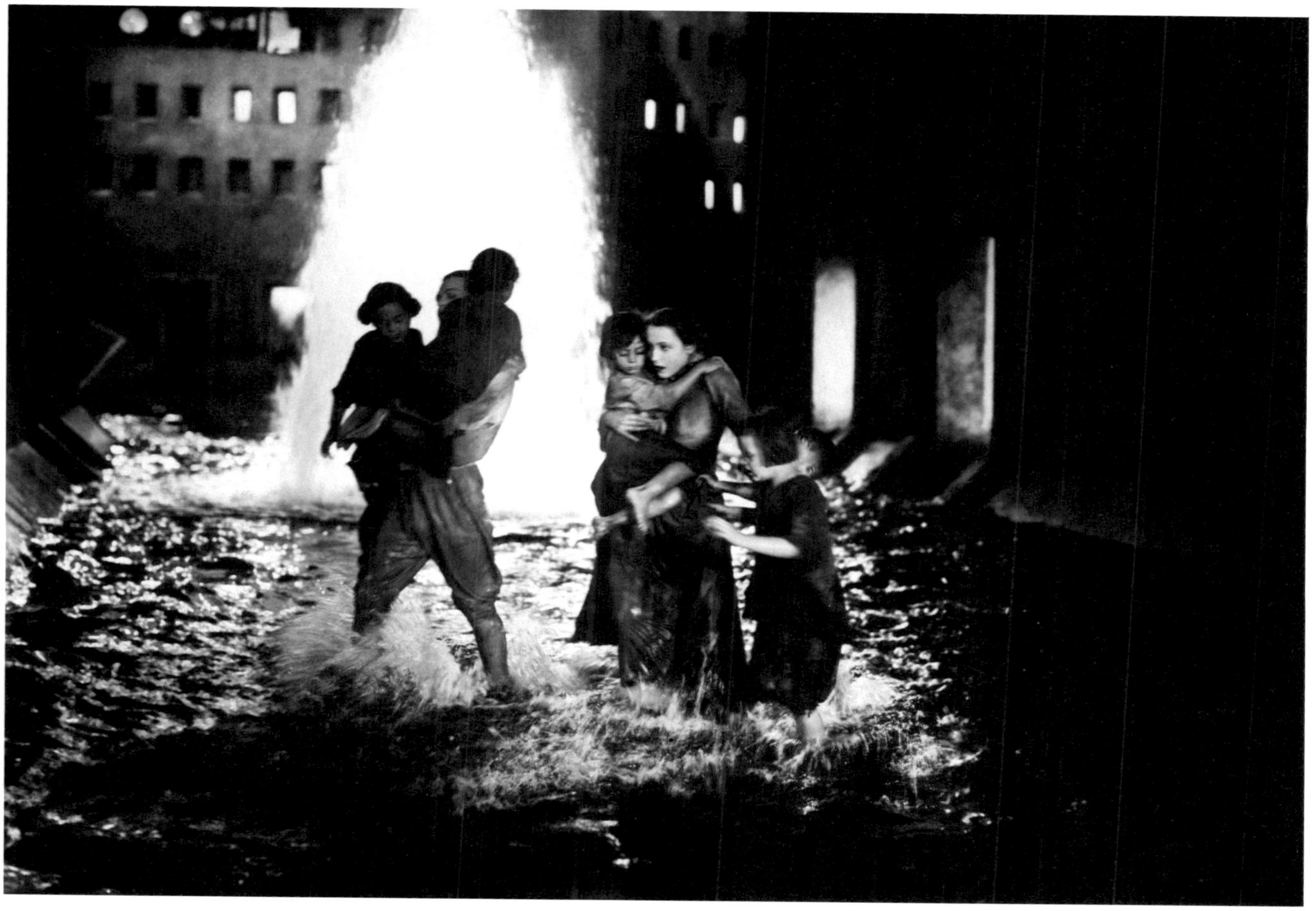

Metropolis, 1927. Director: Fritz Lang. © Friedrich-Wilhelm-Murnau-Stiftung, Distributor: Transit Film GmbH

big eyes? Why have you got such a big mouth?" Only then can she be swallowed, and so she is – quickly and efficiently – in one sentence. In the same way we are in no doubt that the shark must kill, the volcano erupt, the tidal wave wash in over the land, the bacterial culture get loose, the aliens invade etc., but the point is that the disaster doesn't happen right away. We have to be kept in suspense, and in that respect there is often a connection between the film and the film still.

In the film poster the white shark is closing in on the vulnerable woman doing the crawl at the water surface. You could say that the picture has been taken just at what the French master photographer Henri Cartier Bresson calls *the decisive moment*, if it wasn't for the fact that the picture is not a photograph, but a drawing. It's the moment before the shark sinks its razor-sharp teeth in her wet flesh: a fateful and suspenseful point on the timeline, but also a moment that convincingly bears the time before and after within it. Into the picture we read many minutes of undisturbed swimming around and our fearful expectation of the fatal threat. If we have seen the film, we remember it. If we haven't seen it, we go into the cinema with the expectation of being gripped by breathless suspense.

The film poster for *Jaws* is a concentrate of the suspense that is quite central to the film, and I look at it with a shudder, just as I stare with fascination at the still from *The Day After Tomorrow* of the tidal wave that is approaching a small crowd of people from behind as they flee into the doorway of the New York Public Library. Unlike the bathing woman, they manage to escape – we who have seen the film know that – and in this case too the still has been taken at a significant moment. It shows the threat in all its roaring violence, and vulnerable people in imminent danger. *In The Day After Tomorrow*, in fact, the real disaster only comes some way into the film. The film begins with the presentation of the main characters, and slowly builds up to the great climatic disaster. Giant hail falls in Tokyo, tornadoes and cyclone systems move in over LA, there are steep temperature drops in the seas, violent storms and the risk of plane crashes. Besides the almost realistic perspective – the threat of a climatic disaster – it is probably this hair-raising build-up alongside the – admittedly trivial – story of the absent father who has chosen his scientific career over family life that make the film more than just an action film.

Unlike *The Day After Tomorrow, Armageddon* for example begins with a disaster. We immediately witness an asteroid shower hitting New York, and the film has nothing like the same suspenseful build-up.

TRAGICOMEDY

If the stills from these disaster films effectively express fearful anticipation, at the same time the pictures of the dangerous moments have an element of comedy. In the films where there is a plot, the crucial moments become part of an overall development, while in the stills they seem monumental. The still takes on iconic value and in a way exposes what is primitive in our penchant for disaster films, our childish wish to feel we are on the edge of the accident and our urge to identify with those fleeing at a moment when it is being determined whether the enemy will win or lose. The comedy arises because the threat is made so monumental – the tidal wave takes on a fixed (if two-dimensional) form in the Medusa stare of photography – and because we simultaneously identify with the people and remain at a distance observing the stereotypical in this archetypal representation of their struggle against a danger from the outside.

A companion piece to the situational image of the threat is the still of the facial expressions of the characters. The forty muscles behind the facial skin make our features a living narrative that is constantly interpreted by others. In the film still, on the other hand, the muscles are fixed in a grimace which must show an emotion, in this case often fear, with the clarity of a traffic signal. Again there is something monumentalizing about fixing the features in this grimace, but also something comical. We become aware of the intervention of the camera, the fact that the situation is staged, arranged. In this connection it seems meaningful to refer to the American artist Cindy Sherman's fictive film stills, for no one has made the still picture's frozen *mise-en-scène* of facial and bodily expression clearer than Sherman. When Sherman focuses on the fearful, wretched face, we instinctively empathize with the situation of the subject and begin to reflect over the state the person is in – but we also immediately sense the

The Day After Tomorrow, 2004. Director: Roland Emmerich. © Twentieth Century Fox Film Corporation

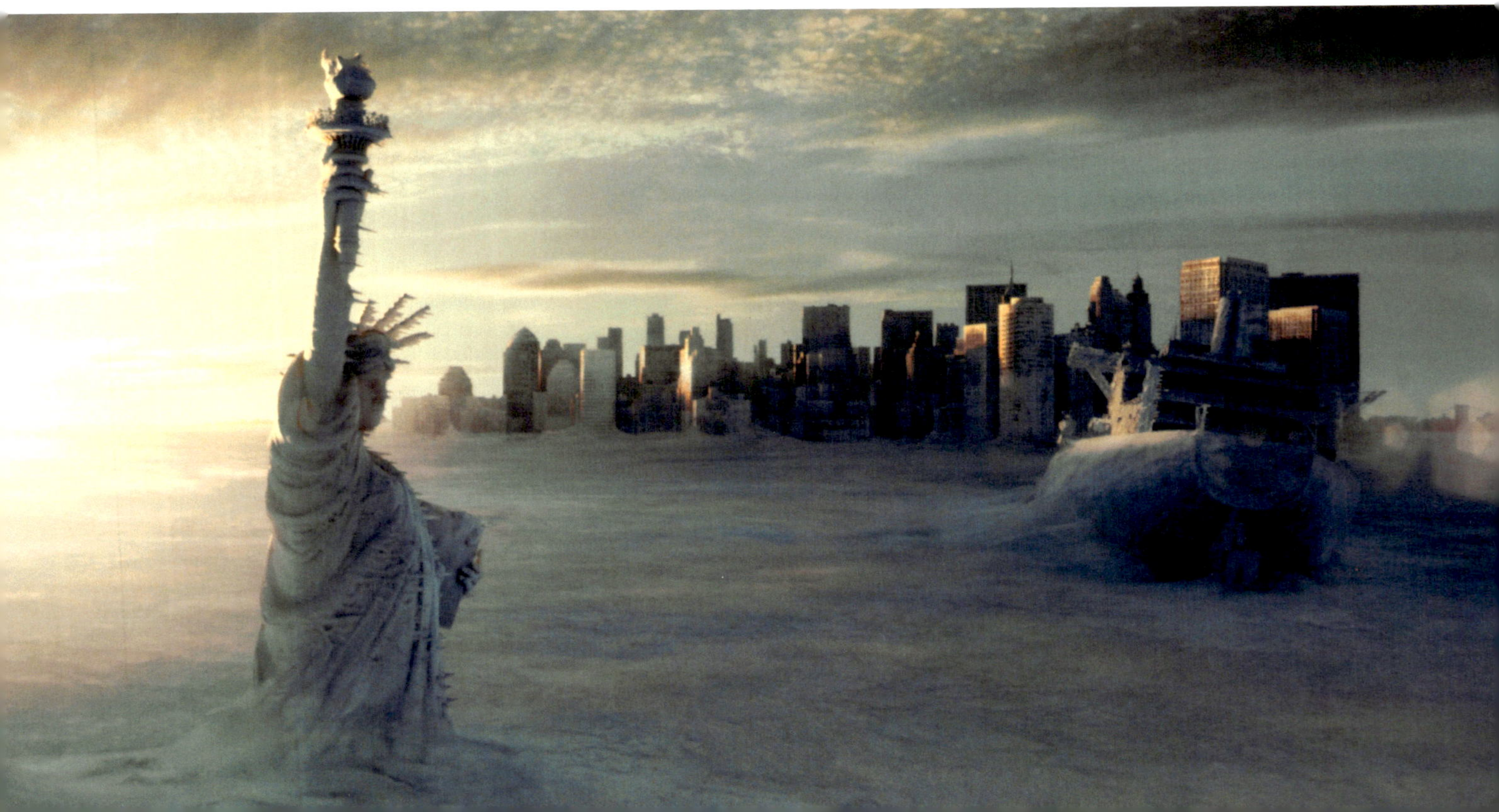

artificiality of the picture, the forced dramatization of the inner life of the emotions in a static, representative image.

Of course the static representation of movement is not solely a photographic matter. Paintings, drawings and sculptures can also be said to freeze various situations, but the photographic "freezing" of time has always been felt as something special, due to the mechanical and realistic character of photography. In a recent work exhibited at the Louvre, another contemporary artist, Mike Kelley, interestingly enough has brought not only images of catastrophy but also the relationship between still images – in the form of paintings - and moving images into focus. In *Profondeurs* vertes the spectator is confronted with a forerunner of the still from *Jaws*, namely John Singleton Copley's *Watson and the Shark* (1777). The painting represents a group of men fighting a dangerous shark shooting out of the water in front of their small dinghy. Interestingly, Kelley has dramatized the work by filming the painting, moving the camera from the facial expressions of the frightened men to the shark's jaws. The filmic sequences are accompanied by music written by Bernard Herrmann, known for his collaboration with Alfred Hitchcock, and shown beside are pencil drawings with detailed depictions of elements from the paintings. Thus the spectator is set out on a journey into a landscape with varied images of the threatening shark.

SCOURGES OF NATURE AND CULTURE

From a psychological point of view one can say that it makes no difference what threat the disaster film dramatizes. We may be terrified by the thought of a dangerous shark at the bottom of the sea, a hostile creature from outer space, a forest fire or a tidal wave, but the fearful anticipation and the sudden overwhelming danger are the same, and that is what is so effectively staged in the film still. From the point of view of cultural history, though, it is interesting to see which threat to humanity is represented.

It is clear to most people that *Jaws, Volcano, Earthquake* and *The Day After Tomorrow* do not show us realistic disaster scenarios. Not many scientists would recognize the zoology, geology or climatology expressed in the films. *Volcano* and *Earthquake* are full of fantastical scenarios of flowing lava and wild quakes, and in *The Day After Tomorrow*, for example, a new Ice Age arrives in less than a fortnight.[2] It is quite clear that the films are apocalyptic and relate to the Biblical story of Judgement Day. *Armageddon* already strikes up the theme in its title, and in Volcano there is a direct reference to Judgement Day when the emergency workers evacuate a number of Hieronymus Bosch paintings from the city art museum, and again when the young geologist Amy Barnes refers to what she calls the geologists' favourite Biblical quotation, the parable of the fool who builds his house on sand.

Nevertheless the films are set in real, recognizable locations, and both *Earthquake* and *Volcano* can take their point of departure in the quakes that hit LA from time to time. In their own way the films give the impression of being docudramas where the ignorant masses and powerful people with political and economic interests battle against scientists who, with their specialized knowledge, can see the disasters coming and call for action. In *Jaws* it is an oceanographer who lives and breathes the study of sharks, the stereotype of the (in this case positively) mad scientist who is in possession of the grim truth about the terrible monster. In *Volcano* it is Amy Barnes and her assistant Rachel who have detected the looming danger. In *Earthquake* we see the young research assistant Walter Russel successfully urging the director of the California Seismological Institute to take a prediction of a violent quake seriously. In *The Day After Tomorrow* it is the palaeoclimatologist Jack Hall from the National Oceanic Atmospheric Administration who tries, at an environmental conference in New Delhi, to warn the US Government of the fateful consequences of global warming. All of them wage a brave struggle against the powers-that-be, who do not want their political careers, economic affairs etc. spoiled.

Despite the fact that the disaster scenarios are unrealistic, it is interesting that they do relate to an aspect of reality, both in the choice of disaster and its setting, and that the viewer reacts to the political manoeuvring presented as a game that has a basis in reality. The system has an inertia and a desire for immutability that renders it unable to accommodate the possibility of the disaster. In that respect the mythological staging of the destructive forces becomes a symbol of the uncertainty that can arise in all sorts of contexts about the handling of dangers and crises.

The Day After Tomorrow differs, of course, from the other films, because it represents the natural disaster as the result of human actions. The tsunami in the film is not the result of a development in the bowels of the earth that has always taken place. The fury of nature is aroused by unthinking overconsumption. The film is therefore also related to films about technical disasters such as *Airport*, where manmade technology shows its demonic face. In the nineteenth century there was a tendency to sing the praises of technology and science. It was the century of inventions, but in the subsequent centuries the negative consequences of both have begun to become clear. Now we fear not only destructive nature, but also the destructive culture we ourselves have created. A further characteristic of many of the films is that the two forms of destruction are mixed. Overconsumption of fossil fuels triggers off a new Ice Age, while earthquakes make skyscrapers collapse, and floating icebergs wreck ships. Once more it is important to point out that the disaster films cannot of course be seen as documentary descriptions. They are fictionalizations of dramatic phenomena that turn death and destruction into a kind of farce, and there is no disaster film about all the dangers that really threaten mankind in what the German writer Ulrich Beck has called 'the risk society'.[3] Industrial accidents or the growing number of allergens and carcinogens in foodstuffs do not make good film disasters.

The films about natural and technological disasters have a broader appeal to our fears of the destruction of civilization, and in these cases too the film stills have a particular symbolic function. In the films, whether we are absorbed or irritated by the simple plot, we are forced to follow it. In *Titanic* we have to watch the ship sink while we think about the class struggle and the love drama on board. In *Earthquake* we watch the hero's dangerous lowering of father-in-law and colleagues into a collapsed office building. With unerring inevitability the fire hose they use succumbs to the strain and the hero comes close to sacrificing himself as the victim of his own heroism. The still of the sinking ship and the office chair hanging free in the collapsed building, on the other hand, take on an emblematic function. They become modern images of Judgement Day that create associations with other apocalyptic visions. In a Christian perspective the tidal wave in *The Day After Tomorrow* becomes a Deluge, the huge sinking ship with the mythological name *Titanic* becomes a floating Tower of Babel, and the collapsing skyscraper the same thing on land. And these disasters also easily come to stand as symbols of a more general critique of civilization and of modern man's more or less justified fear of disasters.

BRIEF SALVATION

Some people might object that I have forgotten to mention the need to see the disaster survived, the wolf cut open and Red Riding-Hood emerge unscathed, but it is quite deliberate that I have left out this dimension of the films. For I consider the struggle against the danger uninteresting, partly because it falls into a quite predictable mould. Good has to triumph over evil, and this must take place over a period of time with setbacks; but it will very certainly happen. Unfortunately the triumph of good over evil has come to take up more and more of the disaster films. *The Day After Tomorrow* is atypical, inasmuch as it slowly builds up to the ultimate disaster, but even in *The Day After Tomorrow* we can't escape seeing Jack Hall and Hall Junior as the strong heroes who, although they cannot stop the disaster, at least know how to survive it. In *Armageddon*, the whole film is about the struggle, in this case not an environmentalist's struggle for the survival of the world and his son, but the space journey and destruction of the asteroid by a deep-core oil driller (played by Bruce Willis). It isn't only dreary because the film gives you a depressing picture of a society where the experts are a bunch of girlie-men and the real heroes are the gritty oil drillers. No, it is mostly the fact that it is so uninteresting to see the danger averted; the way the film ends, as you hear the President celebrating the final conquest of nature by the American people – and humanity – with the aid of science and technology, is only the last straw in what is already a haystack. No wonder most of the stills from *Armageddon* show serious men with hooded eyes signalling strength and heroism.

But perhaps I am after all being too radical in my criticism of the triumph of good over evil. Perhaps I should make it clear that it is the long drawn-out film sequence I consider tiresome, while in the film still I can take pleasure in seeing the danger defeated. In the final analysis there is an element of salvation in the images of the dangerous moments I have described. Hall Junior and the small band are close enough to the entrance to the library for us to know they will reach safety, and the rescue action in the destroyed office building also tells us, in its own sentimental way, about human inventiveness and the will to survive – amidst chaos.

ON TV AND FILM

In many recent disaster films the media coverage of the disaster is an important element in the story. In *Volcano* we hear constant voice-over coverage by news reporters. The introductory sequences with scenes from everyday life in LA are accompanied by a montage of shots from breakfast TV with stories about this and that. The

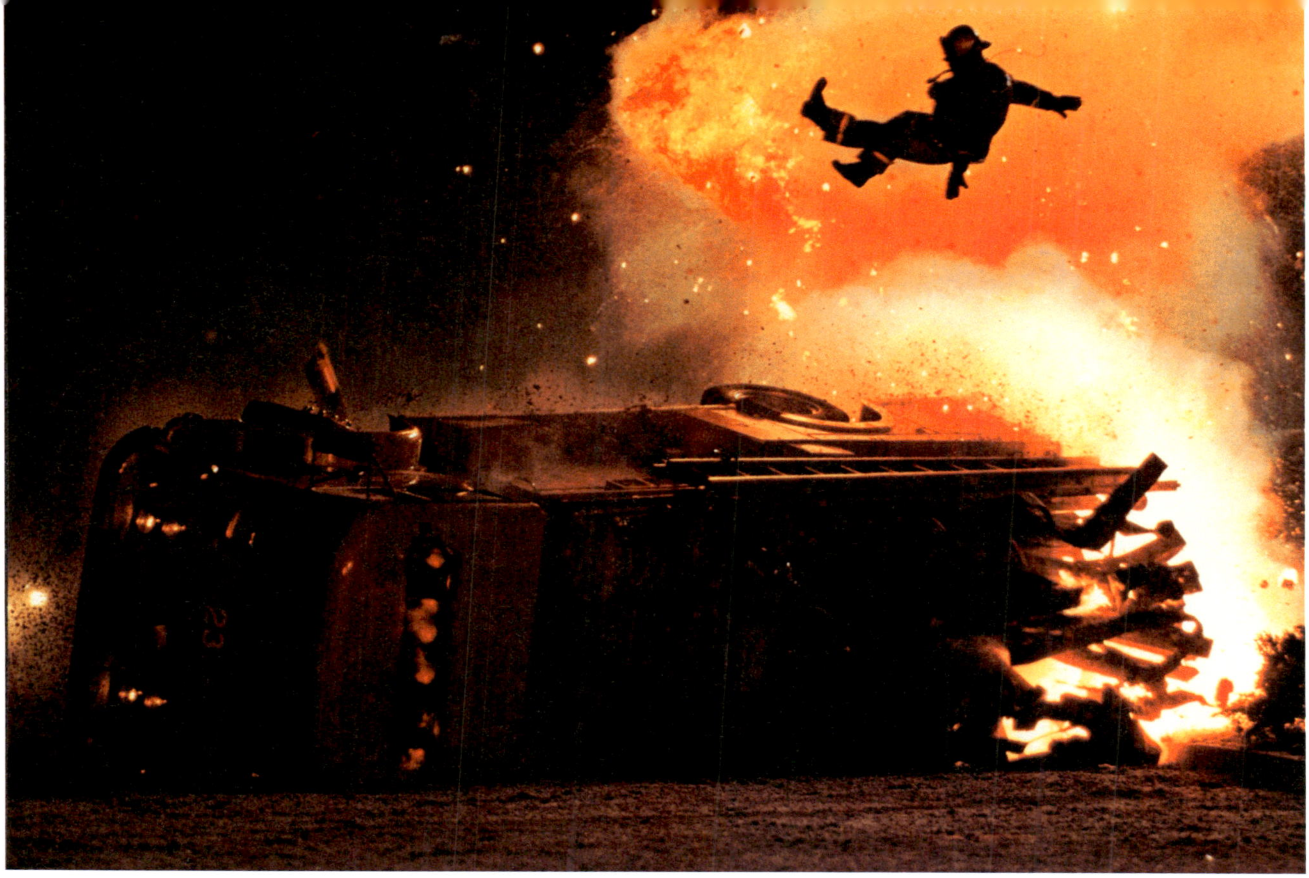

Volcano, 1997. Director: Mick Jackson. © Twentieth Century Fox Film Corporation.

demonstrations against the subway construction are experienced first as part of the round tour of the city, then there is a cut to the main character's kitchen, where the TV churns out a report from the demonstrations.

So it comes as no surprise when the volcano eruption is later presented in a mixture of action scenes and news reports. There is even a satirical version of the 'live' news reports of journalists. Bob Davis from Channel KNX appears as the epitome of the documentary reporter, the travelling eye of the viewers, who turns the disaster into a story on the spot instead of participating in the rescue work. The same mimicry of media can be found in *The Day After Tomorrow*. You constantly see real speakers from Sky News and Fox. A journalist with a film crew reports from a helicopter and waxes indignant about the people down there recording the disasters: "There are people down there taking pictures!" he shouts. Another reporter who is at the focal point of the disaster just manages to note that it looks like a horrible nightmare but is absolutely real before he is hit by a falling billboard with a burning pin-up girl.

When the Titanic sank, the ship's wireless operator sent an SOS. Ships had just begin using the Italian Marconi's invention as a communication system, and a passenger ship 58 miles from the Titanic picked up the SOS. In other words, the news of the sinking of the Titanic reached other ships and land before anyone could come to the rescue. Today we not only send messages about disasters to faraway destinations, we can transmit live from the focal point of the calamity. The disaster films give us a satirical presentation of the media coverage, and sometimes they even reflect on the disaster movie itself. For instance in *The Day After Tomorrow* we see the centre of the film industry, Hollywood, and the well known white lettering on the slopes liquidized by a tornado. On film, the disasters also threaten the production of disaster films.

In the everyday media picture thought-provoking connections arise between the disaster stories. The TV channels repeat the films with fantasies about violent volcanic eruptions that ravage supercivilized societies, while the news programmes tell us about eruptions in Indonesia, where the population is experiencing real devastation and death as a result of the recurrent destructive forces of nature. In many ways the film stills give us a clear illustration of the intricate relationship between reality, the media and film images. On the one hand they point up a contrast between the creations of fiction and the live recordings of the news reports, on the other the viewer experiences grim similarities. In the introductory sequences of *Armageddon* the World Trade Center is for example blasted through by an asteroid, and it gives us an eerie feeling now to see pictures that were shot long before terrorists flew the Boeing 767s into the buildings. As viewers we experience the difference between fiction and reality, while at the same time feeling the shifting of the boundaries between the genres.

The Norwegian crisis psychologist Atle Dyregrov writes that one often hears people who have been involved in disasters saying that in the actual situation they felt dissociated from what was happening. They say they felt as if they were in a film.[4] In a real disaster situation this testifies, according to Dyregrov, to a mental distance, a kind of splitting of consciousness. When you see the news reports and the feature film sequences, you are of course at a distance. You don't need to take protective action, for you know that you are not directly involved. The media images from real disasters leave us as viewers with the feeling that we shouldn't be watching pictures like that. In the film the disaster is transformed into fiction and aesthetic scenarios that can be consumed more painlessly. They exert their attraction unobstructed, which brings us back to the starting-point of this article – our fascination with images of destruction.

PETRIFIED WITH FEAR

In the 1970s there was a tendency to interpret the disaster movies symbolically. It began with the science fiction films of the 1950s, which were seen as images of cold war fears.[5] Russian communists and nuclear missiles were symbolized by green men from Mars and mother ships that attacked American society. This interpretation is convincing. It seems likely that we have a need to convert our mental images of enemies into celluloid, and that the conversion involves a more or less creative interpretation. All the same it can be taken to the point of absurdity. For example I have a hard time accepting eastern European film critics' diagnosis of the film producer and the film viewer as die-hard bourgeoisie living out their fear of revolution in the many disaster films of the 1970s. It doesn't seem adequate to translate natural disasters into popular revolt, and my own fascination with them into an expression of closet anarchism.

At all events I think we have to operate with a broader definition if we want to define the attraction of the film still. To begin with quite direct experience, there is the fascination of the very sight of something huge and overwhelming turned loose; of seeing an existing order threatened by something bigger and more powerful, with its own laws and logic; of feeling threatened, but not really endangered, just part of a game like childhood tag. The film still satisfies the need to experience this kind of threat, because it has an aesthetic, superficial character, because the disaster is staged; but also because it has been reduced to a graphic figure, a pattern. One could say that the film still is paradoxical, because it stops motion, and that has consequences for a deeper interpretation of the picture. True, the moment, as mentioned before, always bears within it the idea of a before and after, but at the same time it makes both impossible. There is only this point, an impossible point where motion has ceased and the threat is constant. In the broader perspective, this cessation forces an interpretation of the picture as a general icon of the eternal threat. It may represent a collective sense of uncertainty and fear of danger from the outside, as experienced in the imagination or the media, or it may represent the sense of an inner, less tangible threat.

Mette Kia Krabbe Meyer, b. 1970, is a photographic historian, PhD and museum curator at the Steno Museum.

Earthquake, 1974. Director: Mark Robson
In the picture: Charlton Heston

1 *See Nach dem Ende. Auflösung und Untergänge im Kino an der Jahrtausendwende. Arnoldshainer Filmgespräche Band 17*, Frölich, Middel and Visarius (eds.), Marburg: Schüren 2001.
2 The environmental activist George Monbiot wrote in *The Guardian* that it was a magnificent film but bad science. George Monbiot: "A hard rain's a-gonna fall", *The Guardian*, 14/5/2004. In Denmark the Meteorological Institute used the unrealistic disaster scenario of the film as the point of departure for a scientific presentation of a series of dramatic weather phenomena. See http://www.dmi.dk/dmi/index/viden/temaer/the_day_after_tomorrow_-_tema.htm
3 Ulrich Beck: *World Risk Society*, Cambridge: Polity Press 1999.
4 Atle Dyregrov: *Katastrofepsykologi*, Dansk psykologisk Forlag, 1994, p. 22.
5 See Manfred Hobsch: *Das grosse Lexikon der Katastrophenfilme*, Berlin: Schwarzkopf & Schwarzkopf 2003, p. 10.

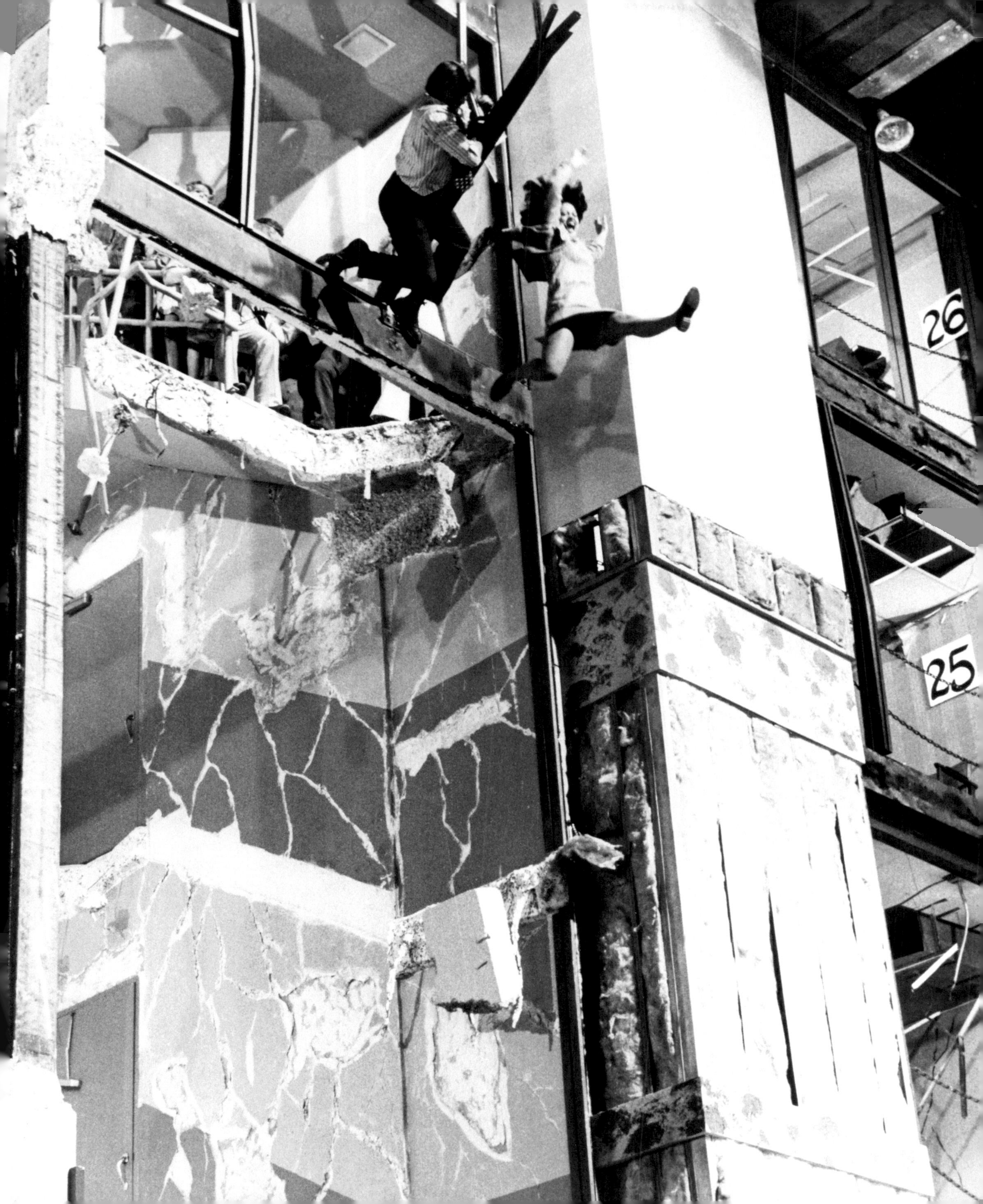
26
25

A FINE ROMANCE

FILM STILLS AND ART HISTORY

By Mette Marcus

Ever since the earliest days of the feature film around the turn of the last century, there has been close interaction between images in films and the subjects of paintings from the history of art, and today there is still an interplay – perhaps more intense than ever – between the genres, with their shared interest in certain medium-specific characteristics. The links between the world of film and the world of visual art are particularly evident in the production of film stills.

CAPTURING THE MOMENT

As we know, films stills are photographs, and of course they take their point of departure in the history of photography. A central thesis in the history of photography concerns the influence that the new medium had on the premises of painting – and more generally on the way one looked at pictures, especially at the end of the nineteenth century. The photograph as a new form of representation clearly nurtured a development in the history of art. Whereas painting had always stood as the epitome of the reproduction of a scene, a subject where temporality had been neutralized or extended, the photograph now made its entry as the medium that could capture and render the moment – and this had several consequences for the painterly tradition. Not only the temporal aspect, but also the cropping or framing of a subject took on great significance, especially for Impressionist painters like Claude Monet and Edgar Degas.

Quite apart from this significance in terms of innovation, the whole way of creating pictures – composing them spatially, showing particular types, subjects or ways of acting – is impossible to look at independently of the history of art. For centuries visual art has created certain templates, and when one looks at film stills the references to art history often present themselves as quite obvious sources. Quite simply, there are ways of composing a picture that seem to find a natural modality in the existing art-historical material. Finally, of course, one must allow for the normal stylistic inspiration that always criss-crosses among the various art forms.

THE EXPRESSIVE CITY

One of these stylistic inspirations from painting can be seen in the fantastic stills that accompany Fritz Lang's *Metropolis*, 1927. The expressiveness one finds most

Metropolis, 1927. Director: Fritz Lang

Distributor: Transit Film GmbH

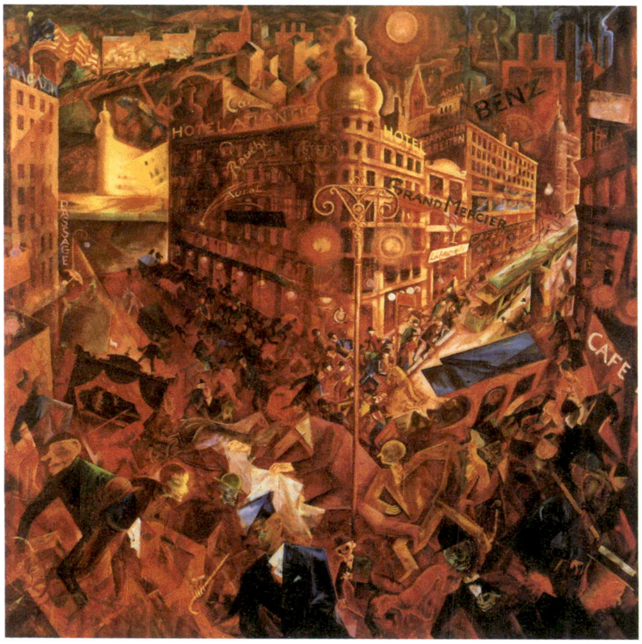

Georg Grosz, *Metropolis*, 1916-17
Museo Thyssen-Bornemisza, Madrid

strikingly in the work of an artist like George Grosz seems to lie very close to the visual universe cultivated in the images from *Metropolis*. One only has to look at his painting *Die Grosstadt*, 1917, where the urban space is rendered with features from the painting style that is otherwise best known from the Italian Futurists – including some very strong lines through the picture surface and a kind of overlap between the various layers of the work. In the same way the *Metropolis* images show the city as an overwhelming architectonic space where the buildings tower like Gothic skyscrapers.

THE SPACE OF THE MIRROR

One way to give a picture dynamics is to use the mirror as a spatializing element. Mirror-images occur in innu-

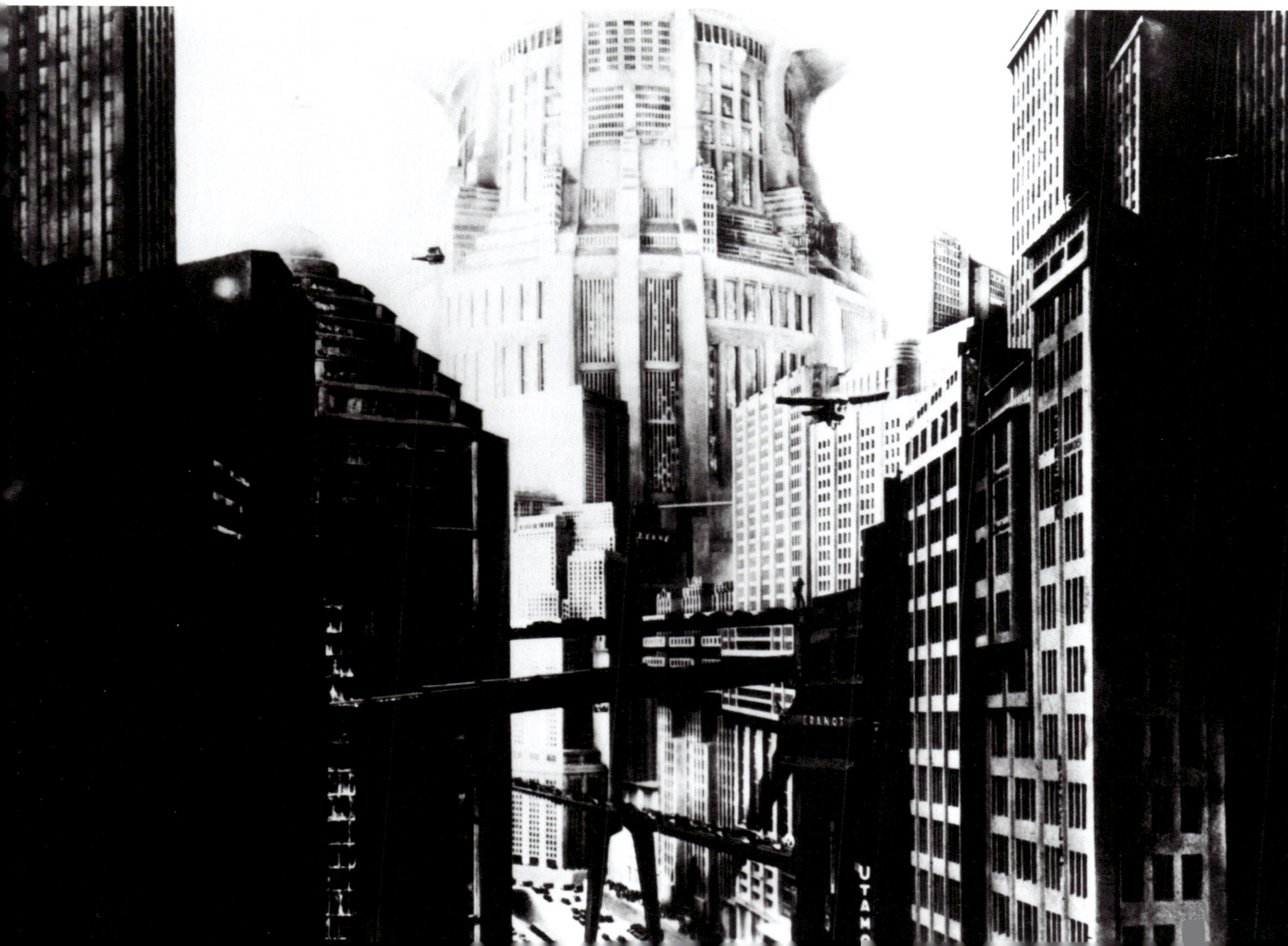

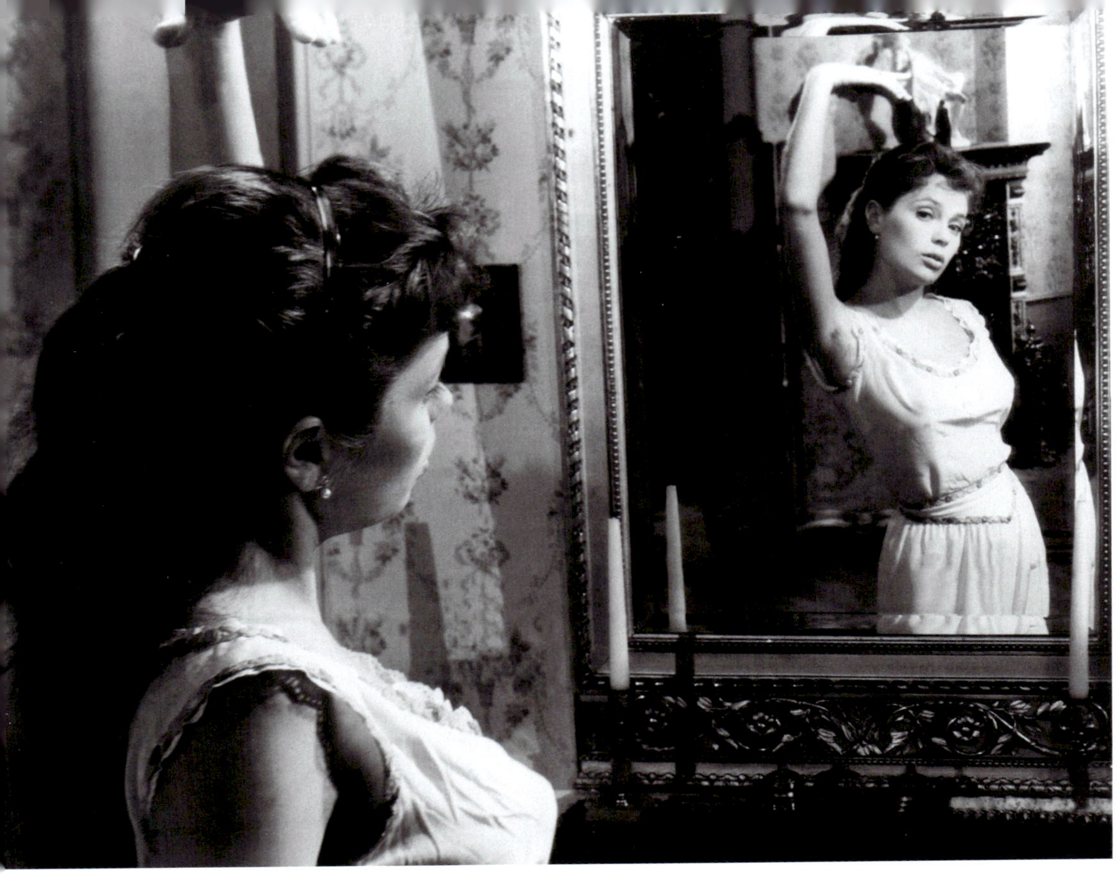

Sommarnattens leende, 1955
(Smiles of a Summer Night)
Director: Ingmar Bergman
Still photographer: Louis Huch

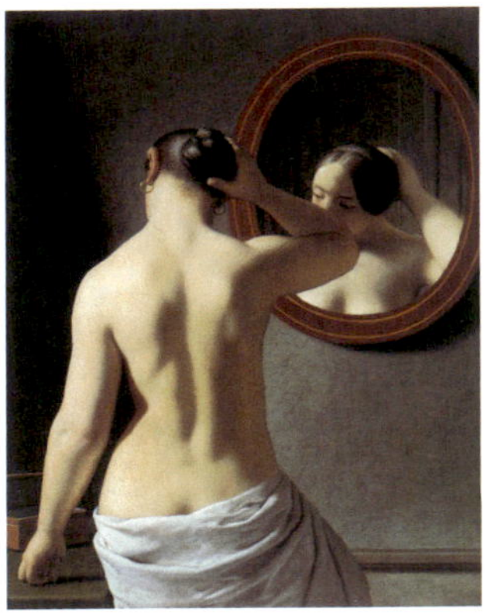

C. W. Eckersberg, *Woman in front of a Mirror*,1841. The Hirschsprung Collection, Copenhagen

merable places in the history of art – used for example to show special details that are only captured by the small mirror in the background, as in the case of the well known painting by Jan van Eyck, *The Arnolfini Wedding* from 1434, where the mirror behind the figures reveals a person otherwise unseen in the picture, positioned in front of the foreground of the picture. Thus the mirror often functions as a way of showing spatial depth in a more sophisticated way, since it makes it possible to show spaces that would normally be outside the viewer's field of vision. So mirrors are an economical way of showing the viewer more facets of the same subject. But the mirror is not only a matter of effect or motivic technique; it also brings out certain psychological aspects. You could say it creates space for self-reflection: the pictorial expression of the encounter with oneself. All these different ways of using the mirror in the history of painting can also be found in film stills – for example in Ingmar Bergman's *Smiles* of a *Summer Night,* 1955, where the mirror shows us Ulla Jacobsen face-on. While otherwise we only have a hint of her profile and body, the mirror reveals – further into the picture – her figure and features. The subject is very close to one of the best known paintings of the Danish Golden Age, C.W. Eckersberg's *Woman in Front of a Mirror,* 1841. Although Eckersberg's use of the mirror has a rather subtler function, inasmuch as it only shows a suggestion of the naked woman's bosom, the posture is the same and is in fact related to a whole succession of Venus figures throughout the history of art.

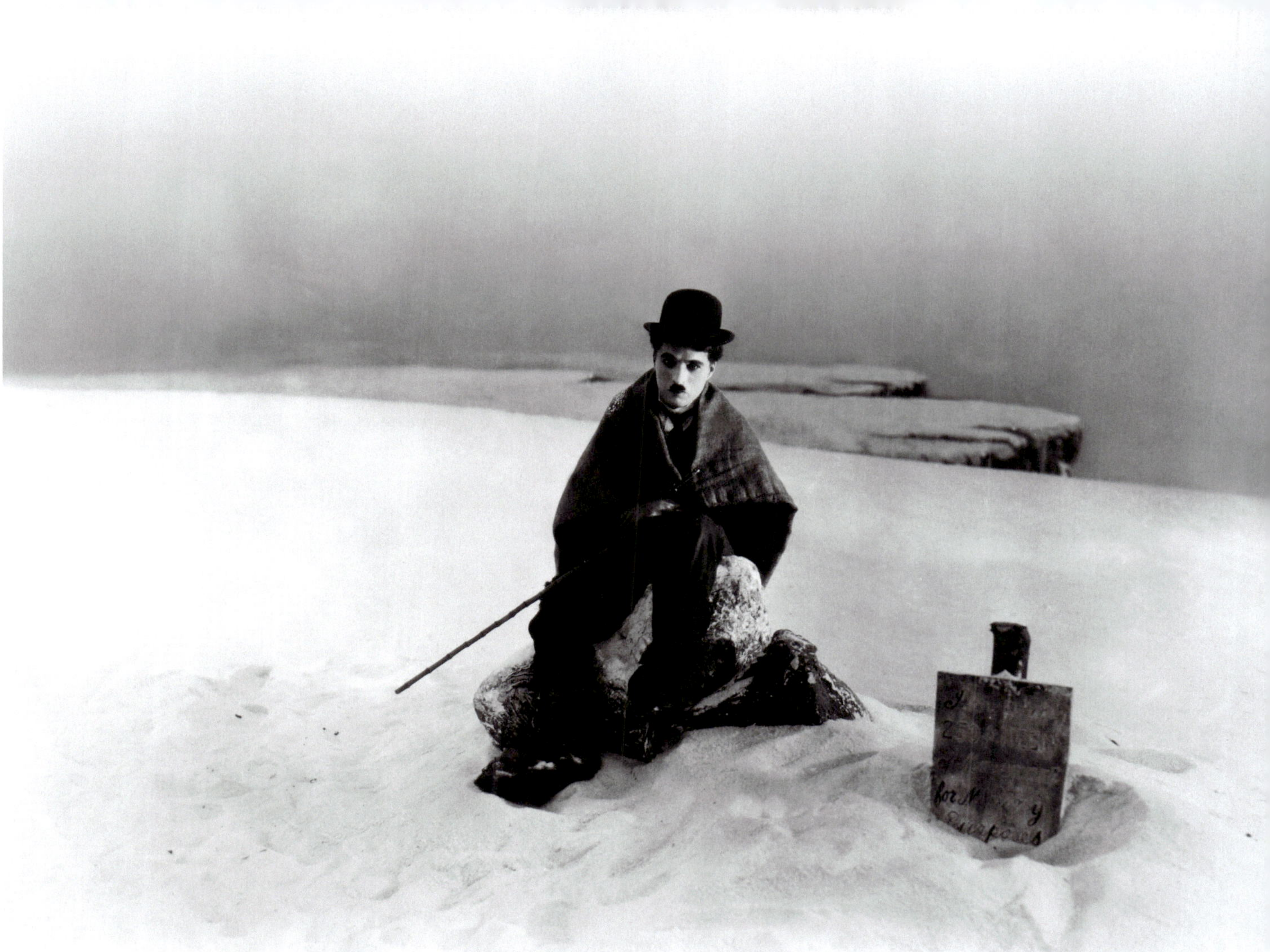

The Gold Rush, 1925. Director: Charles Chaplin
In the picture: Charles Chaplin
Still photographer: Roland Totheroh

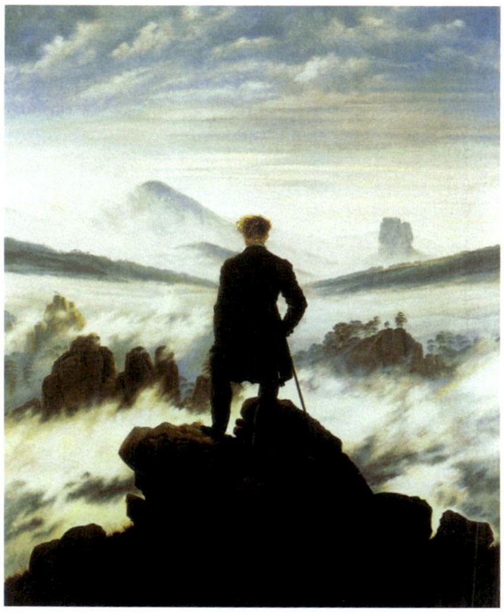

C. D. Friedrich, *The Traveller Above the Sea of Clouds*, 1817
Hamburger Kunsthalle. Hamburg

THE SUBLIME

Films create the space for great emotions and existential situations, like our relationship with the forces of nature; for example in the stills of Charlie Chaplin from *The Gold Rush*, 1925, where we find our (anti)hero alone on top of a snow-clad mountain. It is a typical example of how this feeling of being alone in the world can be depicted as sublime solitude. It is hard not to think of the great painter of Romanticism, Caspar David Friedrich, whose similar rendering of *The Wanderer above the Sea of Clouds,* 1818, directly confronts mankind with all that appears to be beyond history, a world that is beautiful but also indifferent and ungraspable in both senses of the word.

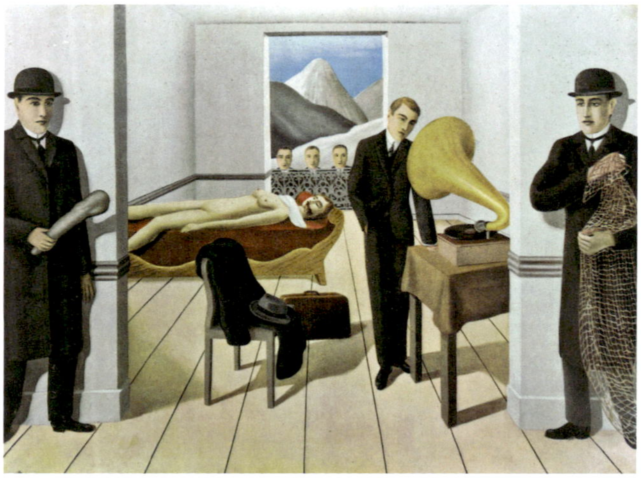

René Magritte, *The Menaced Assasin*, 1927
Musée d'Art Moderne. Belgium

DECISIVE MOMENTS

Film stills typically show the decisive moments of the film; where the plot changes, the code is broken, the mystery is solved or complicated, the murder is committed or revealed. In stills from the crime genre one finds many interior scenes where rather a lot of people are gathered in one room. This is of course due to the primary function of the still – to concentrate the essence of a scene and perhaps at the same time introduce us to the important characters of the film. Often this accumulation of people in space produces an almost surrealistic image, for example in this still from Alexander Mackendrick's *The Ladykillers*, 1955, which is easy to view in the light of one of the masters of Surrealism, René Magritte, whose work *The Menaced Assassin*, 1927, in fact involves a highly peculiar crime scene.

The Ladykillers, 1955. Director: Alexander Mackendrick. © Canal+ Image UK Ltd.

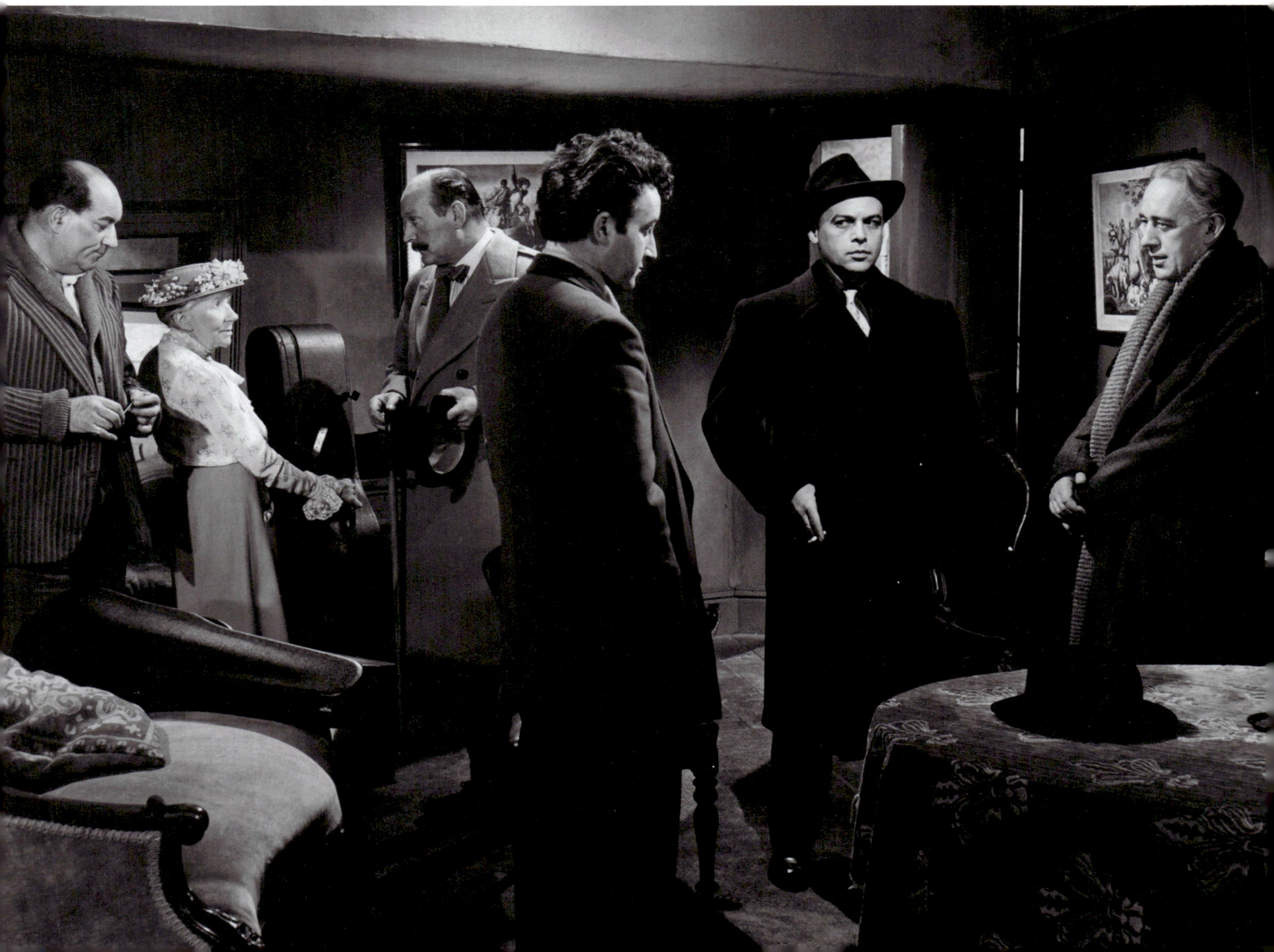

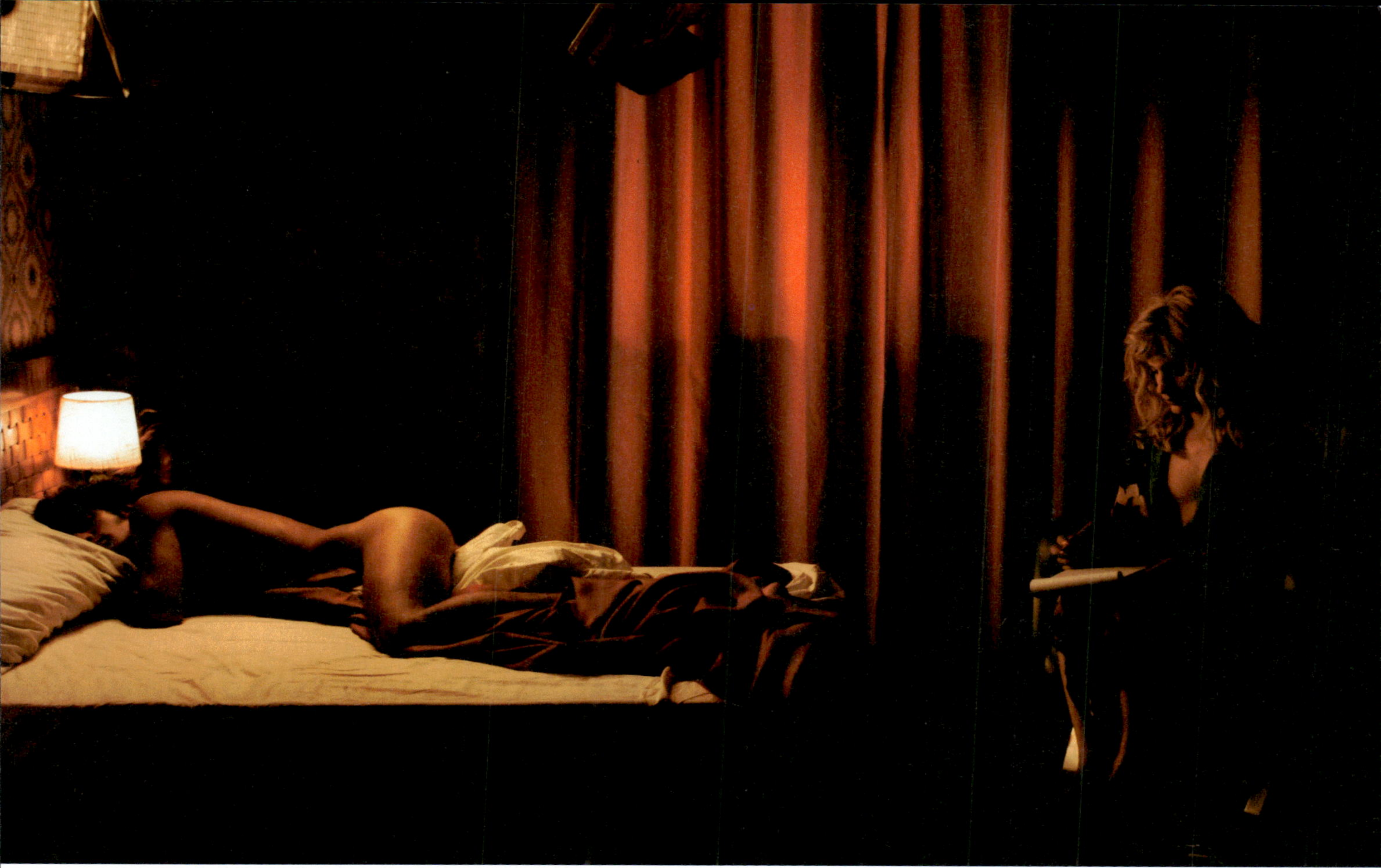

La mala educación, 2004
(Bad Education)
Director: Pedro Almodóvar

THE SLEEPING BEAUTY

In the innumerable film stills that show men watching women in bed – resting, sleeping, sometimes even dead – the pose of the woman is almost always the same. Typically we see the bed from the side, such that the curves of the female body are displayed. If the woman is undressed the subject is very close to a very popular motif from the history of art – the nude Venus figure rendered innumerable times in the visual art of the Renaissance, best known perhaps from Titian's *Venus of Urbino*, 1538. But Ingres, Delacroix, Manet and Matisse too have cultivated this motif, in the nineteenth and at the beginning of the twentieth century. This representation of a naked woman lying on a bed can be seen in a multitude of film stills – exemplified here by a still from the Spanish director Pedro Almodóvar's film *La Mala Educación,* 2004. True, the sleeping woman is in this case in fact a man, but given the way the body lies con-

V.Titian, *Venus of Urbino*, 1538. Uffizi, Florence

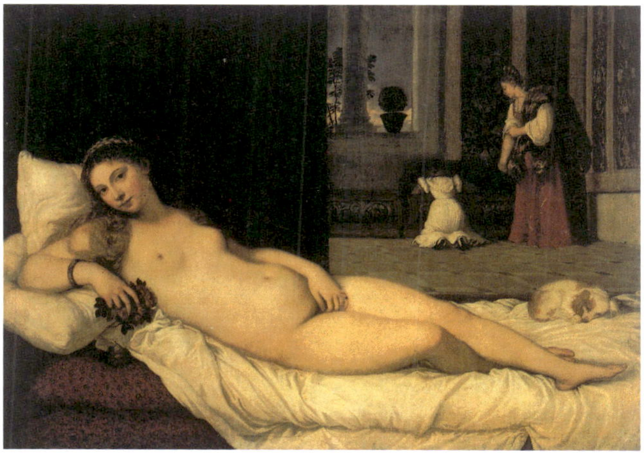

toured in the bed he might as well have been a woman. And there are thousands of film stills that do in fact show women in this role.

VISUAL ART'S FASCINATION WITH FILM STILLS

The film still photographers make use, consciously or unconsciously, of art history, but the exchanges certainly also go in the other direction, and for many years visual artists have drawn very direct inspiration from these special photos. In 1963 the king of Pop Art, Andy Warhol, created a work based on a film still. The use of ready-made transfers from the original medium was after all Warhol's typical working method; but by choosing to base his work on a still from the film *Flaming Star*, Warhol shows us Elvis at the peak of his film career, not as the singer, the King, but as a tough half-breed with the rest of us at gunpoint in a totally authentic film posture.

The visual artist who has probably had the clearest relationship with the film still genre is the American Cindy Sherman. Over a period of three years, in 69 black-and-white photos called *Untitled Film Stills*, she replicated the still's special concentration of the drama of a film scene or even a whole film, as here in *Untitled Film Still #50*, 1979, where, as always, she uses herself as a model – one has to imagine for oneself the non-existent films that form the background against which the pictures resonate, their before and after.

Over the past fifteen years the attitude of the visual artists to the feature film has changed: the film images are to a great extent used as yet another reservoir of material. Photo art – and not only Sherman's – mimes film stills. In 1995-200, for example, the Swedish artist Miriam Bäckström created a series of works under the general title *Set Constructions*, photos of various film sets or locations; and young artists like Lorna Simpson and Thomas Demand create photo works with a strong cinematographic feel. More generally one can say that while in its infancy film grew out of several traditions at once – the new documentary photography, the theatre, visual art, etc. – today it is paying off its debt as the primary source for a whole range of visual art works. While the still photograph is paradoxically the epitome of the filmic, among the younger video artists we also find enormous interest in the forms of the feature film – sometimes, as in Sherman's case, in a kind of mimesis or irony, in other cases as adaptations of existing material or actual films. In particular the re-make phenomenon has gained a firm foothold in video art: the recreation of a film or its direct use as material can be seen in

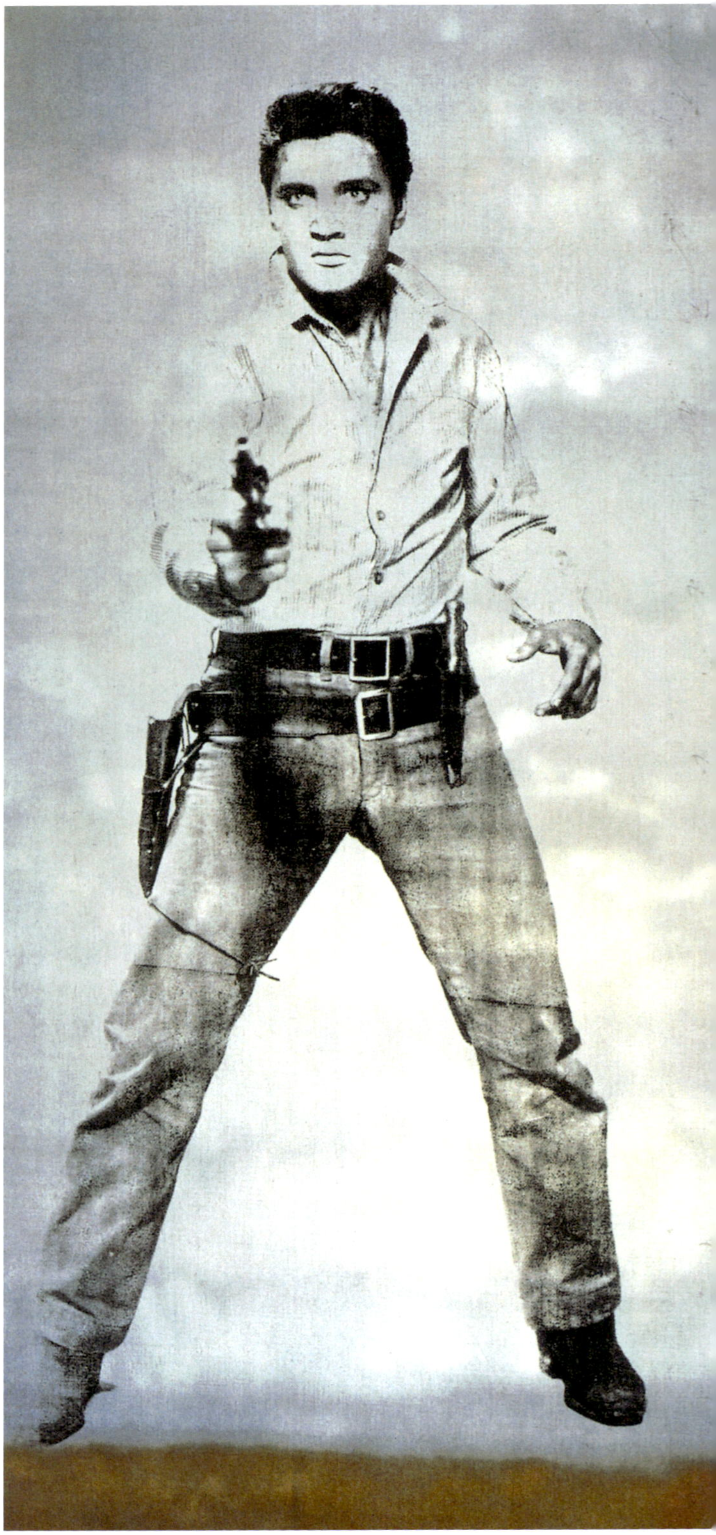

Andy Warhol, *Elvis*, 1963. The Eli and Edythe L. Braod Collection, Los Angeles. © Andy Warhol / COPY-DAN Billedkunst

the work of well known video artists like Douglas Gordon, Susan Hiller, Pierre Huyghe, Christian Marclay and Candice Breitz. They add depth to aspects of the original film by reconstructing the filmic experience as a new aesthetic idiom. But we also see a strong influence in less direct 'translations'. The works of artists like Janet Cardiff, Salla Tykkä and Eija-Liisa Ahtila have a strong narrative feel that lies close to the filmic, and in particular the soundtrack of the work is an element that is used to evoke atmosphere and support the narrative in ways familiar from the feature film. One could continue to reel off names, for the list of artists who work today with their hands deep in the cinematographic material is long, and the inspiration between the genres extends much further than the strictly motivic. There is still a two-way flow between film and visual art.

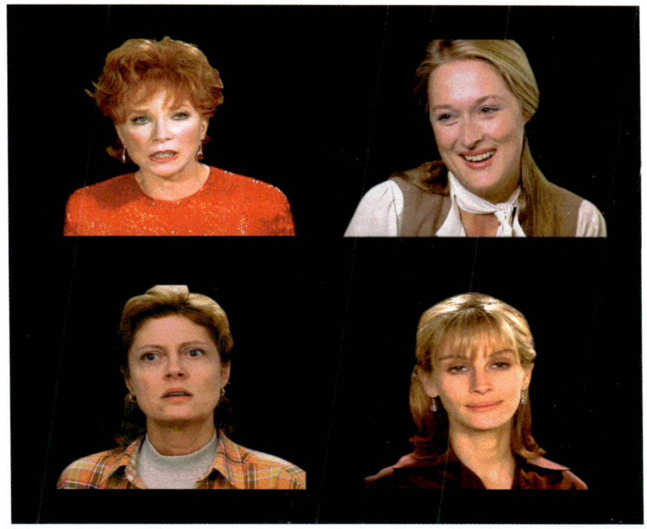

Candice Breitz, *Mother + Father*, 2005
Louisiana Museum of Modern Art

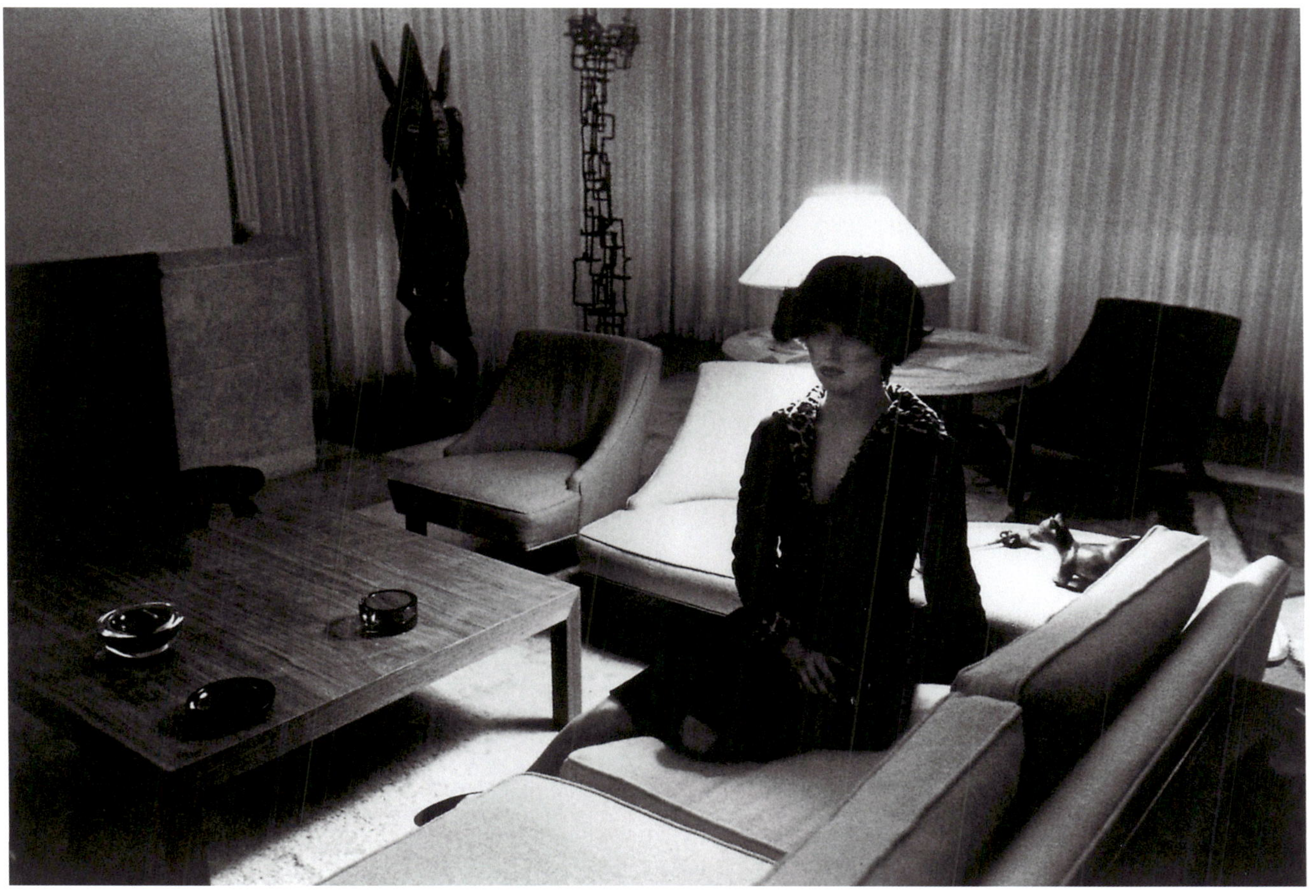

Cindy Sherman, *Untitled Film Still #50*, 1979. The Museum

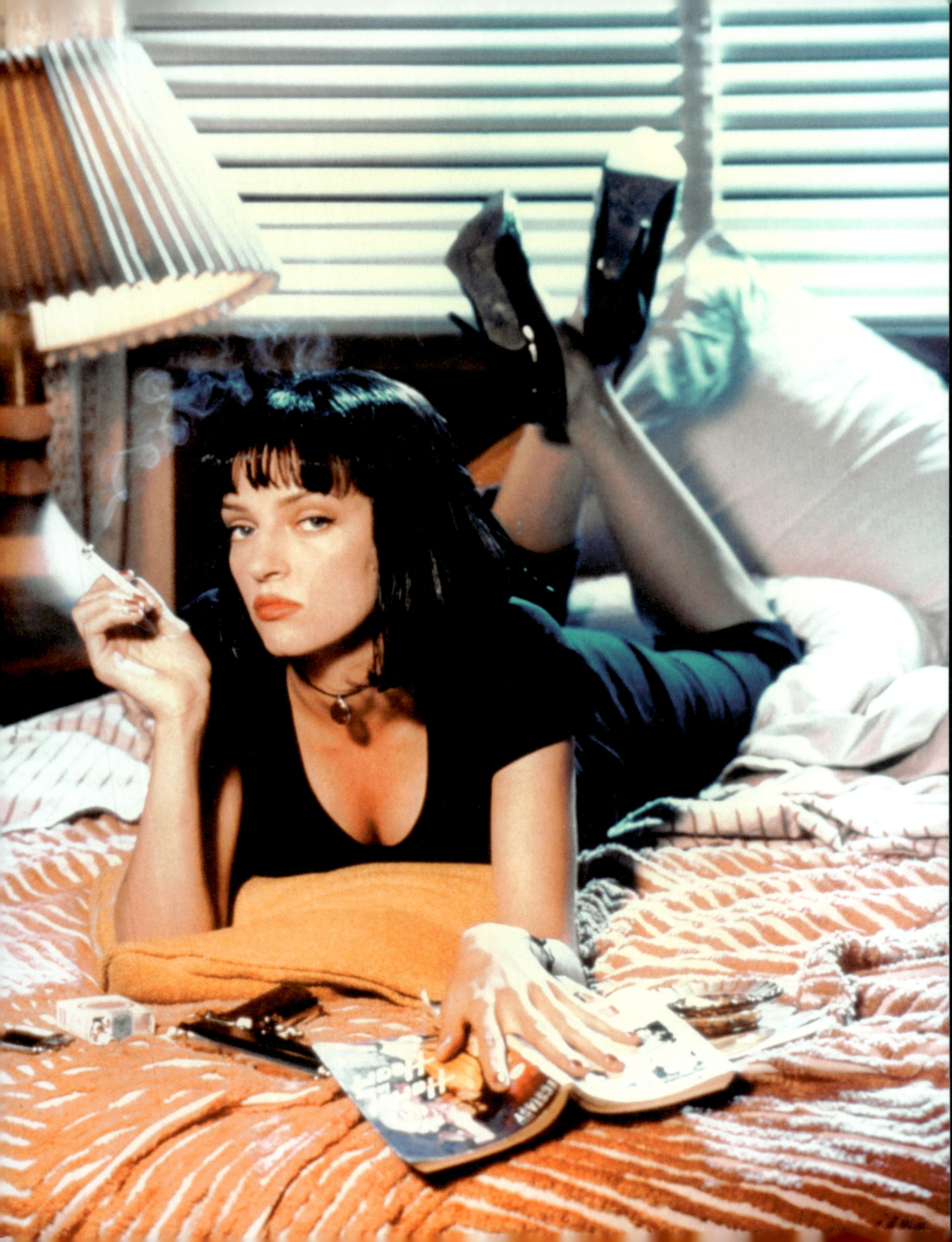